Characters of the Inquisition

CHARACTERS
OF THE
INQUISITION

By

WILLIAM THOMAS WALSH

AUTHOR OF "PHILIP THE SECOND,"
"ISABELLA OF SPAIN"

KENNIKAT PRESS, INC./PORT WASHINGTON, N. Y.

CHARACTERS OF THE INQUISITION

Copyright 1940 by P. J. Kenedy & Sons
Reissued 1969 by Kennikat Press by arrangement

Library of Congress Catalog Card No: 68-8192
SBN 8046-0486-X
Manufactured in the United States of America

ESSAY AND GENERAL LITERATURE INDEX REPRINT SERIES

TO

E. E. W.

Foreword

THE very word "Inquisition," which once enjoyed the connotation, as well as the meaning, of "inquiry," has become almost synonymous in the modern world with "bigotry," "intolerance," "cruelty." Men who are not quite sure what are the essentials of Christian belief are convinced that the burning of a human being for denying certain dogmas is not reconcilable with the teachings of Christ and the profession of a Christian. Men who cannot agree on a definition of the word "God," and are doubtful whether they believe in a God, will declare without hesitation that there is nothing godly about inflicting personal injury, or even deprivation of liberty, on those who do not agree with us. And since the Inquisitors were Catholics, it is clear that the Catholic Church in the modern world has suffered much in reputation on their account; the more so because the histories of the Inquisition have generally been written and disseminated by her adversaries.

A young Catholic sometimes is puzzled not only to answer the accusations of those not of his Faith but to satisfy the questionings of his own heart. He knows some priests, and whatever faults they have as human beings, they are not bloodthirsty men, quite the contrary as a rule; he knows Protestants and Jews, and sees nothing in them deserving of torment, much less hideous death. Some have left the Catholic fold, alleging this reason; others, attracted to her, have been kept outside by this one obstacle. No one sees Catholics today burning unbelievers, even in Ireland and Portugal, where the population is almost entirely Catholic; nor does any man of sense foresee the likelihood of a future persecution involving Catholics—

except, perhaps, as victims. Yet vast numbers of persons continue to associate the word "Inquisition" with vague notions of Catholic dogma; as though the thing were essentially and peculiarly Catholic, and began and ended in the Catholic Church.

It must be obvious to anyone who thinks for a moment on the subject that intolerance, as such, was not the invention, much less the monopoly, of the Middle Ages. It was not the child of Christianity. Centuries before Christ came to the world, Plato set it down as a *duty* of government to show no tolerance toward those who denied the state religion. Even if dissenters were willing to live quietly without proselytizing, their example to others was so dangerous, he believed, that they ought to be incarcerated for five years in a *"sophronisterion,"* or place-for-growing-wise, and there be taught religion every day. Proselytizing dissenters were to be kept in dungeons for life and be denied burial after death. Centuries later we find Jews in Holland, whose ancestors had been victims of the Spanish Inquisition, establishing an Inquisition of their own. "The Amsterdam rabbis," says Graetz, "introduced the innovation of bringing religious opinions and convictions before their judgment seat, of constituting themselves a sort of inquisitorial tribunal, and instituting *autos-de-fe* which, even if bloodless, were not less painful to the sufferers." [1]

This Jewish Inquisition was on a different plane from Plato's, and a higher one. He was a totalitarian who conceded to the State the right to say what religion must be held. The rabbis were men who felt a *certainty* of a higher revelation, more precious to them than any other consideration; and the force they applied was to those who already belonged to the group that had received the revelation—in this instance, the *Torah*. It was not an intolerance in the name of an all-powerful state, representing the mere *opinion* of a group of human beings.

Now, when we examine the Inquisition of the Middle Ages and the Spanish Inquisition more closely, we find certain peculiarities which bring them closer to the Amsterdam rabbis than to Plato. The impulse here is different from that swift blind anger and bloodlust of the mob from which defenseless Jews, women and

[1] *History of the Jews,* Vol. IV, pp. 684-5.

children included, have suffered in pogroms in all parts of the world. It is not like the shootings of children and nuns by Cromwell's Puritans in Ireland; or the lynchings of negroes; or the butchery of civilians, with or without a pretence of legal form, in the French Revolution, in Soviet Russia, and in Red Spain. Here, on the contrary, was a cold, deliberate attempt to set up a judicial instrument of conformity which would eliminate the caprice, the anger and the misinformation of the mob; which would inquire carefully, make distinctions, separate wheat from chaff, proceed not against particular men or members of particular races as such, but against members of the persecuting body—all this in the name of Almighty God, and apparently with a sense not only of representing the highest convictions of the community in general, but of being absolutely right about the whole matter, beyond any argument or need of apology.

There has been too much partisanship in most of the discussions of this subject; too much intolerance in the study of intolerance. The more popular expositions have been in the vein of Prescott's famous comparison of the Inquisitors (unfavorably, of course) to the Aztecs sacrificing human blood to their idol Quetzalcohuatl; or some of Dr. Graetz's angry generalizations, in which the Dominicans of the Holy Office appear as "Calibans" and "foul fiends in monkish cowls," while the heretics punished by them are "victims to the Christian Moloch." Later investigators have been more temperate in their epithets and more cautious in their methods of approach; but too many of them have leaned, with naïve credulity, upon the work of Llorente, a discredited official of the Holy Office, who proved his own bias by admitting that he had burned documents which did not serve his purpose. Lea has depended somewhat upon Llorente, but has also done some good source work, though prejudice has betrayed him into taking some unscholarly liberties with his material. G. G. Coulton has flayed the Inquisition with gusto, but when we look for his authority, we find it is principally Dr. Lea. The same is true of most of the work of Professor Merriman of Harvard on this subject. One great "authority" leans on another great "authority," and so on back to the end of a chain, where often the searcher finds no fact at all, or the very opposite to what has been alleged to generation after generation of trusting readers and students. These modern "authorities," writing with a greater air of scientific detachment, have probably been more effective, on the whole, than Prescott or Graetz.

It is rather startling, on turning from these types of criticism to the literature of Spain and Portugal, to find that men revealing intelligence, compassion, and other normal human traits in most matters, have been capable of writing about the institution, without a word of apology, yes, with unmistakable pride, as of something good, beneficent, holy. It is a bit of a jolt for one in youth illuminated by Dr. Lea and his disciples, to encounter, in the works of one of the most brilliant poets and historians of the Golden Age of Spain, the casual observation that the Inquisition was "the den of the lions of Daniel, which does no harm to the just, though it destroys the obstinate impenitent sinners; heavenly remedy, guardian of the Gates of Paradise." [2] A man as gentle and holy as Fray Luis de Granada could call it "wall of the Church, pillar of truth, guardian of faith, treasure of religion, arm against heretics, light against the deceits of the enemy."

Paramo goes even further, and tells us that the Great Inquisitor was Our Lord and Saviour Jesus Christ; indeed, this author carries his investigation further back, and discovers that the first Inquisitor was our father Adam!

Now, there is no sense in reviving so painful and controversial a subject as the Inquisition, a thing which persecutes nobody today and has not the slightest chance of doing so, if the motive is merely to add fuel to ancient hatreds which still divide man from man, and men from God. To make Catholics, Protestants, or Jews odious one to another, or to the rest of mankind, would surely be a useless, indeed, a wicked performance; and it is one I wish to have nothing to do with. But there is always something to be gained in the search of truth for the sake of truth itself, beautiful truth, luminous and eternal, the Thing that is, and not what hatred or envy, or greed or fear or revenge would like to imagine. There is something, surely, to be gained in saying, "Let us look at the past, not merely to justify ourselves, for we frail mortals have all made mistakes, we have all been guilty one time or another of injustice toward

2 Cabrera, *Felipe el segundo*, t. I, p. 276.

others. Well, then, let us see, if possible, what the truth was, and what can be learned from it—if only to avoid the same mistakes in future."

It would be fatuous to imagine that anything like the complete and absolute truth about so vast and so complicated a subject could be encompassed within the scope of the present study, even if the author were much more capable than he is. A life-time of useful labor is still waiting for some man with the patience and industry of Lea, a far better historical imagination, and considerably less prejudice. All I attempt here is to discuss a few characters through whom the Inquisition is revealed at various critical stages, and to suggest some important considerations that have been generally overlooked.

While I was wondering where this inquisitorial spirit, as distinguished from ordinary forms of intolerance, first made its appearance in the chronicle of man, I happened to notice in the *Book of Deuteronomy* a passage suggesting that what I sought had not originated in Fifteenth Century Spain or in Thirteenth Century France; that Paramo was right, after all, in a certain sense—in the sense in which Christianity is older than the Incarnation, existing as it did in the minds of the Hebrew prophets centuries before the birth of Our Lord. The Catholic Church has always insisted, even in our times and in the face of all opposition, that (in the phrase of Pope Pius XI) "spiritually we are all Semites." And in no flippant, analogical or allegorical sense, but in sober earnest, I came to the conclusion that the first real Inquisitor, as a Torquemada would have understood the word, was Moses. He was quite certain that he had compulsive truth from a higher than human source; he was resolved to keep it and sustain it at all costs; and the means he adopted were essentially those of the Medieval Inquisition, even more irritating if possible to some persons, and not always understood in their own background by later ages. Moses put to death, in the name of religion, a far greater number of human beings than Torquemada did. Yet his name has been venerated by orthodox Jews and Roman Catholics alike, and always will be, while that of the Dominican monk has become a stench in the nostrils of the modern world, and a symbol of something indefensible. All this will bear examination.

Contents

Characters of the
Inquisition

I

Moses

MOSES appeared among the children of Israel (as Christ would appear) in one of the darkest hours of their history.

Jacob had been gathered to his fathers, leaving behind him a prophecy, that was to be quoted for and against the Jews many centuries later, even in medieval Spain:

"The sceptre shall not be taken away from Juda, nor a ruler from his thigh, till he come that is to be sent, and he shall be the expectation of nations, tying his foal to the vineyard, and his ass, o my son, to the vine. He shall wash his robe in wine, and his garment in the blood of the grapes. His eyes are more beautiful than wine, and his teeth whiter than milk." [1]

The children of Israel remained in the land of Egypt, multiplied and prospered. Their numbers aroused the fear, as their prosperity incited the envy, of the dwellers of the Nile, who "made their life bitter with hard works in clay, and brick, and with all manner of service, wherewith they were overcharged in the works of the earth," until at last King Pharao, having failed to impose a sort of birth control on the Hebrews by corrupting their widwives, condemned all their male babies to be cast into the Nile—even as Herod, in his fear and jealousy of Christ, would deal with the male infants of Bethlehem.

It was at this moment of danger that Moses, precursor and prophet of the Messias, was born of a Levitical family, in which there were already two children, a son, Aaron, and a daughter,

---

[1] *Genesis*, XLIX: 10-12. This and all other biblical quotations in this work are from the Douay Version.

I

Miriam (Mary). The mother was a resourceful woman. She hid her baby in a basket of bulrushes, calked and camouflaged with pitch and mud, and laid him in shallow water, among the sedges by the river's brink. The girl Miriam, watching from a distance, saw the daughter of Pharao go down with her maidens to bathe, open the basket, discover the crying infant, and take compassion on him, saying, "This is one of the babes of the Hebrews!"

Miriam stepped forward and said, "Shall I go and call to thee a Hebrew woman, to nurse the babe?"

"Go," said the Princess.

Miriam of course fetched her own mother, who took him and nursed him, as another Hebrew woman, a greater Miriam, centuries later would nurse the Holy Child in Egypt. Pharao's daughter called him Moses, "because," she said, "I took him out of the water;" and when he grew up, she adopted him.[2] He became a powerful lad, strikingly handsome, with a majestic presence, a quick temper, and a great deal of natural wisdom, with a certain diffidence and humility—Moses never could speak, for example, with the burning eloquence of his older brother; he may even have stammered a little. But he had a more profound intelligence than Aaron, and according to Rabbinical tradition, he was well taught in the lore of the Egyptians, the Assyrians, the Chaldaeans and the Greeks. The sufferings and sorrows of his people afflicted him, and he must have brooded long and often on how they could be redeemed from their servitude to a people spiritually inferior, who worshipped false gods made with human hands and had many base customs. One day he saw an Egyptian brutally striking a Hebrew workman. "And when he had looked about, this way and that way, and saw no one coming, he slew the Egyptian and hid him in the sand."

Moses supposed that he was unseen, but the next day, stopping a quarrel between two of his own race, he found that one of them knew what he had done, and in resentment threatened to report the matter, as in fact he did: and Moses, condemned to death, fled to the land of Madian.

There, tired and dusty, he sat down by a well, as a far greater

[2] *Exodus*, II: 10.

Man would sit by the well of Jacob in Samaria: and there came seven maidens, all daughters of the priest of Madian, to draw water for their sheep. Some shepherds arrived, and either out of deviltry, or because water was scarce, began to drive the girls away. To their great surprise, a powerful youth in Egyptian raiment rose up from beside the well, and gave them a thrashing; and after they had fled, Moses gallantly watered the flock for the young women.[3]

The upshot of all this was that he married one of the girls, Sephora, had two children by her, and remained for some years in the land of Madian, until Pharao died, "and the children of Israel groaning, cried out because of the works: and their cry went up unto God from the works. And he heard their groaning, and remembered the covenant which He made with Abraham, Isaac and Jacob.[4]

"Now Moses fed the sheep of Jethro his father-in-law, the priest of Madian: and he drove the flock to the inner parts of the desert, and came to the mountain of God, Horeb. And the Lord appeared to him in a flame of fire out of the midst of a bush: and he saw that the bush was on fire and was not burnt. And Moses said, I will go and see this great sight, why the bush is not burnt. And when the Lord saw that he went forward to see, he called to him out of the midst of the bush, and said, 'Moses, Moses.'

"And he answered, 'Here I am.'

"And he said, 'Come not nigh hither, put off the shoes from thy feet: for the place whereon thou standest is holy ground.'

"And he said, 'I am the God of thy father, the God of Abraham, the God of Isaac, and the God of Jacob.'

"Moses hid his face: for he durst not look at God.

"And the Lord said to him, 'I have seen the affliction of my people in Egypt, and I have heard their cry because of the rigour of them that are over the works: and knowing their sorrow, I am come down to deliver them out of the hands of the Egyptians, and to bring them out of that land into a land that floweth with milk and honey, to the places of the Chanaanite, and Hethite, and Amorrhite, and Pherezite, and Hevite, and Jebusite. . . . But come,

[3] *Ibid.*, II: 15-17.
[4] *Ibid.*, II: 23-24.

and I will send thee to Pharao, that thou mayst bring forth my people, the children of Israel out of Egypt.'"

Moses was terrified in such a Presence.

"Who am I," he said, "that I should go to Pharao, and should bring the children of Israel out of Egypt?"

The Lord replied, "I will be with thee: and this shalt thou have for a sign that I have sent thee: When thou shalt have brought my people out of Egypt, thou shalt offer sacrifice to God upon this mountain."

Moses was a practical person, accustomed to looking ahead. What would the children of Israel say when he told them, "The God of your fathers hath sent me to you?" Would they not say, "What is his name?" What then?

The voice of the Almighty answered,

"I AM WHO AM. Thus shalt thou say to the children of Israel: He WHO IS hath sent me to you."

Moses still hesitated, even after God performed two miracles to convince him—the turning of the rod into the serpent, and the momentary leprosy that whitened his hand and disappeared as it came.

"I beseech thee, Lord, I am not eloquent from yesterday and the day before: and since thou hast spoken to thy servant, I have more impediment and slowness of tongue."

"Who made man's mouth? or who made the dumb and the deaf, the seeing and the blind? Did not I? Go therefore, and I will be in thy mouth: and I will teach thee what thou shalt speak."

"I beseech thee, Lord, send whom thou wilt send."

The Lord now was angry, but He gave Moses one more chance. He suggested Aaron as spokesman for his slow-tongued brother: "He shall speak in thy stead to the people, and shall be thy mouth: but thou shalt be to him in those things that pertain to God."

The last objection having been removed, Moses obeyed. Setting his wife and sons upon an ass, he started on the long journey to Egypt, assembled there the ancients of the people, the earliest known Sanhedrin, and spoke as he had been instructed. "And the people believed . . . and falling down, they adored."

How Moses and Aaron went to Pharao (Moses was then eighty

years old, his brother three years older), and how the King refused to let the children of the promise go into the wilderness:
how he caused them to make bricks without straw, and had them
scourged until they cried out against Moses and Aaron, saying
"The Lord see and judge, because you have made our savour to
stink before Pharao and his servants, and you have given him a
sword to kill us;" how the God of Abraham, Isaac and Jacob smote
the Egyptians with seven plagues—the rivers of blood, the festering
frogs, the sciniphs that came out of the dust, the grievous swarm
of flies, the vexatious murrain on all the beasts of the Egyptians,
the scattered ashes, the devastating and thunderous hail; the insatiable locusts on the burning wind, blackening out the sun; the
three days' darkness so thick it could be felt, and finally the slaying
of all the first children of Egypt by the angel of the Lord, while the
Hebrews celebrated their first Passover feast with unleavened bread,
yearling lamb and wild lettuce behind blood-spattered doors, until
"Pharao arose in the night, and all his servants and all Egypt,
and there arose a great cry in Egypt, for there was not a house
wherein there lay not one dead;" and how the Egyptians begged
the children of Israel to go, lest all die; how the children of Israel,
after 430 years of bondage, trooped forth, taking with them the
sacred bones of Joseph, into the desert where the Lord went before
as a pillar of cloud by day and a pillar of fire by night: how Pharao
and his army pursued, and how the waters of the Red Sea closed
over him and all his men and horses and chariots, while the
Hebrews passed to safety between the walls of water, and went
singing a mighty chorus, while Mary the prophetess and all the
other women danced to the beat of their timbrels; and how the
Lord showed them the tree that would sweeten the bitter waters
of Mara, and fed them for forty years on the manna that fell from
Heaven, a *gomor* of which He ordered kept in the Tabernacle,
as it were a prefiguring of the Blessed Sacrament, until at last
they came to the foot of the holy Mount of Sinai, where they held
their breaths with fear while the Lord God gave to Moses the
Ten Commandments which have been the moral law of the world
from that day to this,—all this is so familiar to us that we are in
danger of forgetting what a sublime epic it is, and how living and

untarnished and valid it is, after thousands of years, in contrast to all the merely human epics of the gentile world, which have no such claim upon our reverence. For the Law of Moses in its essentials is still the basic moral law of the Catholic Church, through which it has influenced, directly or indirectly, the conscience of the whole world; and must be so, in the nature of things, to the end of time. Often forgotten or overlooked nowadays is the oneness and continuity of the revelation on Mt. Sinai with the revelation of Christ: this oversight explains some of the starkest tragedies and blunders of history, and explains, surely, some of the mysteries which set the Hebrews apart from other peoples in ancient times, and set apart down to our own time the comparatively small group of them who are known to us as Jews.

The children of Israel were chosen very explicitly by the Creator of mankind for the loftiest of destinies, of which obviously there were two parts:

(1) To keep the knowledge and worship of one true God alive among all the savage superstitions and vile debaucheries of less favored nations.

(2) To receive, in good time, the Holy One of God, who should come to the earth to save not only the Hebrews but all men; and to give Him to mankind.

This privilege was conferred conditionally:

"Thus shalt thou say to the house of Jacob, and tell the children of Israel: You have seen what I have done to the Egyptians, how I have carried you upon the wings of eagles, and have taken you to myself. If therefore you will hear my voice, and keep my covenant, you shall be my peculiar possession above all people: for all the earth is mine. And you shall be to me a priestly kingdom, and a holy nation." [5]

In this promise lies an explanation of a great deal of the strange history of the Chosen People, with its alternating triumphs and defeats, glories and humiliations, virtues and sins, even to our own day. It was not merely that their great law-giver gave them principles by which all the affairs of life were regulated more intelligently, in a human sense, than those of any other ancient

[5] *Exodus*, XIX: 3-6.

people; that he anticipated modern theories of hygiene, and even the distinction our law books make about burglary, as a crime committed "in the night season"—and with this, the right of a man to kill a burglar, but not a daytime thief.[6] It was not that the Jews had a harsh law of justice alone, contrasting with a Christian law of charity alone—this is a vulgar error, pregnant with conclusions unfair both to Jews and to Christians. The same Moses who, in those rude and dangerous times, told them to exact "eye for eye, tooth for tooth, hand for hand, foot for foot, burning for burning, wound for wound, stripe for stripe,"[7] also transmitted these commands:

"Thou shalt not hate thy brother in thy heart, but reprove him openly, lest thou incur sin through him. Seek not revenge, nor be mindful of the injury of thy citizens. Thou shalt love thy friend as thyself. I am the Lord . . .[8]

"Neither shalt thou gather the bunches of grapes that fall down in thy vineyard, but shalt leave them to the poor and the strangers to take . . .[9]

"Thou shalt not calumniate thy neighbor, nor oppress him by violence. The wages of him that hath been hired by thee shall not abide with thee until the morning . . .[10]

"If a stranger dwell in your land, and abide among you, do not upbraid him: but let him be among you as one of the same country: and you shall love him as yourselves: for you were strangers in the land of Egypt. I am the Lord your God . . .[11]

"You shall not hurt a widow or an orphan. If you hurt them they will cry out to me, and I will hear their cry: and my rage shall be enkindled, and I will strike you with the sword, and your wives shall be widows, and your children fatherless.

"If you lend money to any of my people that is poor, that dwelleth with thee, thou shalt not be hard upon them as an extortioner, nor oppress them with usuries."[12]

[6] *Ibid.*, XXII: 2, 3.
[7] *Ibid.*, XXI: 24, 25.
[8] *Leviticus*, XIX: 17, 18.
[9] *Ibid.*, XIX: 10.
[10] *Ibid.*, XIX: 13.
[11] *Ibid.*, XIX: 33, 34.
[12] *Exodus*, XXII: 22, 25.

The Hebrews, too, then, were told to love their neighbors. But they were not encouraged to confuse charity for fellow men with a sentimental and suicidal toleration for false ideas. Custodians of the holy truth which alone could lead man back to the primal felicity of daily communion with God, which he had lost through the sin of disobedience, they held this higher than any human consideration, holier even than human life itself. Moses, acting under divine inspiration, never hesitated to shed blood rather than let his Chosen People become like the Egyptians, with their corrupting Astarte, or those Phoenicians who sacrificed innocent babies to their idol Moloch. Crimes against God were, in the mind of Moses (by God illuminated), crimes against Being Itself. Hence, when he returned from the holy mount to find that his people had made to themselves (with his own brother's connivance) a molten calf of gold, to which they bowed in adoration, and to which they sacrificed victims, he was so angry that he cast the tables of the Law from his hand, and shattered them, he burnt the calf and beat it into powder, he made the Hebrews drink water containing the dust of it, and assembling all the sons of Levi, men marked for the holy priesthood, "he said to them, 'Thus saith the Lord God of Israel: Put every man his sword upon his thigh: Go, and return from gate to gate through the midst of the camp, and let every man kill his brother, and friend, and neighbor.' And the sons of Levi did according to the words of Moses, and there were slain that day about three-and-twenty thousand men." [13]

Stern justice? It was necessary if the revelation of the Creator of mankind was to be kept alive in the world; if all the human race was not to sink into a state of degradation below that of beasts. It was necessary, this slaughter of 23,000, to prevent the loss of far more, in peace and in war, who would perish if the Chosen People scorned the spiritual and abased themselves before the material. No merely human cause, no liberal reform, no promise for the proletariat, no misty vision of progress in the future, could have justified it. Such punishment could be meted out justly only by the outraged majesty of a patient God, whose only alternative

[13] *Ibid.*, XXXII: 27, 28.

would have been to forsake or destroy a hopelessly corrupted world.

Thus Moses dealt with all offenses against the Almighty: with unnatural vice, which would have made the children of Israel as soft, as foul and as forsaken as the pagans around them; with adultery, which struck at the heart of the family and therefore the foundation of society; above all, with offenses against the revealed Truth itself. Of magicians and soothsayers, of spiritualists, of a man or woman in whom there dwelt a pythonical or divining spirit, he said, "Dying let them die: they shall stone them: their blood be upon them." [14] and if a daughter of a priest was "taken in whoredom," she was to be burned to death.[15] (This form of capital punishment was not invented in the Middle Ages.)

Schism was punished with equal severity, for it challenged a leadership which was divine as well as political. When Core and his friends rose up against Moses, the great prophet called down upon them the anger of God, "and immediately, as he had done speaking, the earth broke asunder under their feet: and opening her mouth, devoured them with their tents and all their substance. And they went down alive into hell, the ground closing upon them, and they perished from among the people." [16] Others were destroyed by plague, 14,700 dying in all.

Moses had toleration for what might be called the *human* weaknesses of human nature, but he had none at all for those which cut the holy cord that bound souls to their Maker. For idolatry, the sin against the first commandment, "I am the Lord thy God . . . Thou shalt not have strange gods before me," he had but one answer. The only good idolaters were dead idolaters. Their portion was the sword, and their lands were confiscated by the Children of Israel. He never forgot the terrible lesson of the Golden Calf. He remembered, too, the feeble excuse Aaron had offered for his share in that abomination, "Let not my lord be offended: for thou knowest this people, that they are prone to evil;" [17] and he

[14] *Leviticus*, XX: 27.
[15] *Ibid.*, XXI: 9.
[16] *Numbers*, XVI: 31-33.
[17] *Exodus*, XXXII: 22.

was constantly on the alert for some repetition of the offense. Moses was aware, doubtless, that those who had received great spiritual gifts would be most tempted by the devil, and if once they fell, would sink lower than less favored sinners.

> For sweetest things turn sourest by their deeds;
> Lilies that fester smell far worse than weeds.[18]

Idolatry, worst of sins, never failed to beget a spawn of other sins, especially those most degrading to human nature. The people of Madian had taken this fatal path, and had become worse than beasts. They adored an idol called Beelphegor, in whose honor they offered up sacrifices, and indulged, like other idolators, in promiscuous orgies. Evidently, too, they had a sort of secret society into which the worshippers of Beelphegor had to be initiated; an old custom among people who have some guilty secret to conceal. They also had an obscene idol named Phogor.

"And Israel at that time abode in Settim, and the people committed fornication with the daughters of Moab, who called them to their sacrifices. And they ate of them, and adored their gods. And Israel was initiated to Beelphegor: upon which the Lord being angry, said to Moses, 'Take all the princes of the people, and hang them up on gibbets against the sun' . . . and Moses said to the judges of Israel, 'Let every man kill his neighbors, that have been initiated to Beelphegor'."

The Hebrews who had not been corrupted took arms, and slew 24,000 of the wretches who had worshipped the false god. Phineas the son of Eleazar, seeing Zambri, of the tribe of Simeon, enter a brothel with a harlot of Madian named Cozbi, went in after them with a dagger, "and thrust both of them through together, to wit, the man and the woman in the genital parts." [19] Nor did the retribution stop then. The Madianites had become so dehumanized that their complete extinction was commanded by God. Moses sent twelve thousand well-armed men against them. "And when they had fought against the Madianites and had overcome them, they slew all the men. And their kings Evi, and Recem, and Sur, and

[18] *Sonnet 94.*
[19] *Numbers,* XXV.

Hur, and Rebe, five princes of the nation. Baldam also the son of Beor they killed with the sword. And they took their women and their children captives, and all their cattle, and all their goods. And all their possessions they plundered: and all their cities, and their villages, and castles, they burned. And they carried away the booty, and all that they had taken both of men and of beasts. And they brought them to Moses, and Eleazar the priest, and to all the multitude of the children of Israel." [20]

"Why have you saved the women?" demanded Moses in anger. "Are not these they that deceived the children of Israel by the counsel of Baalam, and made you transgress against the Lord by the sin of Phogor, for which also the people was punished? Therefore kill all that are of the male sex, even of the children: and put to death the women that have carnally known men." [21]

Moses was growing old, and he himself, because of his sin at the Waters of Contradiction, could never see the Land of Promise; but in a magnificent discourse, after giving the tables of the Law again to Israel, he described it as "a land which floweth with milk and honey. For the land, which thou goest to possess, is not like the land of Egypt, from whence thou camest out, where, when the seed is sown, waters are brought in to water it after the manner of gardens. But it is a land of hills and plains, expecting rain from heaven. And the Lord thy God doth always visit it, and his eyes are upon it from the beginning of the year unto the end thereof. If then you obey my commandments, which I command you this day, that you love the Lord your God, and serve him with all your heart, and with all your soul, He will give to your land the early rain and the latter rain, that you may gather in your corn, and your wine, and your oil, and your hay out of the fields to feed your cattle, and that you may eat and be filled. Beware lest perhaps your heart be deceived, and you depart from the Lord, and serve strange gods, and adore them: and the Lord being angry shut up heaven, that the rain come not down, nor the earth yield her fruit, and you perish quickly from the excellent land which the Lord will give you." [22]

[20] *Ibid.*, XXXI: 7-12.
[21] *Ibid.*
[22] *Deuteronomy*, XI: 9-17.

False gods—this danger was constantly in the venerable old man's mind. He never tired of repeating his warning against the one danger which could be fatal to his people. He gave them all sorts of additional admonitions—a remission of debts every seven years, by what we now call the statute of limitations; care of the poor, and of the widow and the orphan; all manner of laws whereby this Chosen People might keep their personal, family and communal life clean and undefiled, and enjoy the blessing of God's friendship. But always he came back to idolatry. Even if a man's brother or son or wife proposed secretly to him the service of false gods, he must denounce the offender, and be the first to cast the stone of death upon him. Finally, in his anxiety to provide for the spiritual and therefore social health of his people, after he should die, Moses hit upon an idea which in all its essentials suggests a parallel, or rather prototype, of the Medieval Inquisition, in spirit, aim and method.

"When there shall be found among you within any of thy gates, which the Lord thy God shall give thee, man or woman that do evil in the sight of the Lord thy God, and transgress his covenant, so as to go and serve strange gods, and adore them, the sun and the moon, and all the host of heaven, which I have not commanded: and this is told thee, and hearing it thou hast inquired diligently, and found it to be true, and that the abomination is committed in Israel: thou shalt bring forth the man or the woman, who have committed that most wicked thing, to the gates of thy city, and they shall be stoned. By the mouth of two or three witnesses shall he die that is to be slain. Let no man be put to death, when only one beareth witness against him. The hands of the witnesses shall be first upon him to kill him, and afterwards the hands of the rest of the people: that thou mayst take away the evil out of the midst of thee." In any hard or doubtful matter, or if the judges should disagree, the people must appeal to the priests of the Levitical race, and follow their sentence. And "he that will be proud, and refuse to obey the commandment of the priest, who ministereth at that time to the Lord thy God, and the decree of the judge, that man shall die, and thou shalt take away the evil from Israel: and all the people hearing it shall fear, that no one afterwards swell with pride . . ."[23]

[23] *Deuteronomy,* XVII: 2-13.

"Neither let there be found among you any one that shall expiate his son or daughter, making them to pass through the fire: or that consulteth soothsayers, or observeth dreams and omens, neither let there be any wizard, nor charmer, nor any one that consulteth pythonic spirits, or fortune tellers, or that seeketh the truth from the dead. For the Lord abhorreth all these things, and for these abominations he will destroy them at thy coming. Thou shalt be perfect, and without spot before the Lord thy God." [24]

Here, as we shall see, are all the essentials (plus considerably more rigor, to be sure) of the Thirteenth Century Inquisition. If any are suspected of offenses against the revealed truth of God, an Inquiry (Inquisition) is to be set in motion; witchcraft, spiritualism, and superstition in general are to be included: a conviction may be reached if the testimony of two witnesses is accepted: and the death penalty may be inflicted, and in the case of the Hebrews, is mandatory. The Children of Israel, of course, had a theocratic form of government; Church and State were one, and the same authority punished religious and political offenses. This was not the case in the Middle Ages; hence there we find the State, not the Church, imposing the death penalty. But the object was the same, and the results were, as we shall notice later, somewhat similar.

Immediately after this legislation, Moses, at the age of 120, with death approaching in the very sight of the Promised Land, made the tremendous prophecy which alone gives universal significance to all his previous utterances. With the greatest solemnity the splendid old man told the Hebrews what would be the crown and reward of all their fidelity to the revelation he had brought to them.

"The Lord thy God will raise up to thee a Prophet of thy nation and of thy brethren like unto me: *him thou shalt hear:* as thou desiredst of the Lord thy God in Horeb, when the assembly was gathered together, and saidst, 'Let me not hear any more the voice of the Lord my God, neither let me see any more this exceeding great fire, lest I die.' And the Lord said to me, 'They have spoken all things well. I will raise them up a prophet out of the midst of their brethren like to thee: and I will put my words in his mouth, and he shall speak to them all that I command him. *And he that*

[24] *Ibid.,* XVIII: 10-13.

*will not hear his words, which he shall speak in my name, I will
be the revenger.'* The Hebrews would be able to distinguish the
great Prophet from false ones by the realization of his prophecies,
and the failure of theirs." [25]

Shortly after this Moses died, his eyes still keen, his teeth intact.
"And there arose no more a prophet in Israel like unto Moses,
whom the Lord knew face to face . . ." [26]

Centuries passed, and the dying prophecy of Moses was repeated
and strengthened by King David, Isaias, Aggeus, Malachias, Daniel
and other men of God; and in the ripeness of time a star stood
over Bethlehem, and the mighty Word leapt down in the silence of
night. Another slaughter of innocents, another journey into Egypt,
and presently the Prophet predicted by Moses was performing such
miracles as no one had ever performed before, and speaking as none
had spoken; and the world was shaken to its foundations, and
changed forever.

Yet if He was a sign for the rise and fall of many, he was certainly no "revolutionary" in the sense implied by some superficial
exegetes of modern liberalism. As He explained, He had not come
to destroy the Law of Moses, but to fulfill it. In His preaching He
frequently mentioned, and always with approval, the great law-
giver. Upbraiding the Pharisees for evading the commands of
Moses regarding the honor due to parents, He referred to those
commands as the Word of God.[27] When He healed some lepers,
He told them to show themselves to the High Priest and offer "the
things that Moses commanded." [28] "The Scribes and Pharisees," He
declared on another occasion, "have sitten on the chair of Moses.
All things therefore whatsoever they shall say to you, observe and
do: but according to their works do ye not; for they say, and do
not." [29] He cited Moses against the Sadducees who, in their ignorance or neglect of their own scriptures, denied the resurrection of
the dead.[30] A man's attitude toward Moses was likely to determine

[25] *Deuteronomy,* XVIII: 15, 22.
[26] *Ibid.,* XXXIV: 10.
[27] *St. Mark,* VII: 9, 13.
[28] *Ibid.,* I: 44.
[29] *St. Matthew,* XXIII: 3.
[30] *St. Mark,* XII: 26; see also *St. Luke,* XX: 37.

his attitude toward the Just One, when He came, "If they hear not Moses and the Prophets, neither will they believe, if one rise again from the dead." [31] Again, "Did not Moses give you the law, and yet none of you keepeth the law? Why seek you to kill me?" [32] "As Moses lifted up the serpent in the desert, so must the Son of Man be lifted up, that whosoever believeth in him may not perish, but may have life everlasting." [33] Decidedly, He was not like one coming to destroy a house. Rather, as Son of the Owner, He came to perfect and ratify the work which Moses, a good servant, had begun.

His tone was altogether different, too, from that of Moses. He "spoke like one having authority" in His own right. Quite explicitly, on one occasion when the Jews sought to kill Him (not only because he healed on the Sabbath but because He said God was His father, thus "making Himself equal to God") He referred to the prophecy that Moses had uttered concerning Him; and bluntly gave the reason why His hearers had failed to understand that prophecy, "But I know you, that you have not the love of God in you. . . . There is one that accuseth you, Moses, in whom you trust. *For if you did believe Moses, you would perhaps believe in Me also: for he wrote of me.* But if you do not believe his writings, how will you believe my words?" [34] The same prophecy occurred at once to Philip when he first met the Christ. "We have found him," he cried to Nathaniel, "of whom Moses in the law, and the prophets wrote . . . " [35]. Of the distinction between Moses and Himself, Our Lord left no doubt: "Moses gave you not bread from Heaven, but my Father giveth you the true bread from Heaven . . . I am the bread of life: he that cometh to me shall never thirst." [36]—a prediction most literally fulfilled in those mystics, like St. Catherine of Siena, who have subsisted, sometimes for years, on the Blessed Sacrament alone.

During His Transfiguration, the three apostles saw Moses and

[31] *St. Luke,* XVI: 31.
[32] *St. John,* VII: 19.
[33] *St. John,* III: 14.
[34] *St. John,* V: 42, 47.
[35] *St. John,* I: 43.
[36] *St. John,* VI: 32, 35.

Elias conversing with Him; and St. Peter, characteristically impulsive, proposed building three tabernacles, one to his Lord, one
to Moses and one to Elias, only to have his sense of values cor-
rected by a voice from Heaven saying, "This is my beloved Son, in
whom I am well pleased: hear ye him." [37]

By some mystery of human perversity, the authority of Moses,
which should have disposed his followers to recognize and to
adore the Christ, was the very pretext used to reject Him; indeed,
it was the inquisitorial command of Moses, referred to above, that
he was accused, by legal chicanery, of violating. Undoubtedly a
great measure of the blame for this belonged to the High Priests
and the Pharisees. In older times the people had strayed from the
truth, and their priests had been faithful: now it was the other way
about: and the ruling class of Jerusalem, the officialdom and the
intelligentsia, had yielded, partly under foreign influence, to an
empty and insincere formalism on the one hand, and to an even
more deadly skepticism on the other. It was this class, chiefly, that
Our Lord accused of hypocrisy, of preaching but not practicing the
Law of Moses. And it was by this class that the ordinary Jew was
betrayed and kept blind, all in the name of Moses. "Of the people
many believed in Him, and said, 'When the Christ cometh, shall he
do more miracles than those which this man doth?' " [38] The Pharisees, getting wind of this murmur, sent ministers to apprehend
Jesus. The agents returned, saying, "Never did man speak like
this man." [39]

In desperation the corrupted leadership turned to the mighty
name of Moses. To a man whose sight Our Lord restored, they said
scornfully: "Be thou his disciple; but we are disciples of Moses.
We know that God spoke to Moses; but as to this man, we know
not from whence he is." The man answered, "Why, here is a wonderful thing, that you know not whence he is, and he hath opened
my eyes. . . . Unless this man were of God, he could not do anything"—an argument for which the Pharisees could think of
nothing but force, "and they cast him out." [40]

[37] *St. Matthew,* XVII: 4, 5. *St. Luke,* IX: 33, 34.
[38] *St. John,* VII: 31.
[39] *Ibid.,* VII: 46.
[40] *St. John,* IX: 28-33.

Moses was invoked likewise against the first disciple who shed his blood for Christ. Unable to refute Stephen, the High Priests induced false witnesses to say, "We have heard him say, that this Jesus of Nazareth shall destroy this place, and shall change the traditions which Moses delivered to us." In answer to this, Stephen, in his last speech, told the whole story of Moses, and his prophecy of Christ, and ended with these indignant words, "You stiff-necked and uncircumcised in heart and ears, you always resist the Holy Ghost: as your fathers did, so do you also. Which of the prophets have not your fathers persecuted? And they have slain them who foretold of the coming of the Just One, of whom you have been the betrayers and murderers." [41] Hearing this, cut to the heart, they gnashed their teeth at him, and stoned him to death.

Saint Paul likewise had Moses quoted against him, wherever he preached. "Even until this day," he wrote, "when Moses is read, the veil is upon their heart. But when they shall be converted to the Lord, the veil is taken away." [42] Yet he insisted, of course, that the Law of Christ and the Law of Moses were essentially one: and it is interesting to find him quoting the inquisitorial injunction of Moses, and turning it against the Jews who had rejected Our Lord. "A man making void the Law of Moses," he said, "dieth without any mercy under two or three witnesses: how much more do you think he deserveth worse punishment, who hath trodden under foot the Son of God, and hath esteemed the blood of the testament unclean, by which he was sanctified, and hath offered an affront to the Spirit of grace?" [43]

Saint Paul on another occasion was so exasperated at the opposition of his unbelieving compatriots that he referred to them as "the Jews, who both killed the Lord Jesus and the prophets, and have persecuted us, and please not God, and are adversaries of all men; prohibiting us to speak to the Gentiles, that they may be saved, to fill up their sin always: for the wrath of God is come upon them to the end." [44]

---

[41] *Acts*, VI: 14; VII: 51.
[42] *2 Cor.*, III: 15.
[43] *Hebrews*, X: 28, 29.
[44] *Thessalonians*, II: 15, 16.

Yet Saint Paul knew what has often been forgotten: that the whole Jewish nation did not reject Christ, by any means. He himself converted 3,000 Jews on one day, and 5,000 on another. The primitive Christian Church, in fact, was almost entirely Jewish by race. The first glorious Popes and martyrs were generally sons of Abraham and Juda. And the Apostle to the Gentiles refused to believe that God, who had so often forgiven His people when they had erred, would not take them back if they turned to Him in penitence.

"I say then," he went on: "Hath God cast away his people? God forbid. For I also am an Israelite of the seed of Abraham, of the tribe of Benjamin. God hath not cast away his people, which he foreknew. . . . Even so then at this present time also, there is a remnant saved according to the election of grace." He warned the Gentile Christians not to gloat over the spiritual misfortune of the Jews, who were like branches cut off from the tree. "For if God hath not spared the natural branches, fear lest perhaps he also spare not thee. See then the goodness and the severity of God: toward them indeed that are fallen the severity; but towards thee, the goodness of God, if thou abide in goodness, otherwise thou also shalt be cut off. And they also, if they abide not still in unbelief, shall be grafted in: for God is able to graft them in again. For if thou were cut out of the wild olive tree, which is natural to thee, and contrary to nature, were grafted into the good olive tree, how much more shall they that are the natural branches, be grafted into their own olive tree? For I would not have you ignorant, brethren, of this mystery (lest you should be wise in your own conceits) that blindness in part has happened in Israel, until the fulness of the Gentiles should come in. And so all Israel should be saved, as it is written, 'There shall come out of Sion he that shall deliver, and shall turn away ungodliness from Jacob. And this is to them my covenant: when I shall take away their sins'. . . . As you also in times past did not believe in God, but now have obtained mercy, through their unbelief; so these also now have not believed, for your mercy, that they also may obtain mercy. For God had concluded all in unbelief, that he may have mercy on all. O, the depth of the riches of the wisdom and of the knowledge of God! How incomprehensible are his judgments, and how unsearchable his ways!" [45]

The division of the Jews continued, and because they were divided, the world was spiritually divided, and remains so to this day. While the divine plan works toward its appointed end, the wheat and tares grow up together, the net of Peter the Jewish Fisherman drags through the unquiet waters of the world for souls, and Israel remains apart. Meanwhile the spirit of Moses, in its fullest and truest expression, has lived on in the Catholic Church. Yet in this twentieth century of the New Dispensation, a Jewish Rabbi, in the very act of writing, probably with good intentions, the sad blasphemy that "the true Messias is the Jewish people," cannot help slipping into Christian terminology; he must refer to the long "crucifixion" of his people, and their coming "resurrection." [46] In this there is much to grieve at; but is there not also a hope? Not the false Talmudic hopes raised in the hearts of the poor harried Jews after the literal fulfilment of Our Lord's prophecies of the destruction of their Temple and their city, and the passing of the Kingdom from their hands to those of the Gentiles, but the hopes of St. Paul for their final conversion, and a happy, if belated recognition that a prophecy by the great Jew Isaias was realized nearly twenty centuries ago:

"Arise, be enlightened, O Jerusalem: for thy light is come, and the glory of the Lord is risen upon thee. For behold darkness shall cover the earth and a mist the people: but the Lord shall arise upon thee, and His glory shall be seen upon thee. And the Gentiles shall walk in thy light, and kings in the brightness of thy rising. Lift up thy eyes round about and see: all these are gathered together: they are come to thee: thy sons shall come from afar, and thy daughters shall rise up at thy side. Then shalt thou see and abound, and thy heart shall wonder and be enlarged when the multitude of the sea shall be converted to thee. The multitudes of camels shall cover thee, the dromedaries of Madian and Epha: all they from Saba shall come, bringing gold and frankincense and showing forth praise to the Lord." [47]

[45] *Romans*, XI: 21-33.
[46] Kohler: *Jewish Theology.*
[47] *Isaias*, LX: 1-6.

The same Isaias wrote, "Hear ye therefore, O house of David: Is it a small thing for you to be grievous to men, that you are grievous to my God also? Therefore the Lord himself shall give you a sign. *Behold a virgin shall conceive, and bear a son. . . .*" [48]

And this: "Despised, and the most abject of men, a man of sorrows, and acquainted with infirmity: and his look was as it were hidden and despised, whereupon we esteemed him not. Surely he hath borne our infirmities and carried our sorrows . . . he was wounded for our iniquities, he was bruised for our sins. . . . All we like sheep have gone astray. . . ." [49]

Much blood was to be shed in future ages over the denial and the acceptance of those prophecies. "I came not to send peace, but the sword." [50] . . . And Jerusalem shall be trodden down by the Gentiles, till the time of the nations be fulfilled." [51]

[48] *Isaias*, VII: 14.
[49] *Ibid.*, LIII: 3, 6.
[50] *St. Matthew*, X: 34.
[51] *St. Luke*, XXI: 24.

II

Pope Gregory IX

TWENTY-FIVE centuries passed over the secret grave of Moses, and the prophecies of Christ, for whom he had prepared the way by teaching, and if necessary *in extremis* by the sword, had been fulfilled literally and circumstantially. Jerusalem had been destroyed, with the great Temple of Solomon, and the survivors of the Roman terror were scattered as exiles through the world, and presumably would so continue until, in the words of Moses, "they confess their iniquities and the iniquities of their ancestors. . . ." [1] Meanwhile the authority to teach and interpret the divine revelation had passed from the High Priests, who had blinded the children of Israel, to Saint Peter and his successors: and for nearly thirteen centuries the mustard seed had been growing, under their inspired and infallible teaching (though not always impeccable conduct), into the mighty tree of its Founder's prophecy. The Christian Church, incredibly hated by the world, had gone forth to teach all nations; had taken over the civilizing mission and transmitted to the barbarians the culture of Rome: had tamed the Vikings and the Magyars, had given harmony and order to the whole Western world, and was ready to penetrate the East. Conserving the accumulated good of human experience, suppressing gradually and patiently the evil (slavery, for example; divorce, usury, abortion, suicide), the Mystical Body of Christ had woven its gospel into the very fabric of European laws and customs; not by violence, but with the gentle irresistible power of truth, good example, and, from time to time, martyrdom. Now at last the

[1] *Leviticus,* XXVI: 40.

21

mustard tree was about to burgeon into the magnificent century of Dante and Giotto, of Gothic cathedrals and teeming universities; of Saint Thomas Aquinas, Saint Francis, Saint Dominic, Saint Louis and Saint Ferdinand, Saint Elizabeth of Hungary and Saint Clare; the century in which European laws matured and European men became politically free. In every field of human endeavor, Christ, directly or indirectly, had overcome the world.

The achievement was all the more remarkable considering the obstacles. Of these the most constant, perhaps, was the downward pull of human nature itself, even in the Church: a tendency to laxity and corruption, from which the divine organization had to be purged from time to time, sometimes by the providential elevation of some extraordinary Pope; sometimes by the providential appearance of a new religious order. Again, the very presence of unbelieving Jews in various parts of Christendom made certain a dissenting minority, intelligent and irreconcilable, and, as certain Jewish modern writers have noticed,[2] a constant nucleus around which dissident elements in the Christian ranks could be assembled. This was often an additional reason why the Church found so troublesome those internal conspiracies, for such they usually were, to propagate heresies. There was always a considerable intercommunication and cooperation among the various enemies of the Church, even though they might differ radically among themselves on details of their unorthodoxy.

Of the external foes of the Church, Mohammedanism was one of the most dangerous and long enduring. Ideologically it was not external, but one of the great heresies, containing as it did many Christian elements, mingled with some borrowed from Judaism, and much gross and carnal materialism foreign to both; Mohammed taught, for example, the Virgin birth and Resurrection of Christ, yet denied His divinity; treated Him as a great prophet, yet demanded the conversion of His followers by the sword. But the organization of Islam was outside the Christian fold, and its pressure was from without. In its very first century of existence,

[2] For example, Abrahams, *Jewish Life in the Middle Ages;* Rabbi Newman, *Jewish Influence on Christian Reform Movements;* Browne, *Stranger than Fiction,* p. 222; Graetz, *History of the Jews,* III, ch. 15 and elsewhere.

this sect conquered not only large tracts of Asia, but all northern
Africa as far as the Atlantic, engulfed Spain, and invaded France,
leaving there, as on the crest of a highest wave, marks of its own
culture which persisted even to modern times. Nor did the danger
of a Mohammedan conquest of all Europe end with the battle of
Tours in 732. The peril endured for nearly a thousand years, now
menacing France, now Italy, now striking through the Balkans,
now through northeastern Europe: now on land, now on sea. In the
tenth century the Moslems held Sicily, whence they raided the
mainland of Italy, laid waste the country about Rome, profaned
the apostolic tombs, and collected tribute from the Popes. They had
been a threat to the peace and independence of European Christians
for nearly four centuries when Pope Urban II preached the First
Crusade against them in 1096.

More insidious was the danger to the safety and order of Christian life from those who bored from within as heretics. These were
generally people with some perverse or distorted view, which they
held to be the original and unadulterated gospel of Christ, and
tried to propagate under the appearance and guise of Catholics.
Some of these sectaries were pathetic, others were violent, and, like
the Donatists of St. Augustine's time, went about burning Catholic
Churches and persecuting Catholics. The Gnostics and the Aryans
alike made life miserable, when they could, for the orthodox.
Usually such groups of dissenters were organized as secret societies, with passwords, rituals and sometimes even a hierarchy of
their own. There was always some truth in their teaching, otherwise they could not have made any successful appeal to human
nature; yet the attendant falsehood always had the effect of dissolving true Christianity, to which it opposed itself as more plausible and more comfortable.

Now, it is a curious fact that the Church which treasured and
taught the Law of Moses in the New Dispensation of Christ, never
emulated his severity towards the heterodox within the gates for
a good thousand years after the Incarnation. The example of a God
who chose to let Himself be spat upon, mocked and crucified,
rather than invoke legions of angels to destroy His persecutors, a
God who could say in His death-agony, "Father, forgive them, for

they know not what they do!" cried out still from every crucifix that men saw on their churches and altars. The Christian leaders felt, as a rule, that the Church should take no action against her hypocritical members, who mocked her doctrines while pretending to believe them, except to excommunicate them. Some of the later Roman Emperors exiled heretics and confiscated their estates, on Plato's principle that those who opposed the ruler's religion was an enemy of the state; but in general they inflicted capital punishment only on those guilty of acts of violence against Christians. Saint Leo, Saint Martin and others had proclaimed that nothing could justify the Church in shedding blood, and Saint John Chrysostom probably expressed the mind of Christendom when he said, "To put a heretic to death is an unpardonable crime." It is obvious then that there was nothing in the teachings of the Catholic Church to encourage the coercion of dissenters by Catholics; quite the contrary. The rigor of Moses and his successors was felt to have been justified by the stern and peculiar necessities of his time, since God permitted it, but to be unjustified in the community of souls among whom dwelt the suffering God, whose children had sacraments to lead them back when they strayed.

Religion is likely to grow more intolerant when its interests become identical with those of the state, or most nearly so. In the theocracy of the Hebrews, of course, they were fused into one; hence, an offense against God was an offense against society, and vice versa. This tendency of human nature doubtless had its effects upon the minds of Christians as the Church approached the time of her completest triumph, and her doctrines, now unconsciously a part of the very texture of European law, custom and mode of life, were taken for granted by the secular as well as the religious power. There was a real separation of the Church and State in the Middle Ages, but it was a separation of function, not of principles. The average European in any country thought of himself first of all, not as a resident of this or of that country, but as a Christian. His faith was a gift of God, his race or nationality a mere accident. And yet, for the first thousand years, your Catholic man looked upon an occasional heretic as a freak or an oddity;

usually an untaught, unintelligent fellow who perhaps was a little mad, but would do nobody much harm, if left to himself.

To understand how this attitude changed about the year 1000, a modern parallel may be of some service. In the United States, during the nineteenth century and the first years of the twentieth, kidnapping, a crime comparatively rare and motivated by greed rather than violence, was punishable by a term in prison, whose length gradually increased, as the offense became more frequent, until it averaged from 10 to 25 years. If any one had suggested the death penalty, say in 1900, the conscience of the average citizen would have rejected the idea as unjustly severe. Then there occurred some kidnappings ending, by design or accident, in murder; and when the body of the Lindbergh baby, stolen from his crib, was found, public opinion almost universally accepted the view that the menace to childhood, to the home, to society was so grave as to justify the death penalty for such an offense. In several states, laws were passed inflicting capital punishment for kidnapping alone, even if no death resulted. Against this new rigor of the law there has been no protest of importance from public opinion anywhere in the States.

Something very similar happened when the Manichees began migrating to various parts of Europe, taking with them, not an intellectual protest against the tenets of the Church, not a mere refusal to believe or to practise (there were always unbelievers in Europe, and people who did not go to Mass, yet no coercion was applied to them), but something quite positive and quite sinister, which was felt to be a virus injected into the blood stream of human society. As most of them came from Bulgaria, they were called Bulgars, Bougres, and finally Buggers.

The Manichees, originally followers of Mani, were oriental dualists who believed virtually in two gods, one good, the other evil. The Father, or *Spiritus Vivens,* had created the universe, but when he summoned three spirits to carry on the work of creation, one of them, the Great Architect, apparently designed the future paradise, without any thought of man's attaining it. Adam and Eve, on the contrary, were the result of intercourse of the Devil, the creator and master of the world: and though Adam had light in him, Eve was all darkness—a notion which perhaps helped to color the Mohammedan concept of the essential inferiority of women. All life on this planet, being the work of the Devil, was evil. Marriage, since it propagated the curse of life, was evil. Suicide, since it ended the crime of living, was good and desirable. There was a horrible logic in all this, granting the initial premise that all matter was evil *per se*. There was even a germ of truth likely to appeal to a simple-minded person who had noticed that the world was full of miseries and disillusionments, and was either ignorant of or indifferent to the Church's explanation: that man, having sinned, was under the shadow of evil unless he accepted the redemption of Christ: but that all life, all creation, all *being* is good in itself, as the work of an all-beneficent God.

Toward the end of the twelfth century, many thousands of Manichees had settled in the cities of Lombardy and Languedoc. In the latter, especially, they were numerous, and, in spite of their professed aversion to the marriage relation, were increasing in numbers. Perhaps the south of France offered them a more congenial environment than they could have found anywhere else in Europe. It was not only fertile and sunny, but it had long been a refuge for unbelievers. There the Saracens had settled after their invasion of Spain and their defeat at Tours. There, as usual, large Jewish communities had assembled, finding the atmosphere of Islam more congenial, in general, than that of Christendom. There, in the course of centuries, had developed a semi-oriental civilization, easy-going, prosperous, sensual and colorful, with a veneer of Christianity which at times wore very thin. In such surroundings the Manichees probably found more encouragement than in most other lands of the West. "If the truth were known," says Lewis Browne, "probably it would be found that the learned Jews in Provence were in large part responsible for this free-thinking sect. The doctrines which the Jews had been spreading throughout the land for years could not but have helped to undermine the Church's power;"[3] and another modern Jewish writer goes even further, and considers it "indubitable" that the heretical doctrines

[3] *Loc. cit.*

of Southern France "were largely the result of friendly intercourse between Christians and Jews." [4]

Once the dissident movement was under way, however, the Jews quickly dissociated themselves from it. They were too intelligent to give up the sublime tradition of Moses, and their sane and well ordered family life, for any such grotesque nonsense as the various sects of Manichees preached. For grotesque nonsense it was, and vicious nonsense, too, that the Albigenses (the name usually given to the French Manichees, from their populous town of Albi) believed and practised. Nothing could be further from the truth than the theory of certain liberal historians that the "noble Albigenses" were a harmless and highly cultured people, persecuted by the Catholic Church out of sheer bigotry and intolerance.

Although these noble heretics lived in the land of troubadours, they themselves achieved nothing intellectually or artistically noteworthy. They called themselves the Cathari, or the Pure (Puritans). They were a secret society with an inner circle of initiates known as the Perfected. To join their True Church, as they called it, one must promise (1) to renounce the Catholic Faith (for they held that the Mass was idolatry, the Eucharist a fraud and an abomination, since bread and wine were creations of the evil spirit, the Church of Rome the whore of Babylon, and the Pope Antichrist) and (2) to receive, before death, their only sacrament, the *consolamentum*. After a year's probation, a member became one of the Perfected by a curious ceremony. He promised, among other things, never to touch a woman, never to kill an animal, never to eat meat, eggs, milk or any other food that came from animals (to which the souls of human beings might have transmigrated— besides, animals were the result of sexual intercourse), never to take an oath, never to travel or pass the night without a *socius*, never to take off his clothes upon retiring. When he had bound himself to all this and more, he was kissed twice on the mouth by each of the Perfected who were present, and he in turn kissed the next man, who passed the salutation along. If the candidate were a woman, she was not kissed, but merely touched with a book of the Gospels. Indeed, the aversion to women seemed to be the chief

[4] Abraham, *Op. cit.*

and common characteristic of those sects, and the one, naturally, which sane and healthy men were likely to look upon with ribald scorn. The *Cathari* called marriage prostitution, and held that carnal intercourse between the sexes was the original sin of Adam and Eve, and the greatest of all sins, since it begot children. Even perversion, therefore, was preferable, in their eyes, to marriage. Perhaps the prevalence of abnormal vice among them was exaggerated by their neighbors; yet, human nature being what it is, their tenets could hardly fail to lead in that direction.

It was easier to get evidence (and there is a great deal of it) that their fanatical logic translated the dogma that life was evil into the most shocking kind of action, a veritable ritual of suicide and murder. They would ask a sick man, or any other candidate for death, whether he wished to be a "martyr" or a "confessor." If a martyr, he was smothered with a pillow. If a confessor, he was starved to death. Even babies were thus barbarously murdered. Such was the result of a doctrine which regarded a pregnant woman as possessed by a devil, and, if she died in childbirth, certain to go to Hell. The *endura,* in fact, cost more lives than the Inquisition ever did.

The State as well as the Church was repudiated by these anarchists. Holding that it was evil to take life under any circumstances, they considered a soldier who defended his country a murderer, and denied the right of any one to inflict capital punishment, or indeed to administer justice in any way. Their refusal to take oaths struck at the very foundation, of course, of a feudal society. It is not surprising that the various sects of Manichees began to be victims of mob violence, which in itself constituted an additional problem for the officials of both Church and State. Even Lea, who was no friend of the Catholic Church, admitted that "the cause of orthodoxy was in this case the cause of civilization and progress. Had Catharism become dominant or even had it been allowed to exist on equal terms, its influence could not have failed to prove disastrous. . . . It was not only a revolt against the Church, but a renunciation of man's dominance over nature." [5]

All the ordinary machinery of order and of justice seemed futile

[5] *A History of the Inquisition in the Middle Ages,* i, p. 106.

against a secret society whose members, if arrested, would resort to every subterfuge and hypocrisy to conceal their true beliefs. Count Raymond V of Toulouse wrote in 1177 that the heresy had penetrated everywhere, dividing husband from wife, son from father, corrupting even many of the priests, and causing the churches to be abandoned. Wherever it worked, men degenerated into a fantastic state of savagery. Thoughtful persons wondered what could be done.

Even the great, energetic and resourceful Pope Innocent III was unable to put an end to the evil. Fearless champion of the idea that Saint Augustine expressed, that unless men followed the guidance of Christ's Church, the City of God, they could not escape the dominance of the Prince of this world and all the spites and discords of Hell, he persuaded England and France to make peace in 1198 by threatening them with an interdict if they refused; he forced Philip Augustus of France to put aside his concubine and ultimately to take back his lawful wife; he compelled King John of England to accept Langton, the choice of the monks of Canterbury, as Archbishop; and when the King defied him, even after the country was placed under an interdict, he brought him to reason by excommunicating him and releasing his subjects from their allegiance; he likewise excommunicated King Alfonso IX of Leon for marrying a near relative; and he saved Spain from falling anew under the Moslem yoke by proclaiming the Crusade that triumphed in the decisive battle of *Las Navas de Tolosa* in 1212. All this power to move the world, notice, came from the spiritual prestige of the Vicar of Christ: Innocent had no physical force which could have accomplished such results. Yet a great influence he was, not only for order and peace, but for progress. He was a patron of universities. He built the hospital which became the foundation and pattern of the medieval hospital system, on which our modern institutions are modelled.

One of the great trials of his pontificate was the rapid spread of the Cathari. He faced the menace with his usual energy. First he attempted to win back the Manichees to Christianity by reason. He sent some Cistercian legates, chief among them De Castelnau, to debate with the heretics and to impress upon the nobles the importance of stamping out the disease. Unfortunately the legates lived so luxuriously that the Puritan austerity of the Perfected seemed Christian by comparison, and few converts were made. Count Raymond of Toulouse meanwhile was playing a double game, and at last one of his retainers assassinated De Castelnau. Innocent took advantage of the public indignation to proclaim a crusade, which crushed the military power of the Albigenses in a campaign ending with the remarkable victory of Simon de Mont-fort at Muret in 1213, while Saint Dominic knelt in a church nearby and prayed for the Christian host.

The war then degenerated into a struggle for political power, ending in the domination of the French crown over Languedoc; and it did not solve the question which had set it in motion. The heresy, driven out of high places, flourished all the more in secret. When Innocent died at Perugia in 1217—his body looted by night and left almost naked in death—he had failed to destroy the anti-social thing either by persuasion or by the sword. It is inaccurate to say, as some historians have said, that he was the founder of the Inquisition. Like his predecessors, he set in motion investigations by bishops and legates; but not in the distinctive form that characterized the Holy Office of later times. That task was reserved for Innocent's grand-nephew, Ugolino, who, as Pope Gregory IX, is now generally considered the real father of the medieval institution.

Ugolino (Little Hugh) was born under a friendly star at Anagni, about 1170. His father, Matthew, Count of Segni, had ample means to give him a good start in that teeming and colorful world where men lived, fought, loved, hated, worked, studied and prayed with a gusto peculiarly Italian and medieval. All the influence of the Conti family was at his disposal, and like his great-uncle, he was sent to study at the University of Paris. Nature, too, had been generous with him. He was distinguished in form and feature, of excellent mind, unusually good memory, and an eloquence that his contemporaries described as Ciceronian. He understood and loved music. Profoundly Christian, he not only knew the Bible and delighted in explaining it, but he put its teachings into practice, living a chaste life in an age of much laxity, and ministering to the poor.

When his uncle Lothario was made Pope, in 1198, Ugolino, then twenty-eight, became his chaplain, and Cardinal-deacon of St. Eustachius. He was one of many examples of the good side of nepotism. If a Sixtus IV and a Paul IV lived to lament the promotion of their nephews to high office, other Popes found in relatives the loyalty and intelligence they failed to discover in strangers. So, at least, it was with Innocent III, himself the nephew of a Pope. In 1205 or 1206 he made young Ugolino Cardinal-Bishop of Ostia, and almost immediately sent him on a delicate mission to Germany, to make peace between Otto of Brunswick and Philip of Suabia. During the next few years, as he journeyed back and forth from Rome to Germany, Cardinal Ugolino showed himself a man of great skill, tact and prudence; one who never went to extremes; and a born peace-maker.

He was forty-six when Innocent died in 1216. He was immediately taken into the confidence of the next Pope, Honorius III, who sent him to Lombardy in 1217, to preach the Crusade, and, as a step toward that consummation, to make peace between the warring cities of the North. To the people of Pisa the Holy Father described his legate as "the angel of the Lord of Hosts, whose lips guard wisdom and from whose mouth the law may indeed be sought."

Ugolino was eminently successful in this mission. One of the reasons, both in Lombardy and elsewhere, was his gift for friendship. As Cardinal, he won the warm regard of men at such opposite poles of the spiritual, political and economic worlds as the Emperor Frederic II and Saint Francis of Assisi. As for the Hohenstaufen who had been the ward of Innocent III, had inherited Sicily from his mother and the Holy Roman Empire from his father, and lived more like an oriental caliph than a Christian prince, keeping two harems (he made no secret of his preference for Mohammedanism, though it was said he had no belief in anything)—a papal legate could hardly afford to offend a monarch whom a tradition as old as Constantine regarded as the protector and secular arm of the Church. But there was no political reason for cultivating the favor of a poor preaching friar, whom many of the great regarded with suspicion as an enemy of private property. The Cardinal in his scarlet robes and the *Poverello* in his thread-bare serge had something in common. Ugolino, too, must have been humble, and poor in spirit.

He so admired the poverty and simplicity of Francis that he put off his own costly garments, according to Thomas of Celano, and went barefoot, in a coarse habit like that of the Friars Minor, to "entreat for the things that made for peace." Francis was not even a priest, yet the Cardinal bowed before him, and kissed his hands. Once he noticed the contrast his own glittering military escort made with the ragged friars in brown, who had assembled in the huts around the Portiuncula, and cried, "How will it fare with us, who live so luxuriously, in superfluous delights?"

The Saint predicted that Ugolino would be Pope, for he far surpassed all the other Cardinals in virtue and holiness. He used to call him "the right reverend lord Hugo, bishop of the whole world."

The friendship of Cardinal Ugolino probably contributed in no small degree to the final success of his mission. His preaching in Italy had been a triumph. The little group that had assembled around him in 1208 had grown so numerous, and so beloved by the poor and the sick to whom they ministered, that he began to think of other countries: and at the first general chapter of his order in 1217, he divided the whole world into Franciscan prov-inces. Various lieutenants were assigned to teach here and there. He himself resolved to go to France.

Ugolino persuaded him to give up this idea, and to journey instead to Rome. It would be better to make his position at the Vatican more secure before attempting a great expansion.

"Brother," said the practical Cardinal, "there are many prelates who would gladly hinder the good of your Order in the Roman Court. But I and the other Cardinals who love this Order of yours could more readily help and protect it, if you remain within the province."

It was sound advice, as Francis was warned in that famous vision he had of the little black hen trying to gather under her wings an infinite brood of chicks. "I am this hen," he concluded, "small in stature and black by nature. . . . The chicks are the brethren multiplied in number and in graces, whom Francis' strength suffices not to defend. I will therefore go to Rome, that by the rod of her power the ill-disposed may be smitten and the children of God may enjoy full freedom."

Ugolino was in the city when Francis arrived. On the day when the humble Saint spoke before the Pope and the Curia, his friend the Cardinal was "in an agony of suspense, praying to God with all his might that the simplicity of the blessed man might not be despised." It was a decisive moment for the Franciscan order, but Francis was equal to it. He spoke so fervently and so joyfully of his work and his hopes that he began to move his feet as if dancing, "not as in wantonness, but as flowing with the fire of divine love." No one thought of laughing. On the contrary, some of their Eminences were moved to tears "as they wondered at God's grace and the steadfastness of the man." What a scene!

It was Cardinal Ugolino who brought together, in a memorable meeting, Saint Francis and Saint Dominic. The Spanish priest, also father of a new order, was preaching Lenten sermons in Rome that year. Like Francis, he was a flame of love, and sought nothing but the extension of God's kingdom on earth. But as no one man is great enough to express all the approaches to Divinity which are included in the Catholic Church, each saint emphasizes, as a rule, some one or two of the many facets of the truth she presents: and it might be said that Francis sought God primarily through His charity, Dominic through His justice. The Italian's first appeal was to the heart, the Spaniard's to the head. Francis reawoke the love for God and one's fellow man which is the essence of Christianity. Dominic, profound scholar and theologian, was about to provide the Church with defenses against those who sought to destroy her in the realm of ideas. (This is not to deny that the Franciscans had great scholars, and the Dominicans a generous share of what have been called the Franciscan virtues!) From both stemmed movements which, commencing with individual Christian lives, overflowed into society and renewed arts, sciences, civilization itself: from Francis an awakening in poetry (he was a precursor of

Dante), of painting, drama and architecture; from Dominic, the mighty teaching of Albertus Magnus and the angelic philosophy of Saint Thomas, of which the world is still unworthy.

Ugolino helped both saints. He was now father protector of the Franciscans, and, as such, he induced Francis to modify his original rule. In fact, he wrote out the new rule himself, adding not a few things which gave acute pain to the *Poverello*. Ugolino has been much blamed for this. Some have said that he debased the Franciscan ideal, and made possible the division and relaxation that occurred after the Founder's death, indeed started during his lifetime with the election of the low politician Brother Elias. On Ugolino's side it is urged that without his practical sense the work of Francis would have died with him; that the first rule was excellent when monks were few, and under the direct influence of a man whose sanctity and genius no one could resist, but would be quite different when he was dead, and his followers numbered many thousands.

Ugolino was popular with the friars. When he visited them every year during their Whitsuntide Chapter, clad always in one of their brown habits, they would come forth in procession to meet him, and he, dismounting from his horse, would walk back with them to the Church of Saint Mary of the Angels, where he would sing Mass and preach to them, while Brother Francis (who was not a priest) would chant the gospel.

Ugolino was fifty-seven (not eighty, as one tradition has it) when he was elected Pope. He had no desire for the elevation; in fact, he tried to escape when the Cardinals threw the Papal mantle over him, and in seizing him they tore his clothes. He consented, however; and at last, one fine April morning he rode, vested in gold, with the double diadem on his head, through streets carpeted with tapestries from the looms of Egypt and draped with silks from India and the East. Rare incense burned about him. Trumpet answered trumpet from all the walls of Rome. Prelates and nobles made a glitter of many colors, children sang, Greeks and Jews offered homage in their own tongues. Yet the new Gregory IX would rather have been breaking coarse bread, perhaps, with the men in brown who came back singing from sweeping foul hovels

in the slums of antique cities, or from putting alms into the bony
hands of those lepers who howled in the lazar-houses outside the
walls, or pawed over heaps of garbage for some edible morsel. God
had set the feet of Ugolino on a different road, in its own way
a harder test of his poverty of spirit, and he did not flinch from
it again.

It was soon evident, indeed, that he was a strong Pope. He was
one of the great lawgivers of the Middle Ages. He set his Dominican chaplain, Saint Raymond of Penyafort, to work compiling and
arranging all the Decretals of his predecessors and his own—a
monumental collection which became the universal law of Christendom. He remained the staunch friend of the new orders. He was
a father to Saint Clare (though he could never persuade her to
accept property, even as a gift). Contemporary of many saints,
including King Louis IX of France and King Fernando III of
Castile, he had the joy of canonizing, among others, his dear friends
Francis, Dominic, and Elizabeth of Hungary.

In addition to all the ordinary burdens of the Pope's office,
Gregory had to face the three great major problems that haunted
so many of the medieval pontiffs: (1) the conflict, by arms and
propaganda, between Christendom and Islam; (2) the conflict of
Church and State within the confines of Christendom; (3) the
conflict of the Christian Faith against the most destructive of all the
heresies.

The first two seemed one problem in the beginning. For the
State with which Gregory had chiefly to deal was the vast one
ruled by the Emperor Frederic II, and the essential need of the
Crusade at the moment was to get that monarch to undertake it.
Frederic was as indifferent to the menace of Islam as he was to
the lofty concept of his guardian, Pope Innocent III, that the Vicar
of Christ was arbiter over all the kings of the earth. It was not
many months after the accession of Gregory IX that the friendship
between them began to cool; and the break came over the new
Pope's call to a Crusade. Frederic, at his coronation, had taken the
cross from Ugolino, then Bishop of Ostia, and had solemnly vowed
to go to the Holy Land. Now, as Pope, Gregory called upon him
to keep his vow, and "to fight the battles of the Lord." In a second

appeal he begged the Emperor, in virtue of the long-standing affection he had for him, to begin to develop that part of his nature which he had in common with angelic natures, and to repress that which he had in common with the beasts of the field.

Frederic, as it later appeared, was more beast than angel; and he had no intention of rendering any such service to Christendom as the Pope suggested. Not that he was averse to fighting: he was ready enough for that, and could do it as ruthlessly as any Turk, when it came to putting down the democratic aspirations of the cities of Lombardy, for example, or warring against the Pope, or against his son. He had no intention, however, of taking the sword for anything but his own grandeur. This strange man, with the courteous and winning manners of a troubadour, and the dark, crafty, cruel and effeminate heart of an oriental despot, this patron of education who wrote Italian poems, and pried into the secrets of medicine, philosophy, mathematics and nature herself with insatiable curiosity, who loved art and literature (thanks to the training Pope Innocent III had given him), was not exactly the hard-headed rationalist and agnostic that he has been made to appear by some anti-Catholic historians. It would be nearer to truth to call him a mixture of rationalism and superstition. He was dominated by astrologers, and followed their advice as Gregory would have followed the intuitions of prayer. He had a pseudo-mystical concept of his own position, quite different from that of Constantine, or that of Charlemagne. The reverence he often denied to the office of the Pope, he consistently bestowed upon his own: looking on himself as a sort of lay super-Pope, an imperial caliph of Christ on earth, an emanation of the Deity, to be adored as Nero was adored; yet immune from the law of Christ, whom he scorned, as he scorned Moses. Though surrounding himself with Jews, he despised the ancient revelation of the Jews. It was not without reason that some of his contemporaries said that he aspired to be nothing less than *Lord of the World,* a title with which his ruthless grandfather Frederic Barbarossa had been flattered.

Well aware that he was blamed for the ruin of the Fifth Crusade in 1217 (though in truth it must be said that he had the fever prevalent among his troops, and probably was unable to sail), he now went through the motions of answering the call of Gregory, and appeared with an army of Brindisi about three months after a mighty host, including from 40,000 to 60,000 Englishmen (according to various estimates) had assembled there, waiting for him, and dying by thousands from the burning heat and disease. Frederic set sail in September, with Ludwig, husband of Saint Elizabeth, but presently turned back, put in at Otranto, announced the death of Ludwig from fever (though some said it was poison), and went to Puteoli to enjoy the baths. So another Crusade was ruined, and thousands of brave men had died to no purpose. Public opinion ran high against the Emperor, and against Gregory IX also, for it was said he had not prepared sufficiently for the expedition.

Frederic offered neither explanation nor apology. The Pope thereupon publicly excommunicated him for his repeated failure to keep his solemn vow.

The following year Frederic sailed for the Holy Land, to the astonishment of Christendom, with only a few ships and a handful of knights. At Acre the clergy and knights of the crusading orders avoided him, as an excommunicate. It was obvious that he must have had an understanding with Malek, to go with so insignificant a force, and he had hardly landed when the Caliph sent him presents of gold, camels, and elephants. Early the next year the two signed a peace which was to last ten years. Frederic was acknowledged as king of Jerusalem, and there, in the Church of the Holy Sepulchre, he set the crown on his own head, for there was no one else to do it, nor would any priest give him a blessing. Malek el Kemel sent him a harem, however, and Frederic disported himself in oriental fashion until it was time to set sail for home, despised and laughed at by Christians and Moslems alike. The Mohammedans at least could afford to laugh. They took Jerusalem back the following year.

Before sailing for Palestine, Frederic had bought up certain nobles in Rome, who became leaders of his party there, and on orders from him stirred up riots against the Pope, who thus found himself publicly insulted, and in consequence left the city, and went to Perugia. Gregory had been there two years when the Great Flood of February, 1230, overwhelmed Rome to the roofs of the houses in the lower sections, and washed the steps of Saint Peter's. Seven thousand were drowned. The receding waters left everywhere carcasses of dead fish and animals, and even "a great mess of serpents," which rotted and stank. The plague then stole into the stricken city. The people, convinced that they had been punished for permitting Christ's Vicar to be ill-used, begged Gregory to come back, and when he did so, received him with delirious joy.

Meanwhile Frederic, alarmed by the disloyalty and rebellion of his son Henry, who made common cause with his enemies in Germany, concluded a peace with the Pope in the summer of 1230 at San Germano, promising to be obedient to the Church in the things wherein the Church had rights, and was absolved by Gregory, who dined with him afterwards. But when Henry was beaten and safely stowed in an Apulian prison, Frederic decided to crush the Lombard League, knowing, of course, that Gregory, like his predecessors, would be the champion of the free cities against the despotic claims of the Empire; not only because the cities were right, but because the independence of the whole Church would be endangered if the same potentate ruled Italy as well as Germany. When Gregory protested against the barbarity of Frederic's Saracen soldiers in Sicily, who carried off stones from the churches to build their barracks, the Emperor replied loftily that he had not the eyes of a lynx that he could see from Germany what his officials were doing in Sicily, nor had he a voice of thunder, to make his wishes heard there, and he really did not know what they might be doing in his absence. In turn he accused Gregory of instigating the renewal of the Lombard League.

In 1236 Frederic invaded Italy, sacked Vicenza, and the following year defeated the League at Cortenuova. Thus began a war of fourteen years, which put a stop to the Crusade, ruined the trade of Lombardy, and imposed on the Church heavy expenses which Gregory had to meet by unpopular taxation. Meanwhile Enzio, a bastard son of Frederic, gave an historic example of ruthlessness in Sardinia.

Gregory retaliated by excommunicating Frederic a second time on Palm Sunday, 1239, stating seventeen reasons; and he absolved all of the Emperor's vassals from their oaths of allegiance to him.

Frederic was furious. Denying that he was excommunicated, he denounced Gregory as "the so-called vicar of Christ, the preacher of peace, but in reality the author of schism," and urged the Cardinals to call a General Council against him.

Gregory, writing to all the Princes of Europe, compared Frederic to the Beast of the Apocalypse, "coming up out of the sea, having seven heads and ten horns, and upon his horns ten diadems, and upon his heads names of blasphemy;" and answering the Emperor point by point, he gave the lie to "this hammer of the world, eager to crush kingdoms and to make the world a desert."

Frederic retorted by an appeal to the Cardinals. God, he said, had appointed the Papacy and the Empire to rule the world, but Gregory was no other than the Anti-Christ, who had perverted the established order, and had defamed him by quoting him as saying that the world had been deceived by three great seducers, Moses, Christ, and Mohammed. What he really believed, said Frederic, was that Our Lord was coequal with the Father and the Holy Ghost, that Mohammed was in Hell, and that Moses was the friend of God. In opposing Gregory he was not opposing the Church, which he loved and honored, but only a corrupt individual.

In spite of his disclaimer of the cynical epigram about Moses, Christ and Mohammed, men continued, then, and for centuries to believe that Frederic had said it. It sounded more like him than the pious sentiments with which he was trying to separate the Cardinals from the Pope.

While all this was going on, both Gregory and Frederic had learned with deep concern of the rapid spread of many of the Manichean sects; and it is a curious fact that although modern "history" to a great extent has attributed the resulting severity to the Pope and his successors, it was actually the infidel Emperor, surrounded by his Jews and Mohammedans, who first undertook to defend society against them by force.

What Frederic thought of these heretics is set forth in no ambiguous terms in one of his edicts. Here they are "rapacious wolves" who have made their way among the sheep; *"angeli pessimi"* . . . "sons of the father of depravities and author of vileness and fraud, lying in wait for simple minds; these snakes who ensnare the female doves; these serpents, that are seen to crawl secretly, bearing in their tails a virus to spew forth under the sweetness of honey, and while they pretend to administer the food of life, they mix a potion of death, like some most fatal poison." [6]

The Manichees had already split into many secret societies, differing on details, but agreeing in general that life was the work of the devil, and that the Catholic Church was not the door of Salvation. Frederic in another edict denounced the following varieties: "Catharos, Patharenos, Speronistas, Leonistas, Arnaldistas, Circuncisos, Passaginos, Josefinos, Garatenses, Albanenses, Franciscos, Bagnarolos, Commixtos, Waldenses, Roncarolos, Communellos, Varinos and Ortholenos, with those of Aquanigra, and all heretics of both sexes." [7]

The Byzantine Princess Anna Comnena left an interesting description of the Bogomils, or God's Friends, who went about with hair unkempt, heads down, and gloomy faces muffled up to the nose, muttering as they walked. They despised learning, all formal religion, and all prayer except the Lord's Prayer. Contemporary observers (not of their sect) agree that they were full of pride, ignorance and hypocrisy, and although their consciences would not allow them to attend Mass, to marry, or to take oaths, they would resort to every trickery, and all manner of equivocation to escape detection. Nearly all of these sects rejected the authority of the Old Testament, along with a great deal of the New; the Cathari and the Bogomils, for example, asserted that the Old Testament was the work of the Devil. It was the Catholic Church that consistently defended the Law of Moses against them, as in the course of time she would be found defending it against twentieth-century advocates of the racist heresy.

---

[6] Bernard Gui, *Practica,* Douais ed. 1886, p. 307; also in Eymeric, appendix, p. 28.

[7] Gui, *loc. cit.;* Eymeric, *loc. cit.,* p. 29.

Following the spirit of the Roman Law, of which there was a great revival at that time, Frederic, as early as March, 1224, ordered that any heretic convicted in Lombardy be burned alive (the ancient penalty for high treason). In 1231 he applied the same law to Sicily, and in 1233 to the whole Empire, begging the Pope, "to whom it belonged to remove any evil that threatened the Christian religion," to cooperate with him, so that the madness of the heretics might be struck down with the two swords which were in their hands.

Gregory made a very cool reply to this overture. He knew how much real love Frederic had for the Christian religion; but he answered diplomatically that he was very glad indeed to hear that the Emperor was zealous for the Faith, and would certainly give all support in his power to help him "destroy the contagion of so baleful a pest." He hoped, however, that His Imperial Majesty would take care in future not to commit to the flames men who were not heretics, but merely his own personal enemies—as, added Gregory, had already happened, to his great grief and that of others, "and to the scandal of all Christendom and the dishonor of God."

Gregory had already decreed, in 1231, that it was just for the Church to support the State's right to inflict capital punishment for so grave a threat to its own existence; and he had decreed, that year, that Cathari, Patarenes, Poor Men of Lyons, and others might be handed over, after conviction of heresy by the Church, to the secular courts. Some Patarenes in fact were burned in Rome. Catholics were ordered, under pain of excommunication, to denounce heretics, or their secret meetings, and even to point out those who differed from their neighbors in the ordinary habits of life. Gregory commanded the hierarchy to publish his decrees concerning heretics, and to try to induce the local civil authorities to carry out the Imperial decrees.

The stiffening of Gregory's attitude was influenced a great deal by reports from Germany concerning the activities of a sect known as the Luciferians. They were a secret society who had already developed a fixed ritual. During their ceremony of initiation, the novice kissed a sort of toad, allowing its tongue and saliva to enter his mouth. Then he was confronted by "a man of ghastly pallor, all skin and bones," with black piercing eyes, and when he had kissed this apparition, which was icy cold, "all memory of the Catholic faith left him." A banquet followed. Then the ceremony was renewed, with the appearance of a black cat, to which obscene reverence was paid. The following conversation ensued:

Presiding *Magister:* "Spare us!"

Another Brother: "Who has commanded this?"

"The Chief Master."

A fourth: "And we must obey."

The lights were put out, and "unspeakable orgies" were said to have followed. When they were finished, there came forward the figure of a man "all fiery from his loins upward, and thence downward all hairy like a cat." ("So they say," added Pope Gregory.) The Magister offered part of the novice's clothing to this apparition, saying, "Master, what has been given to me, I give to thee."

The Apparition: "Well have you often served me. . . . To your charge I do entrust what you have given me."

In Gregory's account of all this, he adds that the Luciferians often profaned the consecrated Host, doubtless stolen from the altars, or obtained in other ways. Satanists of all periods have manifested hatred, as one might expect, for the Body of Christ.

Incredible? Not to those who have read, in the revelations of certain European converts from Freemasonry, descriptions of the fantastic rituals of some of the continental Grand Orient lodges in the enlightened Nineteenth Century. In some of the advanced degrees of the secret societies that prepared the seeds of the Spanish War of 1936, as they had nourished those of the French Revolution and other modern upheavals, one reads of a hymn to Satan, of a crucifix spat on and trod upon, of a dog presented to the novice for an unseemly kiss; and one wonders whether this is not somehow a survival of one of the grotesque aberrations of the Middle Ages, reported by Gregory IX. At any rate, many of his contemporaries who, as Dr. Mann observes, were neither fools nor knaves, believed all this of the Luciferians of Germany; and it is not surprising that the Pope shared the general indignation, and took steps to cause the deluded wretches or scoundrels who perpetrated such madness to be discovered and brought to justice.

Gregory was motivated by considerations of charity as well as justice. Something had to be done to put a stop to mob violence which often fell most cruelly on the innocent. He had learned a bitter lesson from his mistake in reposing confidence in the confessor of Saint Elizabeth of Hungary, Conrad of Marburg, who had been recommended as a "virtuous and zealous" priest. To this cold and merciless man—zealous to the point of fanaticism, as events proved, and more virtuous in chastity than in charity—the Pope had given a commission to investigate heresy, and to denounce to the secular courts those found guilty of such practices as were reported of the Luciferians. Gregory's instructions were:

"When you arrive in a city, summon the bishops, clergy and people, and preach a solemn sermon on faith. Then select certain men of good repute to help you in trying the heretics and suspects brought before your tribunal. All who, on examination, are found guilty or suspected of heresy must promise complete obedience to the commands of the Church. If they refuse, you must prosecute them according to the statutes that we have already promulgated."

Conrad did not follow these instructions. Instead of working only with "men of good repute," he allowed himself, in his hatred of the vile anti-social thing he was prosecuting, to cooperate with, and to be used by, two rabble-rousers who had no sort of mandate from the Holy See, but took it upon themselves to lead mobs of vigilantes against those suspected of intimacy with the unholy toad. One was Conrad Dorso, or Torso, a Dominican, but not a priest; the other a layman named John, described by a chronicler of the time (not inaccurately, it would seem) as "a one-eyed deformed scoundrel." These two worthies were careful at first to pick out victims who were poor and without influence. Finding themselves well supported by popular indignation—for what sane man would not detest the Luciferian nonsense?—they became bolder before undiscriminating judges who, sensitive to the danger and to the pressure of public opinion, were often willing to condemn a man on their mere assertion; and they managed to suggest to King Henry and many of the nobility the advantages to be gained from denouncing rich heretics and confiscating their goods. This was such a crude and obvious piece of brigandage that they needed some spiritual reputation behind which to hide it. It was a rare stroke for them when they enlisted the help of Conrad of Marburg, who, for all his severity, was known to be incorruptible.

All went well until they accused one Henry, Count of Sein, a man once rich, but now in straitened circumstances. It happened that he was a good Catholic, with all the courage that a clear conscience can give, and that his relatives still had influence enough, if he had not, to get his case tried by the Council of Mainz, and by them referred to Rome. Thus the proceedings came under the eyes of Pope Gregory, who immediately ordered the prisoner set free, and wrote him, "We are astonished that you have borne this injustice so long without reporting it to us. We would not have this state of things go on any longer, and we annul all that has been done."

Before the Pope could punish Conrad, the relatives of some of the other victims took the law into their own hands, and murdered the holy man and his fellow judges. There was no great sorrow in Germany on this account; nor perhaps in Rome. Yet Gregory was not the man to endure the assassination of his own commissioner when he himself had been on the point of taking action against him.

"The Germans have always been wild men (*furiosi*)," he cried, "and now they have got crazy judges!" He ordered the bishops to excommunicate the murderers of Conrad. He decreed also that in all future trials for heresy, the proper forms of law must be carefully observed, and that a cleric who gave any form of consent to, or was even present at, a trial unlawfully conducted, would incur the grave censure of "irregularity."

Yet it was clear that something more had to be done, if the evil of the secret societies was to be suppressed without encouraging some equally grave, or graver abuse, such as mob violence, the reign of cupidity, or imperial political vengeance. The great Pope must have pondered long and diligently over this problem. As Father of Christendom, he did not desire the death of his misguided children, but their amendment. How could he avert the poisoning of all society without permitting injustice to the innocent, or to the heretic himself? How could he steer a safe course between the exasperating indifference of many bishops, or their susceptibility to local pressure, and, on the other hand, the cruelty of the mob or of the Imperial officers?

In his perplexity, Gregory had what seemed a happy inspiration. Why not use the new mendicant orders? Even Lea has acknowledged their usefulness. "The establishment of these orders seemed a providential interposition to supply the Church of Christ with what it most sorely needed. As the necessity grew apparent of special and permanent tribunals, there was every reason why they should be wholly free from the local jealousies and enmities which might tend to the prejudice of the innocent, or the local favoritism which might connive at the escape of the guilty. If, in addition to this freedom from local impartialities, the examiners and judges were men specially trained to the detection and conversion of heretics; if they had also by irrevocable vows renounced the world; if they could require no wealth and were dead to the enticement of pleasure, every guarantee seemed to be afforded that their momentous duties would be fulfilled with the strictest justice— that while the purity of the Faith would be protected, there would be no unnecessary oppression or cruelty or persecution, dictated by private interest or personal revenge."

Gregory, as Lea conjectures, probably had no intention of establishing a permanent tribunal. He was legislating for an emergency; and the Dominicans, with their thorough training in theology, seemed admirably fitted to act as auxiliaries to the bishops. Some of the hierarchy, of course, would not like this: prelates had been known to be a little touchy about outside interference, even from Rome. So Gregory wrote a tactful letter to the bishops of southern France, explaining the situation:

"Seeing you wrapped in the whirlwind of cares, and scarce able to breathe under the pressure of overwhelming anxieties, we think it well to divide your burdens, that they may be more easily borne. We have therefore determined to send preaching friars against the heretics of France and the adjoining provinces; and we beg, warn and exhort you . . . to receive them kindly, and to treat them well, giving them . . . favor, counsel and aid, that they may fulfil their office."

Thus the Dominicans, and to a lesser extent the Franciscans, were sent to the places where heresy most abounded. Some went to Germany, but no formal and permanent Tribunal was established there until 1367. Alberic, a Dominican, was sent to Lombardy, with the title, *"Inquisitor hereticae pravitatis."* One of his successors was killed by a mob; another, Saint Peter of Verona, Dominican son of Manichee parents and founder of the Inquisition at Florence about 1245, was assassinated by heretics on the road from Como to Milan in 1252. It was dangerous business, being an Inquisitor, for the heretics were often rich and influential, with the courage of fanaticism and despair. Hunting them out was not a task that any young Dominican aspired to for its own sake. This was particularly true in southern France, where the Cathari, having survived the Crusade, put up a long and stubborn fight against the new monastic courts. A Dominican convent was sacked by some heretics in 1234. Eight years later the Inquisitor Arnaud and several other Dominicans were assassinated. The Dominicans then asked the Pope (Innocent IV) to relieve them of the mission. This he refused to do. In 1244 an armed force of Catholics broke the resistance of the Cathari by storming Montsegur, whence the murderers of the Dominicans had ridden forth, and burned 200 heretics without trial, even as the Levites of Moses had slain the idolators. After that the Inquisition was accepted by the secular officials. Gregory IX sent Inquisitors to Spain in 1238. One of them was poisoned by heretics.

In his instructions to his emissaries, the Pope created the form which distinguished the Medieval Inquisition from the bishops' investigations and all other previous Christian attempts to deal with the problem of heresy. Into a town, reported to be infected with heresy, the friars were to go and publicly proclaim that all guilty of offenses against the Faith must appear and abjure their errors. Those who did so were to be forgiven. To detect those who did not, the friars were to set in motion an *Inquiry;* and if two witnesses testified that such and such a man was a heretic, they must place him on trial, acting at all times, of course, in cooperation with, and only with the consent of, the Bishop. There was no provision for torture; it was not used for about twenty years.

Gregory apparently had no intention of founding a new institution. He was making use of the new religious orders to help the Bishops in a duty that had always been theirs. Bishop Douais, a profound student of source documents of the early Inquisition, believed he was also trying to forestall encroachments by Frederic II, who had already begun to burn political enemies on the pretext that he was defending the Faith. Gregory proposed to decide by theological experts, not by politicians or soldiers, who was a true Catholic and who was not. Once that question was answered, the Church was free to reconcile or excommunicate the guilty, and the State, if it considered him dangerous enough, could inflict on him the usual penalty for high treason.

Like Moses of old, Gregory desired to protect the children of God from error. Like Moses, he commanded an Inquiry, or Inquisition, to be made with all diligence; and he demanded the evidence of at least two witnesses. Like Moses, he insisted that crimes against God should not go unpunished. So far the parallel is exact, but no further. Moses, under the old dispensation and in a more primitive age, drew no fine distinctions between the penitent and the obstinate, the deceiver and the deceived: let the guilty be stoned to death. Gregory's principal desire was to draw the misguided heretic back into the grace of God; only if he insisted on being God's enemy (and the enemy of society as well) was he to be cut off from the Church, and abandoned to the scantier mercy of the State.

It took some time and effort to get the new arrangement working so that it would accomplish what the Pope desired, and avoid the evils he was trying to eliminate. Most of the judges, it is now generally admitted, were much superior to their contemporaries of the secular courts. Yet now and then, in spite of the watchfulness of Rome, a Conrad of Marburg was bound to appear in the personnel, to cause trouble and injustice. There was, for example, Robert the Bugger, so called because he had been a Manichee, before becoming a Catholic and a Dominican. This heartless scoundrel, as he proved to be, was one of the first Inquisitors. Gregory IX, ignorant of his true character, sent him in 1233 to northern France, where he conducted investigations at Péronne,

Elincourt, Cambrai, Douai and Lille. Then, making no secret of his ambition not to convert the heretics but to burn them, he went, flushed with success, to Champagne, and to his gratification found at Montwimer a large group of Manichees under a Manichee bishop, Moranis. Within a week he had condemned more than 180, all of whom he had burned on May 29, 1239, in the presence of the King of Navarre and other dignitaries.

When complaints of this reached Rome, it was too late to save the victims, but Gregory suspended Robert *le Bougre* at once, and ordered him imprisoned for life.

The Pope was in the last months of his life, wearied with many cares, and engaged in a final struggle with Frederic II for the independence of Italy. The German Emperor, still smarting under the second sentence of excommunication, had decided to show his enemy, once and for all, who was Lord of the World; and at the beginning of 1240 he entered Tuscany with a great army, and made towards Rome. It was not the first time, nor would it be the last, that a Vicar of Christ would stand firm against some tyrant from the north, and Gregory calmly awaited the blow. Meanwhile he had summoned a general council of all Christendom, princes as well as prelates, to hear the matters at issue between him and the Emperor. This was precisely what Frederic had often demanded when he thought it would be embarrassing. Now he fairly raged at the idea, and sent troops to seize bishops and other delegates on their way to Rome from all parts of Christendom. Many of the Lombard and Genoese delegates died in Frederic's dungeons, and the French bishops might have shared the same fate, but for Saint Louis' demand for their release. Thus the Council was made impossible. Although the people of Rome took arms to defend their city and their Pope, it was obvious that they could do little against the overwhelming force that was approaching, with Frederic at its head. On the way the Emperor seized a castle, and finding it full of the Pope's relatives, had them all hanged.

The summer heat of 1241 was terrible. Thus far Gregory, though more than sixty, had astonished every one by his youthful appearance and serene courage. Now, when the news of the murder of his relatives arrived, he seemed suddenly to wither up into a feeble old man. Presently he became a sick old man as well, and a few days later received the Last Sacraments.

As the Hohenstaufen conqueror approached the capital of Christendom, to attack it as he had never attacked any Moslem stronghold, the Teutonic Knights far to the north were being shattered by the sons of Genghiz Khan; and Tartar hosts were again murdering Christians and burning Christian shrines that the man who called himself the right arm of God should have been protecting. But Frederic at last was marching into Rome.

Gregory was beyond his vengeance. This did not keep the Emperor from gloating in the most disgusting fashion over his remains, before he went back to his hawks and his harem. Thanks to his interference with the Council and the bishops, no Pope could be elected for two years. When at last Innocent IV mounted the chair of the Fisherman, he could reckon on the opposition of the Emperor until the day, fortunate for Christendom, when the gifted and perverse man left a world that had been his plaything. One version was that he dropped dead without the sacraments; but the truth seems to be that he died more slowly of dysentery; and according to his son Manfred, who was present, he acknowledged the Holy Catholic Church as his mother, drew a will in which he made such reparation as he could, and with a contrite and humble heart received absolution from the Archbishop of Palermo. His power was already slipping; only seventeen years later the Hohenstaufen empire came to an end with the battle of Tagliacozza, and the murder of his grandson Conradin. It it not permitted to us to know how God judged Frederic, or how clearly the greatest of all poets read the Infinite Mind when he presumed, without hesitation, to place him in the Sixth Circle of Hell, among the heresiarchs:

> *"Qua dentro è lo secondo Federico,*
> *E il Cardinale, e degli altri mi taccio."* [8]

[8] Inferno, canto X, lines 119-120.

III

Bernard Gui

ONE of the most successful of the Inquisitors who carried on the fight begun by Gregory IX—and a long uphill fight it proved to be —was a Frenchman named Bernard Guidonis, or more commonly, Bernard Gui.

All that is known of his early life is that he was born at Royeres, near La Roche-L'Abeille, in Limousin, about the year 1261, or some twenty years after the death of the ninth Gregory, and entered the Dominican Order at the Convent of Limoges in 1279, when he would have been eighteen years of age. Was his family rich or poor, noble or proletarian? These were matters of no importance in the very real community of talents that always flourished within the hierarchical organization of the Roman Catholic Church. All we hear of Bernard is that after he completed the usual course of studies, in what were doubtless the best schools in Europe, he received his tonsure from the hands of Father Pierre d'Astier, later bishop of Perigueux, and became one of that quiet, well-disciplined and intelligent army of men in robes of black and white, who had set in motion, in a few decades, one of those powerful reform movements by which the Church periodically renews and cleanses the humanity of which her children are necessarily composed.

It is hardly likely that young Brother Bernard had any ambition to achieve the dangerous eminence of an Inquisitor of Heretical Depravity, much less see any of his fellow mortals burned to death. He was first of all a priest imbued, like most of the sons of Saint Dominic, with a great and sincere love for Christ, and a desire to see the Kingdom of Heaven prevail through the entire world.

Secondly, he was a born student, whose lucid and concise Latin paragraphs indicate that he was endowed with some literary ability, and probably could preach better than average sermons. Not brilliant, but a good hard-working prudent methodical man, he spent about fifteen years toiling as an obscure teacher and student in various schools of his order, before he began to emerge from the crowd. In 1284 he taught logic at Brives. The next year he studied theology at Narbonne, and during the next two or three years, at Limoges and Montpellier. He worked under several masters of renown—Friar Hughes de Creyssel, Friar Bernard Lamothe, Friar Itier de Compuhac and Friar Guillaume de Quinsac; and at last, in 1291, he himself became a master, and went back to teach theology at the convent of Limoges as *sous-lecteur*.

The following year he received an assignment that was bound to have a momentous effect upon the course of his life. He was sent to be *lecteur* in theology at the Dominican convent at Albi, the stronghold of the *Cathari* or *Albigenses,* and there he was to remain for the next thirty-one years in the very heart of the Manichee country. He taught also at Castres (near that grotto in which Saint Dominic, according to tradition, used to pray), and at lofty Carcassonne. In 1294 he went back to Albi, to serve as Prior for three years. He was prior at Carcassonne (1297-1301), Castres (1302-1305), and Limoges (1306).

He began to play a more important part in the annual chapters of the order. He was *socius* of the prior provincial in 1306, *definiteur* at the chapters of 1307 and 1308; and at the one in 1311 was elected Master General of the order. As Vicar of the province of Toulouse he presided at the provincial chapter of 1314. He was *procureur* of his order at Rome for a considerable time, and so won the confidence of Pope John XXII that he was entrusted with several delicate and difficult embassies in France and Italy. A discreet, tactful, adroit, peace-loving man he must surely have been; an able administrator, who could be energetic and courageous when energy and courage were required.

When there was need of a new Inquisitor at Toulouse in 1306, Brother Bernard was probably the best qualified man who could be found for the position. He had ridden countless miles over those white dusty roads that wind between the mountains and the bluest of oceans, where Saracen pirates of the early Middle Ages used to ravage the Mediterranean coasts of Italy and Spain in slim boats with lateen sails, like shark's fins, such as may yet be seen. In that almost preternaturally clear and limpid air and dazzling sunlight, where everything is as sharply outlined as in a dream, Friar Bernard learned to know the contours of lovely hills and valleys checkered with vineyards, olive groves, and (toward Toulouse) with fields of yellow grain, all cultivated to the last handful of a soil that had been ploughed and harrowed for thousands of years. He learned to know the thrifty stone or brick houses with red tile roofs gleaming in the sun, and who lived in them. He knew the ways of a half-oriental, perhaps never more than half-Christianized civilization, that had been old when Caesar camped his legions on the banks of the Garonne, a civilization that had assimilated the culture of Rome, and afterwards the culture of Islam and the culture of Jewry, but never that of the northern barbarians. It was a warm, passionate, pleasure-loving civiiization in which, beneath the Cross that everywhere rose above old hill-crowning churches, men paid lip service to Moses or to Christ, while they secretly gave their hearts to the dark perversities of the Talmud or of life-hating Manes, or the plausible sensualities of Mohammedanism. There the troubadours who (with the bards of Ireland) fathered the lyric poetry of Europe, gave to lovely woman, long after she had gained respect through the cult of the Virgin, a sentimental adoration just as poisonous, in its way, as the more brutal possessiveness of pagan Rome. In a district where marriage was despised, lust was honored all the more.

Concerning those dark vivacious people with their quick laughter and quick anger, with the blood of many races in their veins, and the broad vowels of the *langue d'oc* on their tongues, Friar Bernard had the inside sort of knowledge that priests have of human nature; and it is evident from his writings that while he hated any inhuman idea that tended to dissolve the faith of Christ, he looked upon most of his fellow mortals with a charitable eye, and was not lacking in a sense of humor. He must have known well enough, too, that the aberrations of many of these people were not wholly their own fault. They had not all been well instructed in the doctrines of Christianity. And one reason for this was the failure of priests to teach them. When Saint Dominic went to Languedoc, he found a pretty widespread contempt for the clergy; and if some of this was due to the incessant propaganda of Jews, Saracens and heretics, it must be admitted that much of it was well earned by the luxurious and easy living of some of the priests themselves, and sometimes by notorious scandals among them. Part of the blame belonged, too, to rich political bishops who had no real interest in their flocks; it was not for nothing that one of the Thirteenth Century councils sternly reproved such prelates for failing to have the truth taught by their priests. The Dominicans and Franciscans were now supplying this need, and waking up the secular clergy to the urgency of their duties. Much more needed to be done; and Brother Bernard, who was an historian of note (he had written, among other works, a complete history of the Christian Era from the Incarnation to the Thirteenth Century) undoubtedly realized that the Church was in the midst of one of her great periodic trials, and that here, in this little earthly paradise of some fifteen thousand square miles between the Pyrenees and the Mediterranean, a profound issue must soon be settled: whether the enemies of Christ would succeed in shattering the unity of Christendom by driving a wedge of heresy between Rome and the West and North, or whether the Church would be free to continue her mission of carrying to all mankind the teachings and commands of the crucified God, who, alone of men since the beginning of time, could repeat, and continue to convey through His Church, the awful words that Moses had heard on Sinai: I AM.

When Friar Bernard rode into Toulouse one day in 1306, he was probably as well prepared for the terrific responsibility that had been placed upon him as a man could be; and from what is known of his later life, it is fair to assume that he quietly and efficiently assumed, as a sacred duty, functions that no normal man could desire for their own sake. He was probably met by an imposing array of clergy, nobles and townspeople, and conducted by them, in a colorful procession, with music, to the edifice around which the town was built, the Cathedral Church of Saint Stephen—a heterogeneous piece of architecture, with romanesque nave and Gothic choir, housing the bodies of Saint Edmund of England, of Saint Barnabas, and (in part) of Saint George; the head of Saint Bartholomew, a portion of the true Cross, and a thorn from the crown of Christ that Baldwin II, Emperor of Constantinople, had given to Saint Louis the King. There, hushed in the presence of such sacred memorials, were gathered most of the people of Toulouse, ready to listen as the new Inquisitor mounted the ancient pulpit from which Saint Bernard and Saint Dominic had preached. It was the will of Christ, he said, that all Christians be as one, under His appointed Vicar, the successor of Saint Peter; and he offered the usual period of grace to any who had been foolish or wicked enough to listen to the wolves in sheep's clothing who sought to divide the flock that they might destroy it. This term of grace extended, according to circumstances, from two weeks to thirty or even forty days, during which time any Catholic who had adopted heretical beliefs, or had conspired with heretics, or had aided and abetted or defended or concealed them in any way, must appear before the Inquisitor and confess. Such a person was regarded not as a criminal but as a sinner, and it is obvious from such records as remain that the object of the Holy Office was not to punish him but to reconcile him with the Church. On confessing and abjuring his sin, he naturally received a penance, as he would in the confessional for any ordinary sin. This penance varied with the gravity of his offense. For holding heretical opinions in secret, he would be told to say certain prayers, or to perform other religious acts, in private. If he had given scandal by openly defying the authority of the Church or leading others to do so, he would be made to fast on specified days, even to undertake a pilgrimage; and for certain crimes which, like heresy, involved some affront to the Divine Majesty (bigamy, blasphemy, sodomy and other offenses thus fell under the jurisdiction of the Holy Office), he might get a term in prison. But the whole emphasis at that stage of the procedure was on the side of mercy.

To prove his sincerity, the heretic who confessed was required to give the name of other persons he knew, who were guilty of similar offenses, and any further information he might have.

Bernard Gui had his headquarters in a house that Peter Cella had given to Saint Dominic, near the Chateau Narbonnais. There had previously been two Inquisitors for Languedoc, but the Dominicans had encountered such powerful opposition from the Manichees, and had sustained so many casualties in the conflict, that they had made Toulouse the inquisitorial capital of the entire province, from whose far corners, therefore, suspects were brought, if they did not come to confess of their own accord. There, for seventeen years, Friar Bernard directed the hunt for heretics, and their reconciliation or punishment. During the whole period he tried 930 cases, an average of about 54 a year, or slightly more than one a week. This conveys an impression of ceaseless activity that is perhaps far from accurate. He presided at only 18 *sermones generales* during the whole period. This suggests that he dealt with his heretics in batches, about once a year on the average. Certain historians have given him the unsavory credit of burning hundreds. The misunderstanding upon which this estimate was based is made clear by the following account of his sentences, found among the records at Toulouse:[1]

Released from obligation to wear crosses	132
Sentenced to pilgrimages, without wearing crosses	9
Released from prison	139
Sentenced to wear crosses	143
Imprisoned	307
Dead persons, who would have been imprisoned	17
Abandoned to the secular arm and burned	42
Dead persons, who would have been abandoned	3
Bones exhumed and burned	69
Fugitives, declared excommunicate	40
Sentenced to be exposed in the stocks or pillory	2
Priests sentenced to be degraded	2
Exiled	1
Houses ordered demolished	22
Copies of the Talmud condemned and burned (two cartloads)	1
Interdict removed	1
Total	930

[1] Douais, *Documents*, I., p. 205.

If we assume that the 307 imprisoned include the 139 released from prison, and if we deduct the condemned dead persons, the houses and the Talmuds, and if, finally, we assume that those 132 released from wearing crosses were included in the 143 sentenced to wear them, we find Bernard passing sentence, at the lowest possible computation, on 527 living persons. If those released from wearing crosses were sentenced by some previous Inquisitor, the number will be 659. To avoid any temptation to "whitewash" Bernard's Inquisition, let us take the lower total, 527. Of this number he reconciled the vast majority; he sentenced 307 to prison, but released 139 of them before the expiration of their terms, and he sentenced 143 to wear crosses, the equivalent of the yellow garments later called *sanbenitos*. The 42 whom he found to be obstinate and incurable heretics, with no hope of reformation, he turned over to the secular officials for the usual penalty. These constitute about eight percent, by the highest possible reckoning, of the total number of the condemned. They would be a much smaller percentage of the total number who were accused or denounced. Of those not arrested for lack of evidence, or released without a trial, we have no accounting, but there were many. Of the forty-two burned at the stake, seventeen were condemned at one *sermon generalis* on April 5, 1310; this suggests that the Inquisition had discovered some unusually large and dangerous conspiracy, and had dealt rigorously with it. During his whole term of office, Bernard failed in eight of every hundred cases that he prosecuted—for the Inquisitor deemed it a failure when he could not win a man back to a sane Christian life, and had to turn him over to the State. The general average for the Medieval Inquisition may have been higher. It has been estimated that ten out of every hundred convictions ended at the stake.

Toward the end of his term, when he had learned nearly all that was to be learned about the ways of heretics and how to deal with them—especially, as he always emphasized, how to make them confess and return to the true Church—Bernard compiled, for the benefit of the Inquisitors under him, a *Practica*. Here, in one large tome, he included all the advice that occurred to his experienced mind, all possible forms that might be needed for investigation, trial and sentence, using letters and documents that he himself had written, with names of culprits or suspects omitted. In this volume, as in a mirror, we behold the famous judge and a great deal of his early fourteenth century stage; and because the portrait is unintentional, it is all the more valuable. Out of the polished but concise and sometimes legalistic Latin periods arise the lineaments of long forgotten priests and archbishops, Jews and Saracens, sorcerers, witches and diviners, heretics of many fantastic varieties, the very form and pressure of that chaotic time.

Bernard arranged his book in five parts. The first contained the formulae for the arrest of suspects, for acts of grace, in general for the merciful part of the procedure. The second dealt with formulae for condemnation of sundry offenses in public *sermones,* and so on. The third contains 47 formulae, chiefly for sentences, the very ones used by Bernard himself. The fourth is a lengthy treatise on the powers of the Holy Office, with many citations of apostolic letters of the Popes defining its functions, limitations, responsibilities and privileges. The fifth contains the texts of Papal bulls dealing with the Inquisition, and of Imperial decrees by Frederic II and his successors; but it deals even more particularly with the characteristics of various sorts of heretics, and how to recognize and detect them.

This last section, of course, is the richest in human interest. It begins with a caution by the author that not every disease can be treated with the same medicine. Therefore the Inquisitor, *"ut prudens medicus animarum,"* must consider each case in its own peculiar circumstances and characteristics, "and circumvent the crafty evasions of the heretical with the bridle of discretion, so that with God's help the winding serpent may be drawn from the cesspool and abyss of errors by an obstetrical hand." [2] After this somewhat complicated metaphor, he passes on to "the errors of the Manichees of modern times." Brother Bernard, as a modern man, found it intolerable that in the year of grace 1307 there should

---

[2] *"Ut, favente Domino, de sentina et abysso errorum obstetricante manu educatur coluber tortuosus."*—*Practica Iquisitionis Heretice Pravitatis,* ed. Douais, Paris, 1886, *quinta pars,* pp. 236-7.

persist in the Christian world believers in an old pagan superstition that paid worship to two gods, one good and one evil, and
went about the business of propagating their dualism with such
crafty hypocrisy that the unskilled layman was likely to be taken
in by them. Besides their two gods they had two meanings for all
their theological terms: one for themselves, the other for outsiders.
They believed in two distinct creations. Everything invisible and
incorporeal (and of course their own sect, as a notable exception)
belonged to the good creation. Everything visible and tangible—
including the Roman Catholic Church, its priests and its sacraments, belonged to the bad creation, the world of matter, the
devil's universe. Hence they found it logical to identify the visible
Church that Christ had established with the scarlet woman of the
Apocalypse. Their own shadowy church of the world beyond was
the true church of Christ, who, in their terminology, became equally
shadowy almost to the point of non-existence; He never had a
human body, they said, and therefore never could have died on
the cross or risen from the dead. They called His Church the
mother of fornications, the great Babylon, the *meretricem et basili-
cam diaboli,* the synagogue of Satan. With singular astuteness, they
said that their own sect was the true Virgin Mary, begetting
spiritual sons and daughters for God; and penance and chastity
alike consisted in joining them, to become first Pure and then
Perfect. Asked whether he believed in Christ and the Blessed
Virgin, a Manichee would answer, "Oh, yes, of course," attaching
his own private and particular meanings to the terms; hence the
difficulty of pinning him down, and making him admit just what
he did believe. Even learned men, if inexpert, were often deceived
by this hypocritical patter which paralleled and travestied the whole
range of Christian teaching. Hence great care must be exercised,
wrote Brother Bernard, to pin them down and make them explain
themselves. "And from then on the task is to exhort them to conversion, and to show them where they were wrong by every
manner of means, through men highly expert and industrious." [3]
Such heretics had better be detained a good while, and questioned

[3] *Ibid.,* p. 239.

repeatedly, "first, that they may often be invited to conversion, for the conversion of such is the most useful of all, because the conversion of the Manichean heretics is commonly sincere and rarely pretended; and when they are converted, they disclose everything and lay open the truth, and reveal all their accomplices, whence follows great fruit." However, if they refused after being given chance upon chance to confess, they were to be sentenced in due course, and turned over to the secular arm.

People were to be suspected of Manichean tendencies who kept three Lents per year, who refused to eat meat or eggs or anything else that came by way of generation or coïtus in animals. A man who would not touch a woman was likewise to be looked upon with suspicion. There were many other signs—such as saying the *Pater Noster* in a certain manner while breaking bread; or bowing to the earth, joining hands, and saying some such formula as *"Benedicite!* Good Christians . . . pray God that he save us from an evil death (by which Bernard said they meant a death with the sacraments of the Catholic Church) and bring us to a good end, or to the hands of faithful Christians" [4] (meaning the *endura* or murder ceremony of the Cathari). Such were the signs by which one might recognize one of the apostles of suicide, the merchants of death who smothered little children to save them from the curse of living.

In preaching, the Manichees of the early fourteenth century would make a clever beginning by declaring that they were good Christians, who would not swear or kill either man or animals; that they held the faith of Jesus Christ and his Gospel, and were the successors of His apostles. They then went on to explain that this was why they were persecuted by the prelates, priests and monks of the Catholic Church, and especially by the Inquisitors, just as Christ and His Apostles had been persecuted by the Pharisees. They went on to inveigh against the alleged evil lives of the Catholic clergy, their pride and greed, and any other faults that occurred to them to mention. They then passed on to the Sacraments of the Church, which they ridiculed and vituperated—espe-

[4] *Ibid.,* p. 240.

cially, says Bernard, the Holy Eucharist, which they declared could not be the body of Christ, "because even if it were as big as one very large mountain, the Christians would already have eaten it all up." The Host was made of the chaff of wheat, which passed through the tails of horses and mares, as when grain is purged *per sedacium*. It went into the *latrinam* of the bowels, and passed out *per turpissimum locum,* "which it could not do, so they say, if God were there." [5] A very literal minded and unimaginative folk, the Manichees, and in their own simple way much more materialistic than the Catholics whom they derided.

The Waldenses or Poor Men of Lyons, wrote Bernard, first appeared about the year 1170, making a claim similar to that of the Manichees, that they were the true Christians and successors of Christ's apostles. They believed in Heaven and Hell, but denied that there was a Purgatory. They would take no oaths, and would obey no authority but that of God, which they claimed to receive directly, as holy and perfected men; by the same token denying the authority of the Church, the validity of her sacraments, and the priestly functions of her ministers. Every holy person, they said (including women), was a priest, and their sect alone was holy; hence they absolved one another of sin. Yet in spite of their aversion to ecclesiastical organization and obedience, they imposed both organization and obedience on all who joined their society, "which they call a fraternity," added Brother Bernard. The members had to promise strict obedience to their superiors. (Some of these dissenters had a hierarchy, even a sort of Pope, of their own.) They promised to live in evangelical poverty, with no private property, and in chastity. Theoretically, at least, they owned all things in common, and lived on the alms given to them; "and he who is greater among them distributes and dispenses to any one according to his need." They were Communists of a sort, these Waldenses, and like many radicals, held somewhat unconventional views of sexual morality. "The Waldenses praise continency to their believers," said Bernard, "yet they grant that one ought to satisfy a burning lust by any manner of shamefulness whatsoever, their

[5] *Ibid.*, p. 242.

apostles explaining this by saying it is better to marry than to burn (*Melius est nubere quam uri*), for it is better, they say, to satisfy lust by any act of shame whatsoever than to be tempted in the heart within; this, however, they keep very secret indeed." [6]

Twice a year the members of this sect would quietly assemble to hold a general chapter or convention in some town where they were met by some believer, and led, as if they were merchants, to the house of a member, where they would elect officers and carry on other business. They made a great point of visiting churches and hearing sermons, and always maintained a very devout exterior. "Commonly they call themselves brothers, and say they are the Paupers of Christ or the Poor Men of Lyons." Those who had achieved perfection never worked with their hands. Married men, on joining the sect, gave up their wives when initiated. [7]

Considering the ease with which these self-canonized saints could pervert the hell fire with which Saint Paul threatened fornicators into the flame of lust, Bernard felt it necessary to warn his readers that the Waldenses were the hardest of all heretics to trap and expose. He furnished the Inquisitors with an account of a typical cross-examination, based upon his own experience:

"When one of them is arrested and brought forward for questioning, he comes as if fearless, and conscious of no evil in himself, and secure. Asked if he knows why he is arrested, he answers very calmly, with a smile, 'Sir, I will gladly tell you the reason.' " [8]

He is never at a loss. When the Inquisitor asks what his faith is, he answers,

"I believe all that a good Christian ought to believe."

"And what do you consider a good Christian?"

"He who believes as the Holy Church teaches to believe and hold."

"What do you call the Holy Church?"

"Lord, what you say and believe to be the Holy Church."

[6] *Ibid.*, p. 249.
[7] *Ibid.*, p. 251.
[8] *"Domine, Liberenter discerem a vobis causam."*—

"I believe the Holy Church to be the Roman Church, over which the Pope presides as lord, and other prelates under him."

"And I believe it," answers the suspect promptly (meaning, "*I* believe that *you* believe it," explains Bernard).

Asked about particular articles of faith, such as the incarnation of Christ, His resurrection and ascension, he replies,

"Firmly I believe it."

Does he believe that the bread and wine are changed in the Mass, at the words of the priest, into the body and blood of Our Lord?

"Ought I not indeed to believe that?" he demands, innocently.

"I do not ask whether you *ought* to believe it, but *do* you believe it?"

"I believe whatever you and other good doctors order me to believe."

The Inquisitor asks if the "other good doctors" are not the masters of the man's sect, and the real dictators of his opinions.

"I believe you also, willingly," replies the prisoner, "if you teach me anything that may be good for me."

Inquisitor: "You judge a thing to be good for you, if I teach you what those other masters teach you. But answer simply, if you believe the body of the Lord Jesus Christ to be on the altar."

Heretic: "I believe." (He means, says Bernard, that "there is a body, and all bodies are of the Lord Jesus Christ.")

Inquisitor: "Do you believe that there is that body of the Lord which was born of the Virgin and hung on the cross, and arose from the dead and ascended into Heaven?"

Heretic: "And you, Lord, don't you believe it?"

Inquisitor: "I believe it absolutely."

Heretic: "And I believe it in the same way (meaning, "I want you to believe that I so believe it.")

Urged again to answer explicitly and directly, he tries another tack. "If you wish to interpret everything I say as otherwise than plainly and simply, then I don't know what I ought to answer to you. I am a simple man, and uneducated. Please don't try to trip me up in my words."

Inquisitor: "If you are a simple man, reply and act simply, without any cloak of words."

Heretic: "Willingly."

Inquisitor: "Then you are willing to *swear* that you have never taught anything against faith . . . ?"

Heretic (trembling a little): "If I ought to swear, I will swear willingly."

Inquisitor: "You are not asked whether you *ought,* but whether you are *willing* to swear."

Heretic: "If you order me to swear, I will swear."

Inquisitor: "I don't compel you to swear, because since you believe an oath to be unlawful, you will try to shift the blame to me for compelling you; but if you swear, I will hear."

Heretic: "What then shall I swear, if you don't order me?"

Inquisitor: "In such a way as to dispel the suspicion that is against you, because you will be counted as a Waldensian heretic, believing and holding that every oath is unlawful and sinful."

Heretic: "How ought I to speak when I swear?"

Inquisitor: "Swear as you know."

Heretic: "Lord, I don't know unless you teach me!"

"Then I say to him," wrote Bernard, forgetting for the moment to be impersonal, "If I had to swear, then, I would raise my hand and touch the holy gospel of God, and say, 'I swear by this holy Gospel of God that I have never taught and believed anything that might be against the true faith that the holy Roman Church believes and holds.'"

The heretic, "shuddering, and almost like a man who does not know how to form even the words," mumbles something rather verbose which he intends to have sound like an oath, but not to have the form of an oath; or something in the way of prayer meant to simulate an oath, such as, "If God will aid me, and this holy Gospel, (to show) that I am not a heretic, or have not been one, or have not said this or that."

Inquisitor: "Well, will you swear?"

Heretic: "Didn't you hear me swear?"

Finally, when the heretic is straitened by questions, and at the end of his resources of evasion, he pretends to weep, or flatters the

Inquisitor, saying that he will perform any penance to free himself from the infamous charge of which he, a simple man, is wholly innocent.

Sometimes, however, he will say he is ready to swear a simple and straightforward oath. At this point the Inquisitor must answer, no doubt with a show of sternness, "If you now swear so that you may go free, take notice that one oath will not be enough for me, nor two, nor ten, nor a hundred, but I shall ask for *tociens quociens,* for I know that among you you dispense from and allow for a certain number of oaths, when necessity compels, to set yourselves or others free. But I will require oaths without number, and especially if I have witnesses against you, your oaths will not be of any good to you, and then you will stain your conscience swearing against him, and on that account you shall not escape."

Bernard adds, "In the anxiety of such a moment I have seen some of them confess their errors, that they might go free." [9]

This page from the great Inquisitor's notebook reads like a scene from a comedy; yet often a man's life, yes, and the fate of his soul, hung upon the outcome of the conversation.

Sometimes the Waldenses pretended to be simple-minded or insane, *sicut David coram Achis,* and they had a thousand other ways of prolonging their examinations, in the hope that the Inquisitor might weary of the seemingly endless task and let them go, or that they might discredit him among the Catholic laity, "because he seemed to trouble simple men without cause, and to seek a pretext for destroying them in a too cautious examination." [10]

One of the most troublesome of the sects with which Bernard Gui had to deal was that of the Pseudo-Apostles. Their doctrine was first formulated, about 1260, by Gerard Segarelli of Parma, who, after a vain attempt to join the Franciscan Order, and a formal abjuration of his errors in 1294, relapsed, and was burned at Parma in July, 1300. His successor as "Pope" of this curious order of anarchists, for such they were, was Dulcinus Novariensis, the bastard son of a priest, says Bernard, who had a woman named Margarita as "his consort in crime and heresy." Clement V

[9] *Ibid., loc. cit.*
[10] *Ibid.,* p. 256.

preached a crusade against them, and they were both burned, but the sect continued to grow, and spread from Lombardy into southern France. Later the anarchists fled to Spain in 1315, and the following year we find Brother Bernard writing from Toulouse to Archbishop Roderic of Compostela, giving an account of their grotesque beliefs, and how they could be recognized and brought to justice.[11]

The fundamental dogma of the *Pseudo-Apostoli* was one that would have made them a menace to any society, ancient, medieval or modern: they owed obedience, they said, to no mortal man. Being in a state of evangelical and apostolic poverty and perfection, they were subject only to God. They claimed, in fact, that the authority which Christ gave to Saint Peter and the other apostles had passed, not to the Roman Catholic Church (which they called "a reprobate church without fruit," the "great whore of Babylon") but through their founder, Gerard Segarelli, to them. They were the only true Christians, and led the perfect life. They had the power, denied even to Catholic priests, of dissolving marriages. A man could divorce his wife, without her consent, or a woman divorce her husband without his consent, to enter their order. Outside their ranks there was no possible salvation. Certainly there was none, according to them, in the Roman Catholic Church; but unlike other heretics, they made some curious exceptions. The primitive purity of the Church had continued in the Catholic Church, they admitted, up to the time of Saint Sylvester. After him all the Popes were "prevaricators and seducers," with the single exception of *"Frater* Pietro de Martone, who was called Pope Celestinus."

Must we infer, from this manner of speaking of Pope Celestino V, that Bernard was one of those numerous clergymen who shared the error that led Dante to place this unique Pontiff in Hell among the pusillanimous? It was in 1294, the very year when Bernard went to Albi to be prior for the first time, that one of the strangest events in the history of Christendom occurred. An emaciated Benedictine hermit, eighty-nine years old, who lived on Monte Morone in the Abruzzi, with an iron chain around his body,

[11] *Ibid.,* pp. 350-353.

emulating Saint John the Baptist, had had a revelation that if the Cardinals, at deadlock for more than two years after the death of Nicholas IV, did not elect a new Pope within four months, God would visit great calamities upon His Church. A sudden desire swept through the Sacred College to make the hermit Pope; and the poor prophet was startled one day in July by the approach to his solitude of three eminent prelates, followed by a huge crowd of monks and laymen, who had come to tell him of his election. He yielded, after many tears, to the will of God, entered Rome clad in sackcloth, on an ass, led by two kings, and was Pope for six months, during which he set a beautiful example of evangelical poverty by sleeping in a little hut on the floor of the Vatican, and on the other hand proved himself a complete failure as an administrator, for he could not say "no," and sometimes gave the same benefice to four or five different applicants. At the end of the year, he resigned and fled to the mountains. His successor confined him to prison, where he died. Dante put him in Hell; but God put him in Heaven. For in 1313, the very time when Bernard Gui was hunting down heretics who considered Celestino the one true Pope of "modern" times, that penniless successor of Saint Peter was being canonized, oddly enough by the rich Pope Clement V; and he is now venerated by all faithful Christians each May 19. All this indicates not only the invigorating scope of the Catholic Church, but the difficulty of an Inquisitor's position, and how important it was to make careful distinctions in an age when saints and heretics both wore sackcloth robes, and had certain superficial appearances in common. San Celestino, like the Waldenses, kept three Lents a year. The essential difference between them was that he was humble, sincere, and always obedient to the will of God, as revealed in His Church.

The False Apostles were often very successful in passing themselves off on simple people as saints. Imitating Saint Francis and his friars, they used to go singing along the roads or through towns. They used to recite in a loud voice the *Pater Noster,* the *Ave Maria* and the *Credo.* They were always saying *Vigilate et orate,* or *Penitentiam agite, appropinquabit enim regnum caelorum.* They even had the effrontery to sing the *Salve Regina.* But their conception of chastity was very different from that for which true Franciscans implored the help of the Queen of Heaven. Dulcinus, second leader of the "Congregation," whom Pope Clement V denounced as "a son of Belial" and an "enemy of the human race," [12] used to call his companion Margarita his "sister in Christ." When she was captured, this "sister" was found to be with child; and she and Dulcinus asserted to their followers that she had conceived by the Holy Ghost. Likewise, according to Bernard's *Practica,* the fellow-apostles of Dulcinus used to take about with them women whom they called *"sorores in Christo,"* and "used to lie in beds with them, asserting mendaciously and falsely that they were troubled by no temptations of the flesh," [13] being of course Perfect. Is it not possible that many of the tales circulated centuries later by other sects, to the injury of true priests and nuns, had their origin in the blasphemous hypocrisies of these false priests and false nuns of the thirteenth and fourteenth centuries?

Of all the fanatics or fakirs who made capital out of the tremendous popularity of Saint Francis and his friars, Bernard had most trouble with those who called themselves Poor Brothers of Penance of the Third Order of Saint Francis, and were commonly known in Italy as the *Fraticelli,* and in southern France as *Beguins* or *Bequins.* Some had actually been members of the Franciscan Order, others not. There has been much confusion about these sects and their names. Usually they went about, both men and women, in brown sackcloth habits, sometimes with hoods, sometimes without. In the district of Toulouse they became numerous enough to attract the attention of our Inquisitor about 1317. Like the Pseudo-Apostles, they had an elaborate and fantastic eschatology, which promised the early destruction of the Roman Catholic Church by King Frederic of Sicily. Like most Manichees, they distinguished between two churches, the material Church of Rome and the spiritual congregation, which of course was their own assembly of saints. (Why they considered themselves more *immaterial* than Catholics does not seem clear—a later inquisitorial document describes them as generally sleek and well-fed!) With the

12 *Ibid.,* pp. 340-1.
13 *Ibid.,* p. 339.

want of consistency common to most heretics, they paid the highest honor to Saint Francis, without noticing, apparently, the love and obedience he always gave to the Catholic Church and all her ministers. Indeed, they said that the rule of Saint Francis and the Gospel of Christ were one and the same thing, and that no Pope or prelate had power to change an iota of the constitution of the Franciscan Order. They were much interested in the Antichrist, whose appearance some of them promised in 1325, others in 1330 or 1335. All would be destroyed, except the members of their sect, and those they would convert from the twelve tribes of Israel. So Bernard described them.

The *Fraticelli* had the sorry distinction of being the first professing Christians in the West to challenge the infallibility of the Pope, and the first to proclaim the modern heresy of the Totalitarian State—though this, actually, was but a reappearance of the worship demanded by the pagan emperors of Rome. After the death of Saint Francis, his followers had divided, on the issue of absolute poverty, into two principal factions, the *Zelanti,* or Spirituals, and the *Relaxati,* later called the Conventuals. A group of the former had been allowed by Celestino V in his short reign to settle in Italy as hermits, in absolute poverty; but the next Pope, Boniface VIII, had revoked the permission. A long and bitter conflict ensued between the leaders of this party and Avignon. Angelo da Clareno, excommunicated by Pope John XXII, defied the Pope's decree, and in 1318, set himself up as general of the congregation of spirituals who had been dissolved by the Pope. He appointed provincials and other officials, established new monasteries, and, in short, founded an independent Francisan Order, known as the *Fraticelli.* He and his followers declared that John XXII, then residing at Avignon, was not truly Pope, since he had abrogated the Rule of Saint Francis, which they considered the same as the Gospel. All his decrees were invalid, they said. All other religions and prelates were damned. By committing mortal sin, a priest lost his sacerdotal powers. Fra Angelo eluded the Pope and the Inquisitors until his death in 1337. His followers split into various groups, each changing the doctrine to suit its leaders. Some still considered themselves

Catholics, others separated completely from the Church. Some have been confused, erroneously, with the Beghards.

Finally the Franciscan Order itself became involved in an unfortunate controversy with Pope John XXII, when Michael of Cesena, General of the Conventuals, convoked a chapter which declared, in 1322, that Christ and the Apostles possessed no property, either separately or collectively, and therefore no Christian should own any. This obvious error, arising from an attempt to make a counsel of perfection into a compulsory rule for all men, was declared heretical by the Pope. Michael of Cesena and his friends then turned a doctrinal dispute into a political quarrel of the utmost danger. Finding a champion in the ambitious Ludwig the Bavarian, they appealed to him to go to Italy and "purge" the Church. Some of them—Ubertino of Casale, John of Jandun and Marsilius of Padua—wrote a manifesto called *Defensor Pacis,* which put forth a democratic-totalitarian program, in which the clergy and people would choose a General Council, which in turn would choose a Pope. The Pope derived his authority, not from Christ, but from the General Council *and from the Emperor.* This, in effect, was a proclamation of the spiritual power of the Emperor, who could of course, through such sycophants as some of the *Fraticelli* were, control the General Council they envisaged. The result of all this was that Ludwig crossed the Alps and had himself crowned Emperor at Rome; whereupon he nominated an Anti-Pope, Nicholas V. Pope John XXII removed Michael of Cesena from office, and the Franciscans themselves repudiated him, returning, under his successor, to complete obedience to the rightful Vicar of Christ. Nicholas V, too, finally cast himself at the feet of John XXII at Avignon, and begged forgiveness. Gradually the quarrel subsided, but not until it had done untold harm both to the Franciscan Order and to the Church. It added infinitely to the difficulties of the Inquisitors; for some of the *Fraticelli* were good and devout men, who had been deceived by fanatical or ambitious leaders, while others were impostors, who used the robes of Saint Francis to gain an easy living, and to cloak the vilest sins. Against these latter, the tone of Brother Bernard was always sharp and contemptuous.

There were two other types of heresy against which he warned his fellow inquisitors. One of these he called "the perfidy of the Jews." Now, in fairness to the Holy Office, it must be noticed that never, in its entire history, did it proceed against the Jews, either on racial grounds as Jews, or on religious grounds as members of the synagogue. Far from attacking the Law of Moses, it defended that revelation against certain sects of heretics, as an essential part of Catholic truth. Over the Jew as Jew it claimed no jurisdiction. It was a Christian tribunal, which concerned itself with Jews only when they were Christians, or when they went out of their way to commit offenses against Christians, either by deriding Christian beliefs or ceremonies, or by persuading Christians to give up the Faith.

That the Jews, scattered throughout Christendom, carried on a continuous and effective propaganda which, while it persisted, was bound to make impossible the complete Christianizing of society, is freely admitted by Jewish scholars, as I have taken note elsewhere. "As a whole," says I. Abrahams, "heresy was a reversion to Old Testament and even Jewish ideals. It is indubitable that the heretical doctrines of the southern French Albigenses in the beginning of the Thirteenth Century, as of the Hussites in the Fifteenth, were largely the result of friendly intercourse between Christians and Jews." [14] Without pausing here to inquire why there should be a distinction between Old Testament "and even Jewish" ideals, unless the latter refers rather to the Talmud and the Kabbala than to the Law of Moses, it may be admitted that the very presence of the Jews in every large community was in itself a challenge to the claims of the Church. This condition the Church was willing to accept; for grace was a gift, and if a man did not have it, he could not be coerced.

If the Jews had confined their activities to the synagogue and their allegiance to the Law of Moses, a great deal of conflict and even bloodshed might have been avoided. Unfortunately, during their dispersion, under all the incredible sufferings and affronts

[14] *Op. cit.* See also similar references above, p. 22, n. 2. It is difficult to understand why Jewish and Christian accounts are usually kept in separate compartments, so to speak, when truth is served by putting them together.

they endured in country after country, they supplemented the revealed teachings of the Torah with others which, judging by their
fruits, had a source quite other than the tables of Mount Sinai.

The Talmud was originally a series of oral instructions by which
the rabbis interpreted the Law of Moses, and applied it to changing
conditions. Early in the Christian era it was committed to writing, and expanded. Most of it has to do with the very exact rules,
covering all contingencies, with which orthodox Jewish life was
always carefully regulated. With this, of course, Christians had no
right to interfere. But by the Thirteenth Century the opinion was
almost universal in Christendom that in addition to all necessary
laws and precepts, the Jews included in the Talmud and Talmudic
books many obscene and blasphemous anecdotes concerning Christ
and His Church, together with curses and imprecations against
Christians, and bits of practical advice for outwitting and exploit-
ing them. This the Jews usually denied. Saint Louis, King of
France, was so disturbed, however, by stories of the harm the
Talmud was doing among them, and the impassable barrier it was
setting up against their conversion to the Faith of Christ, that he
summoned several distinguished rabbis to defend the Talmudic
writings in a celebrated conference; the result of which was that
the rabbis themselves admitted that certain passages insulting to
Christians were in the Talmud; and Saint Louis had copies of the
work seized wherever they could be found and publicly burned.
Modern Jews have made similar denials and similar admissions.
The Jewish Encyclopedia, for example, discussing the obligation
of Celsus to Judaism, remarks that "he asserts that Jesus was the
illegitimate son of a certain Panthera, and again that he had been
a servant in Egypt, not when a child as according to the New
Testament, but when he was grown, and that there he learned
the secret art. *These statements are frequently identical with those
of the Talmud.*" [15]

When Bernard Gui was Inquisitor at Toulouse, he had two cartloads of copies of the Talmud gathered up, and publicly burned.
He himself indicated the motives for this act in the fifth part of
his *Practica*. There he accused the Jews of reciting, in Hebrew,

[15] Vol. III, p. 637. *My italics.*

certain prayers and curses against Christians, and especially against Catholic priests and the Church. They named Christians, he added, only by circumlocution, but the reference was plain, and three times a day, he insisted, the Jews asked God to destroy all the followers of Christ. On their feast of propitiation in September, he went on to say, they recited a special malediction called the *cematha,* in which (again by circumlocution) "they call Christ the illegitimate son of a whore, and the Blessed Virgin Mary, an abominable thing to say or even to think, a woman of heat or lust, and they curse both, and the Roman faith, and all its members and believers." In a book "whose author is called Salomon" there were many statements from the Talmud, he went on, including the assertion that Christ was not God, nor the promised Messias; and in this work all those who professed Christ were called heretics and infidels. Another book called *The Gloss of Moses of Egypt,* said "that Jesus erred worse than Mohammed did, and had deceived the greater part of the world, destroying the law God had given."

Another offense with which he charged the Jews was that of proselytizing among Christians, particularly among Christians of Jewish descent. A certain number of the Jews in every age had become Catholic, some of them, in fact, saintly Catholics of the sort that the author of the Apocalypse, himself a Jew, had considered *true* Jews, as distinguished from those "who say they are Jews, and are not." The Catholic Jew, in short, has accepted his full spiritual destiny, and has regained the stature of a Chosen People, which his ancestors of the synagogue lost through their rejection of the Christ. There was another class of Catholic Jew, however, and probably the more numerous, to whose difficulties many men who dominated affairs in the Middle Ages seem to have been singularly blind. This was the sort of Jew who was compelled, at the sword's point, or under the sickening fear of social and economic ostracization, to accept baptism. Granted, the Church forbade this, and various Popes sternly reminded Christian folk that baptism must never be imposed upon anybody. But human nature being what it is, there were always fanatics who were "more Catholic than the Pope," and who could be counted upon, in any grave crisis, to make a scapegoat of the Jew, and to insist upon his immediate baptism or death.

One of these periodic crises arose when Pope Urban II preached the First Crusade at the close of the Eleventh Century. Urban was setting in motion a vast defensive warfare which was to last a full thousand years, a warfare necessary to the very existence of Christian Europe, and one which, with all its failures and its uncalculated miseries, was to prevent, on many occasions, the conquest of the West by Islam. Perhaps it was to be expected that when the Crusaders began to move toward the Holy Land from every corner of Europe, the Jews were in for a rough time. The battle line had been drawn between the friends of Christ and the foes of Christ; and it seemed obvious that the Jew was on the side of the enemy. His opinion of Christianity was well known; it was known, too, that he belonged to an international race, with strange and secret ways of communication; and it was suspected, not without some grounds, that when Christian clashed with Mohammedan, the Jew often sent information to the latter which would help in a military way against the former. Again, he was an alien in every country; and aliens fare badly in time of war everywhere.

Finally—let us be realistic about the matter—there is a quality in the Jews which does not exist in any other race. Some Jewish writers, almost in despair to account for the determined animosity of other races, have had recourse to the term "their Jewishness," a characteristic under which many a Jew has squirmed, and grown either defiant or servile, as men must, and suffered in the depths of his soul. Yet, if Jews are different from other races, it is in such intangible and indefinable ways that no Jew-baiter has been able to put his finger on the precise point of difference. No one who has noticed the generosity of Jews, their love of family, of music, of art; their gratitude to those who have befriended them, their pity for the unfortunate and the oppressed, and better still, their willingness to show their compassion in costly acts of mercy which put or ought to put many a Christian to shame—no one who looks at this unique and gifted people critically, realistically, without hatred on the one hand or sentimentality on the other, can accept the vulgar calumny that they are in any human sense inferior to any other group of Adam's progeny. Is it not possible, is it not indeed obvious, that the elusive difference is spiritual? A people set apart by the Creator for a lofty destiny, time and again disciplined and penanced and restored to favor; finally blessed with the presence of the Prophet that Moses had foreseen, but blinded by a growing materialism, indifference, moral confusion, yes, even by a formalistic loyalty to the memory of Moses himself until, in a tragic moment, their leaders made the great rejection which surely was the turning point of all history— how could such a people, cast off once more by a just God whose divine Majesty they had affronted, fail to experience an inner dislocation of the spirit, which, as the core and animating principle of their whole being, must inevitably extend disharmony, discontent and futility to their outward acts, bodily and mental? And how could this necessary operation of cause and effect desist, unless the Jew, like his ancestors of old, turn from his error to the arms of that all-merciful God who is only waiting, as in ancient times, to enfold him once more in His love, to brush from him the stains of a mortality unworthy of his secret destiny, and to raise him once more to the exalted humanity of Moses, of Abraham, of Isaac and of Jacob, even to communion with the Holy One Himself?

Now, all this is evident to any one who begins his survey of history with a sincere belief that Christ was exactly what He said He was—the Son of God. That is still, and must always be, the crucial question in human affairs: *What think you of Christ?* The Christians of the Middle Ages logically began with an affirmation of His divinity. To such a man as Bernard Gui, for example, the divinity of Christ seemed so clear that he could think of no fouler injustice than to try to wheedle into forgetting it, and losing his hold upon it, any Jew who, by God's grace, had come to accept it. The convert Jew was fortunate, and he had a right to hold on to his faith, which for him meant the salvation of his soul. Therefore, any one who tried to persuade the convert to turn his back on the Redeemer was guilty, in the eyes of the Inquisitor and of most good Christians, of the greatest possible crime.

If it was wrong to steal a man's money or his wife, what could be said of one who stole another's immortal happiness? Hence Bernard wrote rather bitterly of the baptised Jews *qui redeunt ad vomitum Judaysmi*.[16] Here surely he was thinking, not of the divine law of Moses, but of the Talmudic insults to Christ. He considered himself the champion of the right of a Jew to be and to remain a Christian, if he chose, without interference. And he went to great trouble to explain to his fellow Inquisitors, out of his long experience, the methods by which the Jews of the synagogue and the Talmud would try to "rejudaize" the Jew who had been baptized. They actually had a ceremony of reinstatement, he said, for the brethren who had so outraged their feelings. They would ask the Christian Jew if he wished "to make *tymla,* that is to say, take a bath in running water, that he might wash away the stain of baptism and become a Jew again." If he said Yes, a leading Jew would say in Hebrew, *Baaltussuna,* meaning, as Gui translates it, "Thou shalt return from the state of sin." The Christian was then stripped and washed in hot water, after which the Jews rubbed him vigorously all over his body, especially on his forehead, his breast and hands, with sand, giving particular attention to any part touched by the water of baptism or the holy chrism. Then his fingernails and toenails were cut away to the quick, even unto blood. Finally, with suitable prayers, he was immersed in running water; and all the Jews kissed him and gave him a name, usually the same with which he had been baptised; and he confessed the Law of Moses and promised to keep it, and to deny his baptism and the Christian faith.[17]

When Bernard Gui got hold of such a wavering son of Abraham, he did his best to bring him back to the faith of Christ. And if his net closed upon a Jew who was zealous in drawing Christian Jews away from the Faith, he made him promise to do so no more, and to take an oath to that effect upon the Law of Moses. There is no indication in his list of sentences that he caused any Jews to be put to death.

To some modern Catholics it seems as if the Inquisitors over-

16 *Practica,* p. 288.
17 *Practica, loc. cit.*

looked one very important matter in dealing with the judaizers: the fact that many Jews had been compelled to accept baptism. This was clearly against the law of the Church; and though we may admit that Bernard was defending the personal rights of a voluntary convert, we can understand also the indignation Jews must have felt when one of their number was forced at the point of the sword to submit to baptism, and their burning desire to get him back into their own fold. No distinction is made in the *Practica* between these two classes of converts. A Jew who reverts to Judaism is a heretic, and a Jew who induces him to do so is a heretic, and that is all there is to it.

Yet there is no doubt that some of these Jewish converts had been forced to become Christians, under circumstances which make it impossible not to feel the strongest indignation against those who wronged their free will. The Crusades, as we have noticed, had the cruelest consequences for the Jews. Until then, throughout Europe, they had enjoyed the greatest prosperity, indeed, the control of the trade of the civilized world. This had its advantages, but it had the disadvantage of making them the target of envy, and sometimes of just resentment. Now, in the armies bound for the Holy Land, there were always some fanatics, some criminals escaping from the law, some adventurers with no more belief in Christ than the Jews themselves had, some debtors eager to escape from the crushing burden of high interest. All wars produce a certain mass hysteria, ruthless and blind, discriminating only between Our Side and Their Side; and when the issue was For Christ or Against Christ, it was inevitable that the Jews, popularly looked upon as growing rich at the expense of Christians while they plotted constantly to destroy the Christian order, should be regarded with more than the ordinary wartime animosity against what are now called "fifth columns." Crusaders massacred Jews, in the summer of 1096, at Trier, Worms, Mainz, Cologne—wherever they advanced along the Main and the Danube; and when they took Jerusalem, they soiled their victory by a hideous butchery of Jews. The Second Crusade was marred by similar atrocities in Cologne, Mainz, Speyer, Strasburg and elsewhere. In 1171 the Jews of Blois were accused of having used Christian blood in their Passover, and were burned. Philip Augustus confiscated the immovable goods of all the French Jews, and banished them. In the Third Crusade, corpses of defenseless Jews were scattered all the way from London to Vienna. Englishmen slew them on the eve of the coronation of Richard *Coeur de Lion;* Germans slew them along the Rhine. During the Albigensian Crusade, the Jews of Southern France endured their usual bloody fate. King John of England confiscated their wealth; Edward I expelled them from that kingdom, in 1290. In the Spanish Crusade of 1212 the Jews of Toledo were slaughtered.

The Thirteenth Century bore many glorious fruits, but not for the sons of Abraham. And the decadent fourteenth had even worse things in store for them. It began with their plundering and expulsion from France by Philip IV in 1306; their slaughter by the *pastoureaux* in 1320 and even bloodier persecution in 1321, when the lepers accused them of having poisoned the wells and rivers—this about the time when Bernard Gui was composing his *Practica.* The Crusades had brought to the Jews the same punishment that their ancestors had meted out to the idolaters, the blasphemers, the worshippers among them of the gold calf. Their ancient prophets would have said that they were being chastised for not walking in the ways of God. But what a mockery that this should be done in the name of Him who said, "Love your enemies; do good to them that hate you," and murmured, as He gave up His life for the Jews and all men, "Father, forgive them, for they know not what they do!" What an injustice, too, that the survivors of the pogroms were often granted their lives only on condition that they accept baptism. Some of course sought it themselves in their fear of future massacres, confiscations, and social and economic discrimination. Many of the conversions, therefore, were insincere and temporary.

Modern Jews—Dr. Cecil Roth, for one—have acknowledged that the Popes and most of the hierarchy pretty consistently stood between the Jews and all this mob violence, and protected them from extermination or other barbarities in countless instances. Pope Alexander III was a friend to the Jews. The Third Lateran Council in 1179 defended their right to refuse baptism. Innocent III, although he frowned on the tendency of many Christian rulers to give the Jews power and preferment over Christians, issued a constitution, when the Jews appealed to him against the Crusaders, in which he forbade mob violence and compulsory baptism—a measure that Gregory IX confirmed in 1235. It is true that the Fourth Lateran Council in 1215 had urged the exclusion of Jews from public offices, and had compelled them to wear a circular badge. But later Popes mitigated the severity of this legislation, and when the Jews were accused of all manner of crimes in 1247, Innocent IV wrote a famous letter to the bishops of Germany and France, in which he said, "Certain of the clergy and princes, nobles and great lords of your cities and dioceses have falsely devised certain godless plans against the Jews, unjustly depriving them by force of their property, and appropriating it to themselves; . . . they falsely charge them with dividing up among themselves on the Passover the heart of a murdered boy. . . In their malice, they ascribe every murder, wherever it chance to occur, to the Jews. And on the ground of these and other fabrications, they are filled with rage against them, rob them of their possessions without any formal accusation, without confession, and without legal trial and conviction, contrary to the privileges granted to them by the Apostolic See. . . They oppress the Jews by starvation, imprisonment, and by tortures and sufferings; they afflict them with all kinds of punishments, and sometimes even condemn them to death, so that the Jews, although living under Christian princes, are in a worse plight than their ancestors were in the land of the Pharaohs. They are driven to leave in despair the land in which their fathers have dwelt since the memory of man. . . . Since it is our pleasure that they shall not be disturbed, . . . we ordain that ye behave toward them in a friendly and kindly manner. Whenever any unjust attacks upon them come under your notice, redress their injuries, and do not suffer them to be visited in the future by similar tribulations."

The poor bewildered Jew, plundered, despised and in fear of his life, was not capable of making fine distinctions. He knew that the men who wronged him called themselves Christians, and he hated them and the Catholic Church, and the very name of

Christ. Blinded by unbelief, he still considered himself to be of a Chosen People; and where usury, for example, was concerned, he regarded the Christians as his ancestors had the Egyptians—as legitimate subjects for spoliation, and deserving of what they got. He was not likely to see the other side of the picture.

There was, of course, another side. When William of Normandy conquered England with money borrowed from the Jews of Rouen, he took many Jews with him to gather taxes for him. His successors farmed out the taxes to the Jews, and William Rufus went so far as to farm out vacant bishoprics to them. This caused an unfavorable reaction, of course, against all Jews. Most of the nobles, under King John, had mortgaged their estates to Jews. Some of the great Cathedrals were built with the money of Jews, who thus in exile helped to build temples to the God they had rejected. Often the interest was so high as to increase the popular resentment felt against the alien race. Richard of Anesty, who borrowed from Jews in the middle of the twelfth century, to finance a necessary journey to Rome, paid 3d. to 4d. in the pound per week for the money—something like 85 per cent per annum.

Bernard Gui was a human being, whose writings reveal a spirit of prudence and moderation, above all, a sense of humor. Can it be that he had no compassion for the sufferings of the Jew, no understanding of the difficulties of the Jewish convert? If the Church forbade compulsory baptism, and if some of the Jews had been compelled at the sword's point to accept baptism, how then, one wonders, could the Church permit the Inquisition to punish such a Jew for relapsing into Judaism?

The Church had to permit it, or follow an alternative incompatible with her mission as the teacher of truth. The alternative, as Menendez y Pelayo has pointed out, would have been to condone apostasy. Could the teacher of God's revealed truth wink at the repudiation of that truth? The Jew who had accepted baptism under the threat of death had wronged his conscience in so doing. Well, what did the Catholic Church command her own children to do under similar circumstances? She told them to die as martyrs rather than accept Mohammedanism, or any other religion than the teaching of Christ. If through weakness they apostatized, she could not justify the evil, even though she might pity the victims: she cut them off from the body of her communicants. If they died for the Faith, she raised them to her altars as martyrs. The essential thing, she taught, was to be true to one's own conscience. Death was a trifle by comparison.

Teaching this heroic code to her own children, could the Church logically demand anything else from the Jews, or for that matter, from all God's children? If the Jew sincerely believed the true religion false, he could die rather than accept it, and it was his duty to die. The Church forbade her members to inflict such a fate upon him, or to use any force to wrong his conscience. Never-theless there were wicked men, sometimes calling themselves Christians, who would put a Jew to the cruel test. Alas, then, the Jew, like a Christian, must follow his conscience, which was the voice of God within him. If he could not do this, if he weakly chose baptism rather than death, that was his misfortune, and he must abide by it; at least the Church could not condone his giving up God's truth for any denial of that truth. This is a stern code, "a hard saying," as the Jews said of some of Christ's teachings; but nothing less could be worthy of a God of truth, and of the Church representing Him among men. Moses would have understood this. King David would have understood it. Christ Himself taught stark truths: "The brother also shall deliver up the brother to death, and the father the son, and the children shall rise up against their parents, and shall put them to death. And you shall be hated by all men for my name's sake: but he that shall persevere unto the end, he shall be saved. . . The disciple is not above the master, nor the servant above his lord. . . And fear ye not them that kill the body, and are not able to kill the soul. . . Do not think that I came to send peace upon earth; I came not to send peace, but the sword. . . He that findeth his life, shall lose it, and he that shall lose his life for me, shall find it." [18]

This was the code of the Christian. Could the Church ask anything less of the Jew? "Come to me, all ye that mourn—" Yes; but invariably the mercy of Christ insisted upon the recognition of His justice. It was not merely that He forgave the woman taken

[18] *St. Matthew*, X: 21-39.

in adultery; she was to "go, and sin no more." This was the attitude that the Inquisition sought to take toward the revealed truth, and those who approached it. A Bernard Gui might be a very merciful man by nature, and still insist that the most important thing was the revealed truth of God. Without grasping this point of view, it is impossible to understand the mind of such a man.

Finally, the Inquisitor of Toulouse had a keen professional interest in those who preyed upon the superstitious hopes and fears of simple people. He furnished forms in the *Practica* for dealing with wizards, fortune-tellers, magicians who in any way invoked demons, held commerce with the spirits of the dead or pretended to do so, or with the souls of the damned; those who for a consideration would endeavor to promote peace or discord between married people; those who professed to cure sterility; those who sold love potions, charms, strange herbs to be taken facing toward the east, with certain spells and incantations; those who baptized wax figures, or made lead images of those they wished to harm; above all, those who manifested "any superstition or irreverence or injury toward the sacraments of the Church, and especially concerning the sacrament of the Body of Christ." [19] Evidence exists, unfortunately, that in every age there were men and women who would steal a consecrated Host from a church, with the purpose of insulting the Redeemer, or using It in certain rites of black magic, to gain various ends. Such persons were excommunicated and otherwise punished; but could be reconciled if penitent.

The spirit in which Friar Bernard approached all these problems is best illustrated, perhaps, by his famous instruction, setting forth what the ideal Inquisitor should be:

"First, it is obvious that the Inquisitor should be diligent and fervent in his zeal for the truth of religion and the salvation of souls, that he may detest and wipe out the heretical depravity; but he should so carry on amid displeasing circumstances and accidental occurrences that he shall not be distracted by indignation or the fury of anger, for such fury carries one on headlong; nor, on the other hand, should he be overcome with torpor by any

[19] *Practica*, p. 293.

laziness or negligence, for such torpor weakens a man's power to go ahead.

"Second, let the Inquisitor be steadfast; let him stand firm among dangers and adversities even unto death, suffering all things for the righteousness of faith, that on the one hand he may not yield impulsively to any intimidation whatever, for this disables and weakens the mind for carrying on; and on the other hand let him be constant among the prayers and blandishments of sinners, who seek to have delays granted for trials, or to have imposed penalties mitigated according to time and place, because this introduces severity.[20] And let him not be yielding and pliant by too great a desire to please, for this destroys the virtue and vigor of actions; for God loves all those who please men *justly*. (Prov. XVIII: 'He that is loose and slack in his work is the brother of him that wasteth his own works.')

"Third, let him be vigilant among doubtful matters, that he may not believe easily everything that seems probable, for such a thing is not always true; nor should he obstinately reject the opposite, for often the thing that seems improbable happens to be true; and so the cases heard are to be discussed and examined with all care, and the truth sought out.

"Concerning this last, indeed, which is a kind or form of judging or punishing, care is to be taken that the function here assumed is manifest in the bearing or in the countenance of the presiding magistrate. The Inquisitor, therefore, like a just judge, must so hew to the line of justice in passing judgment upon crimes that he shall keep a spirit of compassion not only inwardly, in his mind, but shall manifest it also in his outward bearing, so that in this way he may avoid the reproach of indignation and anger, which exhibits the mark and evidence of cruelty. So, also, in imposing pecuniary fines, let him follow the very truth and spirit of justice . . . that the trial may not be disfigured by any element of greed or of cruelty." [21]

---

[20] "*Sit etiam constans inter preces et blandimenta peccantium, ut sive in dandis dilationis terminorum, sive in penis impositis pro loco et tempore mitigandis, quia hoc crudelitatem importat.*"

[21] *Practica*, pp. 232-3.

Of torture Bernard had very little to say. In only one of his 930 cases is it certain that he used it. He probably employed the method in vogue throughout Languedoc: starvation. A few days without food generally made a prisoner more willing to talk. It is not impossible, of course, than on occasions not recorded, the Inquisitor of Toulouse permitted the application of some of the more revolting forms of torture; for these had been allowed by the Inquisition, though very sparingly, for several years.

Through all the centuries when the Catholic Church was creating a better civilization in Europe, torture had not been used in the secular courts. It had gone out of fashion during what are called the Dark Ages, and it had come back into fashion with the Renaissance, more specifically with the revival of Roman Law throughout the West during the twelfth century, at the very period when the Popes—particularly Innocent III, Honorius III and Gregory IX— were doing their best to put an end to the trial by ordeal. The courts of Frederic II used torture to extract confessions as a matter of course, when the judges had reason to believe the prisoner was concealing the truth. It was natural that when Frederic made heresy a capital offense, worse even than *lèse majesté* (since, he said, it offended the majesty of God), the ordinary machinery of justice should be invoked. The tortures commonly employed were the rack and the strappado. The rack was a triangular frame on which the arms and legs of the prisoner were slowly pulled by ropes, until he signified his willingness to tell what he knew. The strappado was a rope tied to the wrists of the victim, behind his back, and attached overhead to a pulley and windless, by which the poor wretch was hoisted in the air and then let fall with a frightful jerk to within a few inches of the ground. This was the torment to be inflicted upon Savonarola, not once but many times.

Now, although Gregory IX had committed the Church to a cooperation with the state in the prosecution of heresy, and encouraged the secular magistrates to inflict the death penalty on the unrepentant, he apparently took it for granted, as most churchmen did for several years, that the Inquisitors were to act only as specialists in theology, and not in any sense as police officials. Canon law had previously condemned confessions extorted by pain, and it was generally felt that clergymen should have nothing to do with torture. As time went on and the secret enemy remained unvanquished, nay, boldly took the lives of Inquisitors here and there, those engaged in the perilous business felt more and more that they were locked in a desperate warfare with implacable and resourceful cohorts of the powers of darkness; and as in all wars, they tended to become more ruthless as to means. It was not until 1252, however, that Pope Innocent IV, in his bull *Ad Extirpanda,* opened the door for the introduction of torture in the Inquisitorial courts, by demanding that heretics be treated as ordinary criminals. To be sure, the Pope did not use the word "torture," as several translations have made him appear to do. What he actually said was, "Moreover, the *podestá* or ruler is required to compel all heretics whom he has arrested (short of injury to limb or danger of death) to confess their errors plainly, and to accuse other heretics whom they know, and their property, and followers and shelterers and defenders, as thieves and robbers of temporal goods are forced to accuse their accomplices and to tell what crimes they have committed; for these are truly robbers and homicides of souls, and thieves of the sacraments of God, and of the Christian Faith." [22]

There is nothing here about the rack and the strappado, and strict confinement and deprivation of food were the only methods used in Languedoc more than half a century later.[23] In other places the permission of Innocent was certainly understood as *carte blanche* for the Inquisitors to obtain information by the customary tortures, which, however, were applied by secular officials. This latter restriction made for delay and inefficiency, and presently the Inquisitors were complaining against the canon law which forbade clerics, under penalty of irregularity, even to be present in the torture chamber. In 1260 Alexander IV permitted them to grant one another dispensations from the irregularity so incurred. This permission, confirmed by Urban IV in 1262, was plainly a consent to evade the canon law, and therefore must be considered one of

[22] The exact words of Innocent were, *"Teneatur praeterea potestas seu rector omnes haereticos quos captos habuerit, cogere citra membri diminutionem & mortis periculum, tanquam vere latrones, & homicidas animarum, & fures sacramentorum Dei,"* etc.

[23] Douais, *Documents,* vol. II, p. 115 *et seq.*

the abuses of the Inquisition. It was still understood, however, that torture was to be used only when the Inquisitor was convinced that the prisoner was concealing the truth, and when all other means of obtaining a confession had failed. The prisoner was then shown the instruments of torture and urged to confess. If he still refused, he was given a slight *vexatio,* which was gradually made more severe if necessary.

Obviously there were abuses of this dangerous privilege, and in 1311 Pope Clement V, who made many reforms in the Holy Office (insisting, for example, on cleaner and more humane prisons instead of the dark holes in which prisoners were sometimes kept), decreed that no Inquisitor could ever use torture without first obtaining the permission of the bishop of the diocese. This was a tremendous limitation in favor of mercy. Another restriction was that no prisoner might be tortured more than once, or more than half an hour at a time. Overzealous Inquisitors found a way to get around this, by describing a second torment as a "continuation," not a repetition. It is difficult to say just how common this practice was. Probably Lea and Vacandard have exaggerated it. Lea asserts that "usually the procedure appears to be that the torture was continued until the accused signified his intention to confess;" yet he admits also that "in the fragmentary documents of inquisitorial proceedings which have reached us, the references to torture are singularly few." [24] He might have added that some of the documents that have reached us were evidently intended for the use of the Holy Office alone, not for publication, and made no bones about mentioning torture when it *was* used. Is it not to be inferred, then, that in some cases at least, the absence of any reference to torture means that no torture was employed?

The procedure laid down by Bernard Gui in the *Practica* probably became the norm for most of the tribunals of southern France, if not elsewhere. First he proclaimed a term of grace. Then he began to receive complaints and voluntary confessions. The heretic who came forward of his own accord was told to perform some light penance, and to go and sin no more. A man denounced by another was investigated carefully. If only one witness accused him,

[24] *The Inquisition of the Middle Ages,* Vol. I, pp. 424, 427.

nothing further could be done; as in the "Inquisition" of Moses. If there were two or more, he received a summons, either through his pastor or through one of the *familiares* of the Holy Office, directing him to appear on a certain date to answer the complaint, a complete statement of which was furnished him. If he appeared and confessed, or satisfied the Inquisitor that he was innocent, he had nothing more to fear. If not, and if the Inquisitor had reason to believe that he was a heretic, or was concealing some heretic, an order was issued for his arrest.

Names of the witnesses against him were withheld from the prisoner; but this had been found necessary under the circumstances. The Cathari assassinated many persons who denounced them, in the time of Gregory IX; and the Inquisitors decided that they could not count on the cooperation of the public unless they protected the denouncer by rigid secrecy. To offset this disadvantage for the accused, they permitted him to make a list of his enemies, and the testimony of any among them was rejected. A false denunciation, furthermore, was punished with the utmost rigor. The examinations were conducted with the greatest secrecy, to protect the reputations of accused persons, in case they might be innocent.

Another important safeguard was the custom of submitting the evidence, when it was all assembled, to a very large jury, not chosen at random as our juries are, but picked from among the most respected and learned men in the community—*periti et boni viri*. This was the practice from the time of Gregory IX on; we find Arnaud summoning a jury of good and expert men in Languedoc, at the very inception of the Holy Office. The number was decided by the Inquisitor, but seems never to have been less than twenty; in one jury at Pamiers, in 1329, there were thirty-five, of whom nine were lawyers; at another there were fifty-one, including twenty lawyers. These "experts" considered the evidence for several days, and then advised the Inquisitor what they thought the sentence should be. He was not bound to follow their recommendations, but in practice usually did so. The jury did not know the names of the accused. This probably led to some injustice, as Vacandard points out; on the other hand, it probably saved some unpopular prisoners from the effects of prejudice or personal animosity. At any rate, the consultation of good and expert men, with all its faults and merits, was the beginning of our modern jury system.

Such was the judicial machine which Bernard Gui strove for seventeen years to perfect, believing all the while that he was doing his best for God and for human society, and that he was rendering the greatest service he could to the hundreds of heretics whom he restored to communion with the Church of Christ. When his task was finished at last, the Church had won her desperate battle in Languedoc, and the Manichean poison, though still secretly existent, no longer threatened to destroy all order in church and state. Bernard had labored successfully. He had the reputation of being a just, incorruptible, yet merciful judge. His *Practica* was in great demand as a guide to Inquisitors. But if this is his chief claim to our attention, his contemporaries knew him for many other works of erudition: for his *Chronicle of the Emperors,* covering the history of the entire Christian era; his *Chronicle of the Kings of France,* his *Lives of the Saints, Mirror of the Saints, Historical Treatise on the Dominican Order,* a *Treatise on the Mass,* and other works then widely read. He was sixty-three years old now, and perhaps a little tired. At any rate, his superiors thought it was time he received some reward; the necessary words were spoken, and he was made Bishop of Tuy, in Galicia. The following year he was transferred to the more congenial See of Lodève (Hérault).

It was 1323 when Bernard left Toulouse and the Holy Office. Petrarch was then nineteen years old. Dante had died two years before, soon after bringing his *Paradiso* to its glorious end. Saint Thomas Aquinas, who had left this world when Bernard was a stripling, was canonized in July of that same year by Pope John XXII, exiled at Avignon; and Saint Thomas, like most of the best men of his time, had considered the Inquisition a just and necessary institution, and went back to the Old Testament for an example to defend it: the house of David could not obtain peace, he said, until Absalom was killed in the war he waged against his father; and he reasoned that if coiners and other criminals were put to death, it was only right that heretics who persisted in their errors after a second admonition ought to be handed over to the secular arm. Lesser philosophers reminded their readers of the fate the sons of Core had suffered justly at the command of Moses.

If we had lived then, most of us would have taken the thing as a matter of course, as they did. If they could survey our scene, they would be scandalized at the number of innocent human lives we sacrifice every year, needlessly, to careless driving and the quest of pleasure: and they would deem our wars an incredible hell on earth, presaging the Last Days. Their world tolerated the Inquisition; but it was at Toulouse, the very year after Inquisitor Gui left, that the poets of Languedoc began to compete in the *jeux floraux* for gold and silver flowers, and Arnaud Vidal won the first award by a song in honor of Our Lady.

We hear very little of Bernard Gui after 1324. He was probably earnest and conscientious as a bishop, as he had been in the professor's chair, and in the dread seat of the Inquisition. He died, full of years and honors, at the age of seventy, in the town of Louroux.

IV

Nicholas Eymeric

WHEN Bernard Gui was leaving Toulouse forever, to take up the happier duties of a bishop, a little boy of three years was playing in a town near the eastern coast of Spain, without any intimation perhaps that he too would be an Inquisitor, and that his particular task in life would be to carry on the work of the French Dominican, and give to the jurisprudence of the Holy Office its complete and almost final form. This boy would expand the *Practica* into a far more imposing and voluminous *Directorium Inquisitorum* which, for centuries to come, would be to all Inquisitors what Blackstone would be to Britons, a guide, a precedent, a treasure of practical advice. He would probably be the most hated man of the Fourteenth Century; but this may have troubled him very little, even in his childish dreams.

Nicholas was born in 1320, at or near Tarragona,[1] where it is almost a liberal education merely to have eyes and ears. To see the wild mountains to the west, and at one's feet a harbor cluttered with ships from all the world, and in between the snowy peaks and the vast blue of the Mediterranean, a thousand memorials of all the races of men who had inhabited that hoary city from the dawn of antiquity—a child growing up there could hardly fail to be a bit of a poet, and somewhat historical-minded; and this is one way of beginning to understand the present, and perhaps even a little of the future. It was from that corner of the peninsula, that breeding ground of ancient races, that the Iberian culture

[1] So says Pegna, in his introductory biographical note to the *Directorium*, ed. Venice, 1607. Espasa's *Encyclopedia Ilustrada* has him born at Gerona.

very early spread. There, later, the Phoenicians exchanged silks from the east and tin from England, worshipped strange gods, and possibly sacrificed children to Moloch. There the Romans had a metropolis of something more than a million souls, and left memorials that travelers still wonder at: the great aqueduct, the forum, the amphitheatre, the palace of Augustus, the so-called Tower of Pilate (who, according to a local legend, was born there), the sepulchre of the Scipios, the arch of Sura, the Aurelian Way. There Saint Paul and Saint James may have first preached the Gospel of Christ in Spain, there Christian blood was shed like water for the Faith, there the Visigoths held sway, there the Moslems built a mosque on ground saturated with the gore of Crusaders, there finally the Cross returned to triumph over the crescent. On the site where the mosque had been, the Christians were beginning to build, while Nicholas was a child, the fine Romanesque cathedral that now stands there. And to that ancient city, in the early years of the Fourteenth Century, certain Waldensian, Manichee and other heretics of Southern France, who had escaped the nets of Bernard Gui and the fires of the Inquisition of the Toulouse, were already beginning to flock, bringing with them the same half-oriental ideas that were religion to them, and poison to orthodox Christians.

What did Nicholas Eymeric think of all this? Even Inquisitors were once little boys who bumped their heads, had their fingers bandaged, and were spanked. Did this one, born to speak a tongue as much like French as Spanish, have parents rich or poor? Did he sail on the Mediterranean? Did he climb the mountains? Did he ever imagine he saw the ghost of Pilate on the ruins of the temple of Hadrian, of a moonlit night? Did he ever fall off the aqueduct? It would be interesting to know. But the boyhoods of Inquisitors are generally shrouded in mystery, for Inquisitors were friars, and of Eymeric, like most medieval friars, we learn only, after his birth, that he entered a monastery, when he was fourteen years old, and in the course of time became a priest, under the rule of the Order of Preachers.

Surmise is not history; but of Eymeric, as of all the men and women born in his generation, one thing may fairly be surmised:

in his late twenties he passed through as harrowing and as exhausting an experience as perhaps is possible for human nature to endure and survive. The times, at best, had been unsettled enough. In Spain, many racial and religious animosities slumbered under the peace imposed by strong kings, or broke forth into fire, bloodshed, and anarchy under the weak ones. Italy, from which the rest of Europe more or less took its intellectual and moral color, had been torn by the strife of Guelf and Ghibelline, of pagan German Emperor against Christian Pope. Bands of *condottieri* lived off the countryside. Rome was a place of violence and sudden death, from which the Popes had fled to Avignon, to dwell in shameful dependence upon the bounty and the political will of the Kings of France. The Hundred Years' War had begun to bleed England and France white; the English in 1347 had got Calais, and much good would it do them. In the same year Cola di Rienzi came to power in Rome, and proclaimed his republic. Yet all such matters, and the occasional hanging of a murderer or burning of a heretic here and there, were dwarfed by the most terrifying and most universal catastrophe that had fallen on the race of man in centuries, perhaps since the Flood.

Imagine what it must have been to live through the nightmare of the Black Death. A young priest like Eymeric gets up before dawn, happy and tranquil and carefree; reads his office, says his Mass, has his breakfast, and is about to start his morning's study or other work, when he meets Brother So-and-So, one of his best friends. This brother is ordinarily as brisk as a lark at that hour, but today something has happened to him. What seems to be a small black boil has appeared on the palm of his hand, or perhaps under his arm-pit. He thought little of it at first, but now he is becoming feverish, has a headache, dizziness and deafening noises in the ears. When evening comes this brother is dead, his strong young body has become a corpse, black and grisly. Another monk gets the same mysterious disease, and another, and another. Nothing can be done about it; the victim almost always dies, and usually within two or three days at the most.

As for the city on whose outskirts the monastery stands, the people are in a panic. There is a black corpse in every house;

whole families lie dead, with no one to bury them. Half crazed mothers flee from their sick children, leaving them to die alone. Maniacs run shrieking or sobbing through the streets, gibbering at the black faces of the dead who lie there grinning at the sun. Everywhere the church bells are tolling, tolling.

There is a great demand, of course, for priests to hurry to countless bedsides, to hear confessions, to give *Viaticum,* to anoint the dying or the dead, to console the living. What a test for a man! Among priests, too, there are cowardly souls, and some flee for the deserts and the mountains, there perhaps to encounter the same ghastly terror. But most of them apparently meet the challenge as good priests ought: the fact that there is a higher mortality among them than among the lay population at large, indicates how many of them, carrying the Body of Christ to sufferers, are laying down their lives for their sheep. And it is not only the sick who demand their attention. Hysterical sinners come running to the churches and monasteries, as if pursued by Death himself, to scatter ill-gotten gold at the monks' feet. Others rush to the opposite extreme. Despairing of God's mercy, they fling themselves into a delirium of the senses, they dance and sing like idiots, they drink until they fall down drunk, or stagger into brothels whence even the harlots have fled. In all this welter of sin and repentance, epicurean madness, and universal stench of sickness and death, the only remaining centre of sanity is the stricken Church of Christ; and presently there can be seen on the streets little processions of men and women in black robes, singing penitential psalms and carrying stretchers; these are voluntary members of burial societies, who are willing to risk their own lives to render a last Christian service to the dead who lie about in houses or on the streets.

Society was shaken almost to its foundations by this visitation. Within two years some 25,000,000 persons died of it in Europe; probably half, possibly more, of the entire population. There was, of course, a great scarcity of priests. This of course opened the way to much corruption and laxity. Better a poor priest here and there than no baptism for infants, no confession for the living or the dying, no giving of the Body of Christ, without which "you shall not have life in you."

Whether Nicholas Eymeric was one of the few priests who could not look upon the face of black death, or one of those who braved it and survived as if by a miracle, history has not recorded; but it would be strange indeed if a man passed through such experiences as he must have endured in his late twenties, and saw the half-naked flagellants scourging themselves on the roads, without having a different set of values from ours, nor would it be surprising if there remained in him something of the fanatic. When he was sent to be an assistant to Nicholas Rosell, Inquisitor General for Aragon, he was so convinced that the joys of this life are fleeting and illusory, and that the only goal worthy of a man's attention was the saving of his immortal soul, that he flung himself unreservedly into the task of hunting out the miserable persons who had fallen into the spiritual sickness of the Manichees, to draw them back to what he firmly believed to be their only hope of salvation. He was so eminently successful, in the opinion of his superiors in the Dominican Order, that when Nicholas Rosell was made a Cardinal in 1356, Eymeric became Grand Inquisitor in his place. It was an extraordinary honor, considering that he was only thirty-six, for even an ordinary Inquisitor, as a rule, had to be forty. Allowing for the toll the Black Death had taken among the Dominicans, it must be inferred that Eymeric, to attain such a responsibility at his age, was noted for scholarship, judgment, prudence and common sense.

He was certainly no respecter of persons. The more important a man was, the more fearlessly and ruthlessly he tracked him down, if he had reason to suspect him of heresy. By the time he was forty, he probably had more enemies than any other man in Spain. Finally he alienated one of his most powerful friends, Prince Juan of Aragon, by attacking the works of Ramón Lull, then very popular in eastern Spain, and accusing some of the prominent Lullists of heresy. Eymeric's superiors relieved him of his office, doubtless at the request of the Prince. How many heretics had he caused to be burned, imprisoned, penanced, reconciled? There are no reliable statistics.

Certain it is, however, that he proceeded to Avignon, where the Frenchmen who then ruled the Church were enduring an all-too-comfortable "Babylonian captivity," and appealed to Pope Gregory XI. The Holy Father may have found him a considerable problem. Eymeric was not an easy man to get rid of, particularly if he thought he had a just grievance. Furthermore, he was a brilliant theologian, and perhaps the Pope was not sure whether the fault lay with him, or with his adversaries and critics in Aragon. At any rate the eleventh Gregory kept him as his chaplain, sent him now and then on some difficult mission concerning the Holy Office, and gave him leisure to study and to write.

During his middle age at lovely Avignon, Eymeric wrote prodigiously and well. He was the author of no fewer than thirty-seven books, works on the physical sciences, codices of logic, commentaries on the Gospels, sermons, and eleven volumes of theology, these last unpublished to this day. The crown and flower of his activity, however, and the one which brought him admiration in the Middle Ages, and scorn and misunderstanding in later times, was his *Directorium Inquisitorum*.

This is by no means a mere "handbook" for Inquisitors, like Bernard Gui's fairly bulky volume. In the great tome wherein the scholarly Cardinal Pegna has transmitted it to us, with his own commentaries and additions, we have perhaps the best contemporary record of the ideas and methods of the medieval Inquisition in its heyday, and with it a full compendium of the whole range of Catholic thought on God and man, as interpreted chiefly by Saint Thomas Aquinas.

Eymeric divided his work into three parts. The first sets forth what Catholics are obliged to believe, first by divine revelation, then by the apostolic letters of the Popes, the decrees of the Church Councils, and the canon law, with the interpretations of the Church Fathers. Here, protected by subtle and careful scholastic reasoning that marches, with almost endless commentaries, from definition to definition, is set forth in orderly fashion almost the complete story of God's communication with man: the Law He gave to Moses and the other great Hebrew prophets, all pointing to the Incarnation of the Messias; the Crucifixion and Resurrection of the Son of God, a belief in whom, says Eymeric, logically implies and includes a belief in the doctrine of the Trinity; and the interpretations of the teachings of Christ through the centuries by the one, holy, catholic and apostolic Church whose bindings and loosings He promised to ratify in Heaven, and to which He said, "Lo, I am with you all days, even to the consummation of the world." All this must be accepted by a Christian, because it is God's revelation. A heretic is a professing Christian who takes the parts that he likes, and rejects what he dislikes, without considering that truth is not a subjective thing, but has an objective and eternal validity outside of him and independent of his very existence.

Eymeric makes clear who are to be considered heretics, and who not. The simple, for example, are not to be examined on *subtleties* of faith, unless there is a suspicion that they have been corrupted by heretics, who have a way, he says, of preying upon the simple; otherwise they are not to be troubled. In this part also, Eymeric propounds twelve weighty questions concerning faith, and gives answers generally following the opinions of Saint Thomas. *What is faith?* Eymeric and Saint Thomas base their answer upon the famous one of Saint Paul: *Fides est substantia sperandarum rerum, argumentum non apparentium*. Merely to *doubt* an article of faith is to be a heretic; one must have certainty about it. Jews and Gentiles (and Eymeric does not fall into the modern error of calling Catholics "gentiles") are not heretics. And so on.

Part Two of the *Directorium* is an elaborate catalogue of all the errors and heresies by which the faithful, conceivably, could be entrapped. Here Eymeric lists first of all the errors condemned by Christ Himself. (1) Christ condemned the errors of the Pharisees: that the traditions of men were divine decrees; that it is better to offer one's goods to the priest than to help one's parents; that divorce is permissible, etc. (2) Christ condemned the error of the Sadducees, who denied the resurrection of the dead. (3) Christ condemned the errors of the Herodians; the one that John the Baptist rebuked in Herod, and the denial of His divinity.[2]

Eymeric points out the errors of the philosophers, too, even those of ancient times. Aristotle, for example, had said that the world always existed, that the sun had generated planets and animals

2 *Directorium*, p. 242.

from eternity, that God could not have made any other world, that resurrection from the dead is impossible. Averoës and Avicena had followed certain of the errors of the Stagyrite. Then there was "Rabbi Moysis" (Maimonides?) who denied the dogma of the Trinity, ridiculed Christians who believed in it, and declared that some things were possible to God, others not.[3]

The errors condemned by Christ's vicars include the simony that Saint Peter rebuked in Simon Magus, and the aberrations of the Gnostics, from which so many subsequent heresies stemmed.

There are also the errors of the Greeks, of the Tartars, of the Turks, of the Saracens, of the Jews,[4] all of which Eymeric names and distinguishes.

Finally, he sets forth at great length the sixty-nine different heresies condemned by the Council of Tarragona. Most of these are variations in one way or another of the half dozen heresies, chiefly of Manichean origin, to which Bernard Gui paid most attention in his *Practica;* and we find Eymeric confirming and enlarging the observations of his forerunner in Toulouse on the most troublesome sects: Manichees, Waldenses, Pseudo-Apostles, Beguins or Fraticelli, Judaizers, and various types of Magicians, Sorcerers and Devil-worshippers.

The Manichees seem to have kept in Spain most of the characteristics that Bernard Gui had recorded of their parents or grandparents in southern France. They believed in the essential wickedness of the world, but considered themselves Perfect; they professed to love Christ, but hated the Blessed Sacrament; they would take no oaths, but did not scruple to lie and equivocate to escape detection; they denied the authority of Church and State, but set themselves up as religious authorities; they resented the discipline of the Church, but kept four Lents a year.[5]

The Waldenses were still defying the Vicar of Christ, but had a sort of Pope of their own, whom, according to Eymeric, they called their Mayor; and these perfectionists still taught that "it is better

[3] *Directorium,* pp. 238 *et seq.*
[4] *Ibid.,* pp. 303-307.
[5] *Ibid.,* p. 440.

to satisfy any sort of lust by an act of shame" than to allow temptation to ruffle inward purity.[6]

The Beghards, Beguins or Fraticelli still went about in burlap robes, like those of Franciscans, with faces partly covered. They were likely to have yellowish countenances, but generally looked plump and well-fed, ate and drank lustily when they could, were inclined to lechery, yet went about making holy exclamations (such as "Blessed be Jesus Christ!"); refused to kneel in churches, like other Christians, but sat on the ground, turning their faces to the wall; considered the rule of Saint Francis more holy than the Church itself, and venerated as martyrs the four Franciscan friars burned as heretics by the Inquisition of Marseilles in 1316, saying that Christ was crucified in them spiritually again. Finally, they were always setting fairly exact dates for the appearance of the Antichrist.[7]

The Pseudo-Apostles were industrious, as before, in denouncing what they chose to call the great Whore of Babylon exiled to Avignon, but claimed for themselves the plenitude of Papal powers. In Spain they wore long white tunics, with mantles over them, and very long hair, uncovered to the elements. They sang blessings as they sat to eat, or arose. Their code of sexual morality was as vile and perverted as ever. They held, according to Father Eymeric, that "a nude man and woman can lie together without any sin in the same bed, and can touch each other in all parts, and kiss, without any sin." [8] To lie with a woman and not have intercourse with her was a greater achievement, they insisted, than to raise the dead to life.

A consecrated church was no better for praying to God, in their opinion, than a stable of horses, or a pig-sty.

Eymeric carefully enumerated all the signs by which the various classes of heretics might be detected, and distinguished from one another. Of heretics in general, he remarked that they all tended toward the same end—the corruption of others and the damnation of themselves.[9]

[6] *Ibid.*

[7] *Ibid.*

[8] *Et quod coniungere ventrem suum cum ventre mulieris ad nutum, si quis stimuletur carnaliter ut cesset tentatio, non est peccatum.*—p. 270. See also 440.

[9] *Ibid.*, p. 181.

The eastern seaboard of Spain must have been a favorable breeding ground at that period for the Black Arts of sundry descriptions, if we may judge by the attention Eymeric gave to necromancers, fortune-tellers, astrologers, and downright diabolists and satanists. He took pains to make a distinction in favor of "mere magicians and diviners, such as those who work only with the *arte chyromantiae,* who divine from the lines of the hand, and judge from natural effects and conditions of men." These were not heretics, and the Inquisitor was not concerned with them, nor of course with those "magicians" who dealt in mathematics, alchemy or other sciences. Magicians were heretics, however, when they taught heresy, parodied or mocked the sacraments, invoked devils, offered sacrifices to devils, rebaptised children in their name, asked them to reveal the future, or offered any service to the powers of darkness.

There were three ways, according to Eymeric, of invoking devils. The first was the method of the prophets of Baal: promising obedience to the demons in prayers, praising them, promising them reverence, observing chastity for their sake, fasting in honor of them, wearing black clothes in reverence for them, using characters, signs and unknown names to invoke or worship them, lighting lamps in their honor, sacrificing birds, beasts, or one's own blood to them. Secondly, as King Saul consulted the pythonical spirit, there were sorcerers in Spain who attempted to gain something from dark powers of evil by drawing a circle on the ground and putting a boy in the midst of it, by weaving spells with mirrors, swords and flasks, and so on. The third way of foul questing was to interpose the names of devils between those of saints, as the Saracens, said Eymeric, invoked Mohammed, and some of the Beghards invoked their Peter John.[10]

Is all this the fantasy of a warped and bigoted mind, as historians of the liberal school have made such medieval apprehensions appear? There was plenty of evidence that only too many of the enemies of Christianity—principally Jews and Arabs,[11] who had come from Africa to dwell in those old cosmopolitan cities

[10] *Ibid.,* p. 338.
[11] *Ibid.,* p. 317. This is Pegna's opinion.

along the east coast—made their living by preying upon the credulity and superstition of the simple. They wrote books instructing their readers how to invoke the aid of demons, to gain health and prosperity for themselves, to bring sickness, failure or death on their enemies. They taught how to mix love potions by which girls could be seduced, and they played cunningly upon the emotions of women, "whom the demons deceive," observed Pegna, "on account of the frailty of their sex, and their great curiosity." [12] Whether the sorcerers and their victims ever obtained the powers they sought from such a source, is beside the question. Eymeric apparently had his doubts about it, for he listed among the errors of the sorcerers the belief that it was possible, by black arts, "to coerce the free will of a man to the will and desire of another." [13] But he knew, unfortunately from evidence, that the *poculum amatorium* purchased from one of these wretches by a love-lorn youth might be composed of a relic of a martyr, an Agnus Dei, even a consecrated Host. Unfortunately, too, there was a considerable traffic in books of black magic that played a useful part in the perpetual conspiracy to dissolve Christian belief. Eymeric confiscated large numbers of such works. He had the pleasure of burning publicly an opus in seven parts entitled *Liber Salomonis,* which gave a complete course in making sacrifices, oblations and prayers to the demons.[14] One of the famous impostors he exposed was Raymond of Tarragona, a Jew by birth who became a Catholic, joined the Order of Preachers, and under cover of the habit of Saint Dominic, wrote and disseminated books containing not only heresies but a great deal of more or less thinly disguised satanism. One of his works of diabolism began with the pious words, *Misericordia et veritas*— Eymeric, jointly with Archbishop Peter of Tarragona, asked and received the permission of Pope Gregory XI to burn all the books of this Raymond the Neophyte, as he was called, and to punish the author. By an edict of Pope John XXII, *in perpetuum valituro,* all who invoked demons, or made images, prepared phials or had any other dealings with the

[12] *Ibid.,* p. 338.
[13] *Ibid.,* p. 347.
[14] *Ibid.,* p. 316.

Black Art were excommunicated *de facto;* and all excommunicated persons who remained so a year without taking steps to be reconciled to the Church were held under "vehement suspicion of heresy" by the Inquisition.

Are we to dismiss all this with a superior shrug as medieval superstition, or a *cosa de España?* A murder in Pennsylvania, in the 1920's, disclosed the operations there of numerous "wizards" and "hex doctors," whose advice led some simple men to commit a violent crime. No age or country has been free from this sort of thing.

As for Jews, Eymeric followed the opinion of Saint Thomas, which was also the consistent teaching of the Church, that they must not be compelled to accept Christianity, "for to believe is of the will." They could be restrained, however, from interfering with the practice of their Faith by Christians, or persuading them to do evil, or blaspheming Christ, or persecuting the faithful in any way. The same was true of infidels; and in Eymeric's opinion the Crusades were justified not as a means of converting the Mohammedans, but to make them stop persecuting and impeding the faith of Christ. Christian Jews who gave up the Faith, and Jews who induced them to do so, were regarded by Eymeric, following Bernard Gui, and citing the decree of Nicholas IV, as heretics. A Jew who sinned against the Law of Moses was a sort of heretic, also. "We Christians and Jews hold certain high things in common," wrote Eymeric: a belief in God the Father, for example. If Jews sinned against such truths, they were heretical, and the Pope, as Vicar of Christ, could judge them, "if their own prelates do not punish them." However, the Popes consistently upheld the right of the Jews to follow in their own way the beliefs and rites of the Old Testament, which the Church indeed regards as revealed by God, and prefiguring her own ceremonies.[15] Taking advantage of this, some of the Cathari of Leon used to circumcise themselves, so that they might propagate heresy as "Jews."

Gentiles who had only the natural law were heretics if they sinned against that law. Hence the Inquisition could punish a

[15] *Ibid.,* p. 348 *et seq.*

sodomite, for example, even if he was neither a Jew nor a Catholic.[16]

Eymeric's ideal of his office was as lofty as Bernard Gui's. The Inquisitor, he said, ought to be "modest in his bearing, circumspect in prudence, firm in his constancy, eminently learned in the sacred teaching of the Faith, and abounding in virtues." He ought to love God so much that he would lay aside all fear of men.[17] He should be at least forty years of age (though bishops need not be more than thirty), to make sure of his bringing seasoned judgment, based upon experience and observation, to his tremendous responsibility. His power came directly from the Pope. He had equal authority with a bishop, when they were proceeding together on a case. He and his *socius* could absolve each other from excommunication or irregularity (a faculty conceded by Pope Urban IV in 1261) except in certain cases reserved to the Pope, as for example if the Inquisitor extorted money illegally. He could proceed against any individual, in any rank of life, except a Pope or a Bishop. He could prosecute other priests, kings and nobles, even dead persons. He was allowed to have an armed guard or *familia* for his own protection and the apprehension of criminals, but he must be careful not to abuse this privilege. He could invoke the aid of the secular arm, and secular officials could be excommunicated for refusing to aid him. He could maintain his own prison, preferably in common with a bishop; and he must visit the prisoners therein at least twice a month, and ask if they needed anything and were decently lodged or not. He must not imprison any one without sufficient *indicia* of guilt.[18]

Eymeric carefully outlined the procedure of his officials and provided form letters for every contingency. On arriving in the country to which he had been sent, the Inquisitor must first present himself to the King or secular lord of the place, show him his apostolic commission, and "exhort and supplicate" him to aid in the holy work, to grant safe-conducts to him and to his *socius,* notary and *familia,* and to protect their persons and their goods.

[16] *Ibid.,* p. 353.
[17] *Ibid.,* p. 534.
[18] *Ibid.,* pp. 534, 536, 556, 558, 559, 571, 583-85, 587-91.

For the convenience of the secular lord, a form letter was presented, which he was to send to all his officials. It began thus:

"N——, by the grace of God King of such a kingdom, to our beloved and faithful officials, one and all, wherever they have been appointed, or shall be appointed, to hold places within our dominion, to whom these presents come: *Salutem et dilectionem.*" The officials were then directed to give every possible aid and favor to "Our Religious and Beloved Brother N—— of the Order of Friars Preachers, Inquisitor of Heretical Depravity." [19]

The Inquisitor then sent the same officials a rather tart letter notifying them that he expected prompt obedience. If he felt any lack of coöperation, he could ask an official to place his hand on the Gospels and take a formal oath to obey him and the Church. Any one refusing or neglecting to do this, after three days, would be excommunicated and denounced, under a form provided by Eymeric.[20] This of course was no light matter; and before receiving absolution, the excommunicated politician would have to kneel and swear to obey, after which, to make the occasion more impressive, the Inquisitors and others present would recite a psalm, *Miserere mei, Deus,* or the *Deus misereatur,* followed by the *Kyrie* and the *Paternoster.* The Inquisitor would then ask forgiveness for the culprit in a special prayer, and finally absolve him.

If the official, after absolution, should suffer another lapse of coöperation and obedience, there was a special form for denouncing him yet more vigorously. This was made as public and as ominous as possible. The Inquisitors and their *sequaces* would appear before the populace, carrying lighted candles, which they extinguished in the sight of all by plunging them into water or otherwise, while bells were rung. A denunciation was then read, warning all Christians to avoid the recalcitrant, for he was a moral leper who would corrupt every one. Whoever supported him would likewise be excommunicated. Solemn High Mass was then held, and the people were warned not to eat, drink or talk with the excommunicated man, or have anything to do with him.[21] There was nothing half-hearted about Brother Eymeric.

[19] *Ibid.,* p. 390.
[20] *Ibid.,* p. 396.
[21] *Ibid.,* p. 399.

Now and then, in the early days of the Inquisition, all the officials of a city would refuse to cooperate, even after the candle and bell ceremony. In that case the whole community was placed under an interdict. This meant the complete cessation of their religious life. There could be no Mass, no baptisms, no marriages, no confessions, no blessings for the dying and the dead until the guilty made amends, and took the oath. If they still persisted, however, they were declared relieved of their offices.

Generally there was no need of proceeding to such extremities. Except in a few strongholds of heresy where the most important elements of the population had forsaken the Church for the weird teachings of the Manichees, the Inquisition was welcomed as an instrument of peace and security, and received the full support of officials and people. Once this was assured, the Inquisitor was ready to announce the *Sermo generalis*. All the people and clergy of the town were summoned to meet in the cathedral church on a given day, usually a Sunday, when all would be free to attend. The Inquisitor read to them, in the vulgar tongue, a form explaining the purposes of the Holy Office, and calling upon all who knew of any persons guilty of speaking against the Faith or the sacraments of the Church, or sacrificing to or invoking demons, to come forward and denounce them, or be excommunicated. For this they were granted a time of grace, usually a month or more. All guilty persons who confessed within that time would be treated as leniently as possible; otherwise they could expect to be prosecuted with vigor.

Toward all who came forward voluntarily, without being denounced, Eymeric advised that "the Inquisitor ought to be more gentle." He should first find out how they came by their heresy. If they desired to tell him in sacramental Confession, he should not allow it, "for Inquisitors are not judges, as Inquisitors, in the interior penitential forum, but judges in the exterior forum." There was danger, too, that he might be deceived in the confessional, in which case the sacrament would be dishonored. Moreover, he would be placed in a difficult position, as confessor, if he had to prosecute the penitent later, for he would be bound to secrecy by the seal of the confessional, and would not be free in the exercise of his duties as Inquisitor. Always be easy, however, Eymeric repeated, with the voluntary penitent. Such a person perhaps doubted some article of faith, but told nobody, "infected" nobody. In this case he must be absolved secretly, with salutary penances; urged "to stand firm in the Catholic Faith, avoid such and such a temptation," and so on. If others were involved, however, the Inquisitor must know, and must speak with them too—always being lenient, if they come voluntarily.[22]

If many denunciations came in during the period of grace, the Inquisitor wrote the names of the denouncers, the denounced, and any witnesses, with their addresses and occupations, in a small notebook. A separate book was kept for each diocese, and Eymeric warned the Inquisitors never to let any one see it, or reveal the names of the denouncers; "for danger threatens them." Many an Inquisitor carried around with him in his little book the lives of numerous men who, if he made a slip, might be found in dark alleys some morning with knives between their ribs. The Inquisitor himself walked in daily danger of such a fate.

After the term of grace expired, the Inquisitor settled down to the more disagreeable part of his work. He would look over his little notebook and select the complaints "which have the appearance of truth," especially the more serious crimes, and those most hurtful to the Faith. Then he would cite the denouncer to appear before him, and place him under oath. If the man's story did not ring true, he would tell him to come back some other day. If on the other hand it seemed to carry conviction, the Inquisitor could proceed in any one of three ways: (1) by the *accusatio;* (2) by the *denunciatio;* (3) by the *inquisitio.* These were three methods employed in Roman Law for criminal cases.

Under the *accusatio,* one man accused another of a crime, and offered to submit to the *poenam talionis* (that is, he himself would undergo the legal punishment for that crime) if he failed to prove his case. If one citizen accused another of being a relaxed and impenitent heretic, his failure to prove this would result in his being sent to the stake in place of his victim. In 1304 the Inquisitor Fra Landulpho fined the town of Theate 150 ounces of silver

[22] *Ibid.,* pp. 407-411.

because its officials had accused a citizen of heresy, and had failed to substantiate the charge. But in general this method had become rare, for obvious reasons. Eymeric urged that it be avoided if possible, on account of the danger in which it involved the accuser. However, if the accuser insisted, the Inquisitor must acquiesce, and tell the man to put his complaint in writing. This done, the Inquisitor proceeded not *ex officio,* but *ad instantiam partis.* A notary and two religious persons, or at least two honest men, were summoned, and in their presence the trial began. One of the last men accused in this manner was Martin Luther.

Under the *Denunciatio,* the accuser denounced another without offering to prove his case. This method, too, had been found unsatisfactory in general for heresy trials, and with the development of the monastic Inquisition, had gradually yielded to the *Inquisitio,* which experience had found most effective. The Inquisitor, unlike the judge under the Roman Law, was seeking not to punish the offense, primarily, but to heal and reconcile the offender. As a priest, he was not interested in the prosecution of crime—that was the state's business. What he desired was the spiritual health of the offender, and this involved his reconciliation with the Church of God, and some sort of penance to test his sincerity and help him gain the strength to persevere in his reformation. For this reason the earlier Inquisition was not very hospitable to lawyers and advocates as counsel for the accused. There has been a great deal of misunderstanding about this; it has been made the ground of a strong indictment of the Inquisition, as unwilling to give the accused the fair chance that he is allowed in modern criminal practice. But the Inquisitor did not have this juridical point of view. He was a specialist in the science of the things of God, the doctor of souls, as Bernard Gui said, whose aim was not to punish but to heal and save. If the heretic fell into the hands of the state, he was burned without getting a second chance. The Inquisition saved him from this fate, if he would abjure and be reconciled, and there is no doubt that large numbers of heretics escaped the faggots and the stake because patient Inquisitors induced them to abjure, or frightened them into it. For all this the best method seemed to be the *Inquisitio.*

In this form the entire initiative was taken by the Inquisitor, who was both prosecutor and judge. His first task was to examine the accused and the witnesses. For this purpose Eymeric developed a technique as elaborate and painstaking as anything in the history of jurisprudence. He provided a form for every conceivable emergency. He even suggested the questions that the Inquisitor should ask each witness concerning the accused. For example:

"Do you know so-and-so? How long have you known him? How well? When, and how often have you spoken to him? Did you hear him say anything against the Faith, the sacraments, etc? What did he say? Did he say it *trufatorie,* or *recitative?* Deliberately and seriously, or did he seem to be joking? Was he laughing? Angry? Arguing with any one?"

If the witness replied that the remarks were made in jest or in anger, the Inquisitor must not be too gullible, but must investigate further to make sure, "for almost all modern heretics excuse themselves in this way." Let him find the truth, so far as possible, and then proceed. If the accused really was angry or joking, he was not to be prosecuted for heresy. He ought to be punished in some way, however, "for a man should not speak against Faith in levity or anger."

It was the general policy of the Inquisition not to convict a man for a slip of the tongue, but to warn him gravely to avoid it in future. Likewise heretical statements were not to be taken seriously if they came from a person who was drunk, talking in his sleep, senile with age, or too young to know the significance of his remarks.[23]

To avoid any possibility or suspicion of fraud, all witnesses had to be examined in the presence of a notary, preferably some public official of importance, two religious or at least reputable persons, and the Judge.

The next step was the examination of the accused. He was put under oath and asked many set questions about himself, his parents, and so on. He was not to be arrested until he confessed, or until the Inquisitor had strong reasons, from the testimony of at least two witnesses (as in the Inquisition of Moses) for believing him prob-

[23] *Ibid.,* p. 420.

ably guilty. To commit him to prison, however, the Inquisitor must first obtain the consent of the Bishop.

It was the understanding of all the great jurisconsults of the Inquisition that the Inquisitor, in all his examinations, should deal with people "humanely, remembering that he himself is a man, who could commit similar offenses, if he were not borne up by the grace of the omnipotent God, and that he should deal with the culprit according to his quality and dignity." [24]

In these formal instructions for Inquisitors, the person on trial is never called "the accused," "the suspect" or "the defendant," as in modern law. He is always "the criminal" (*reus*); "the guilty." The difference here was one of method rather than of justice. We place a man on trial while there is still a legal presumption of his innocence. The Inquisitors would have considered that unfair, and hurtful to his reputation. They virtually convicted a man before they began to proceed formally against him. If they could not convict him, they did not even arrest him. Some never knew they had been suspected.

Not a conviction, but the truth is what Eymeric repeatedly demanded of his Inquisitors. And to get at the truth, he admitted, there was no infallible formula. In fact, it was better not to have a general rule, for "the sons of darkness will find a way to avoid" such; they cared nothing for truth, and would resort to every evasion and sophistry.[25] Eymeric, in his long experience, noticed ten different methods by which the heretics tried to slip out of the net, and with characteristic thoroughness he set them down, somewhat in this fashion, but at much greater length:

(1) Some heretics use equivocal words, which enable them to pay lip service to any Catholic dogma, but in a sense different from that understood by Catholics. (2) They will change the sense of a question by adding . condition. For example: Is marriage a sacrament? "If it please God," answers the heretic, "I believe it indeed;" meaning, "It does not please God, so I don't believe it." (3) They will answer a question with a question (as Bernard Gui also noticed). (4) They will pretend astonishment. Q. Do you believe

---

[24] *Ibid.*, p. 422; Pegna's comment.
[25] *Ibid.*, p. 428.

God is the creator of all things? A. Why, shouldn't I believe it?
(5) They will resort to tergiversation of words. Q. Do you believe
that one swearing a legal oath commits a sin? A. I believe that
if one speaks the truth one does not sin. (6) They will change the
subject, *per verborum manifestam translationem*. (7) They will
seek to justify themselves. Q. Did Christ ascend into Heaven?
A. Sir Inquisitor, I am a simple man and illiterate, who loves God
simply, and don't know these questions. (8) They will feign weakness or sickness when trapped. They will ask to lie down. The
women will often plead *se pati muliebrem passionem*. (9) They
will pretend to be foolish or mad, and answer laughingly, or inco-
herently. If they prove to be truly insane, adds Eymeric, they must
be restored to mental health, if possible, and are not to be punished.
Finally (10) many of them feign sanctity, casting down their eyes,
wearing Franciscan cords or robes. Yet they are like white sepul-
chres, all gilded without, but inside full of all uncleanness; for
inwardly, says Eymeric, these heretics are found to be full of pride,
lust, appetite, ruin and vainglory.

For every *parade* of the wary heretic, however, the trained Inquisitor has a feint and thrust of his own, ready to use with
deadly effect. Pin him down, says Eymeric, by explicit questions
and demand explicit answers. Or be bland with him, profess sympathy that he has been deceived in his simplicity, and offer to be
his teacher. Have some of the testimony of the witnesses read to
him, without names, and watch his reactions. Glance at the process
with a look of astonishment, as if to say, "It is clear you are not
telling me the truth." Pretend you have to go away and don't
know when you will be able to return. Meanwhile what a pity it
is that he has to remain in prison! He is a delicate man, and may
get sick, and you are very sorry for him. If he would only tell
all he knows, and get it over with! Yes, this is a subterfuge, admits
Eymeric; but as usual he has a good precedent ready to justify
himself: did not King Solomon trick the two women who were
disputing over the child, that he might do justice? If no other
way will serve, leave the prisoner alone, and have some person
"not displeasing to him" bring him food and drink and get into
a conversation with him, talking of other matters until his confi-

dence is gained. Then the confidant must say he knows the Inquisitor well, and will ask him to be merciful. At the right moment the Inquisitor enters and, as if overhearing the conversation, says that of course he will be merciful. Anything is good, says Eymeric in effect, that brings about the conversion and penitence of a heretic. It is even justifiable to lodge a spy with the heretic, a man who pretends to belong to the same sect, and draws him into conversation—particularly at night, when people are more communicative, adds the sage Inquisitor.

Once the accused begins to confess, the Inquisitor must let nothing—dinner or supper, or the need of sleep—interfere with his getting a complete confession; lest the heretic, having begun to purge himself, "return to his vomit." [26]

Many silly things have been written about the Inquisition, but none sillier than the charge, recently repeated by Mr. G. G. Coulton,[27] leaning heavily upon the researches of Lea, that no verdict of acquittal was ever given by the tribunal. The Inquisitors did not use the term "acquit," but they certainly did grant the equivalent, as many famous historical cases demonstrate. Eymeric gave two special forms for making out a *certificate of innocence,* which the Bishop and the Inquisitor signed together, and presented at the end of a trial to an accused person against whom nothing had been proved.[28]

There was also a ceremony by which a man, publicly defamed for heresy, might clear himself of suspicion, when no real proof of his guilt was to be found. He was cited to appear on a certain day, with seven, ten, twenty, or even thirty other men of the same rank in life, and take oath, with his hand on the four Gospels, that he was not then, and never had been, guilty of holding the opinions for which he had been defamed. The *compurgatores* were then required to lay their hands on the Gospels, and swear that they believed he had sworn truly. If they did so, he was publicly declared "purged," or as we should say, acquitted. If they would

---

[26] *Ibid.,* p. 435.

[27] In his *Medieval Panorama,* for example, Mr. Coulton makes this and many other statements that will not stand up under critical examination.

[28] *Ibid.,* pp. 474-5.

not swear, he was then excommunicated, and unless he was reconciled within a year, would then be condemned.[29] What is obvious in all this legal machinery, however, is that the Inquisitors were not the sadistic ogres they have been made to appear in the Protestant-Liberal traditions, but conscientious judges, trying to be both just and merciful according to the best legal standards of their time—standards far higher, it must be repeated, than those of the secular courts.

The same state of mind is evident in the safeguards and limitations with which Eymeric hedged the use of torture. If, in spite of every effort to have the right personnel, a Conrad of Marburg or a Robert the Bugger got himself into an inquisitorial office, he was not free to indulge his cruelty as he might choose. For a prisoner could not be tortured, in the Fourteenth Century Inquisition, without (1) the advice of a large jury of "good and learned men" (2) the consent of the Bishop, and (3) the existence of *indices* of guilt, unconfessed, when all other means of getting a confession had been tried in vain. Eymeric had no illusions about the efficacy of torment, and warned his Inquisitors not to rely on it. "For some are so soft-hearted and foolish," he wrote, "that they will admit everything, even though it be false, under light torture: while others are so obstinate that no matter how much they are tormented, the truth is not to be had from them . . . In putting men to the question, the greatest prudence is to be exercised." [30] First of all, the torture was not to be thought of unless the accused had made conflicting confessions and would not tell the truth; or if he was reputed to be a heretic and had one weighty witness against him (this made two *indicia*, explained Eymeric); or if he had one or more "vehement or violent *indicia*" against him.

After all other means, including the intercession of relatives and friends, had been exhausted, the prisoner was usually notified in writing that he would be put to the torture. If he still refused to satisfy the curiosity of the Inquisitor, he was taken to the torture chamber, where the ministers of the Holy Office were instructed

29 *Ibid.*, p. 476.
30 *Ibid.*, p. 481.

to take off his clothes, "not joyfully, but as if somewhat perturbed," with a view to getting him to confess without the necessity of employing the instruments. If further threats or promises did not induce him to tell the truth, the sentence was carried out, gently at first, and never with "new or unusual" torments, for that, said Eymeric, would be cruel. The Inquisitor would ask questions, while the notary wrote them down, with the answers. If these last were satisfactory, and the *"reus"* repented, he was reconciled and given his penance. If impenitent, he was handed over to the secular arm, even if he made a full confession. If he was a relapsed heretic, there was seldom any hope for him, in either case.

A man who had been "decently" questioned and tormented, without revealing anything, was to be allowed to go free, unless there were some new *indicia* against him; if, for example, he made some contradictory statement in his answer to the questions. If he made a confession under torture, he was then to be taken to another room, out of sight of the ghastly instruments, and there have his confession read to him; after which the Inquisitor would ask, not once but several times, whether or not it was true. If he repudiated it, the torture could be applied again—not as a repetition, for that was illegal, but as a continuation (!), provided that he had not been properly questioned, in the opinion of the Inquisitor. If, however, the Inquisitor felt that the questioning had been sufficient, the man was to be allowed to go free. If he confirmed his confession, he was asked to abjure and be reconciled.

Boys and old persons could be tortured if necessary, but lightly. Pregnant women could not.

A confession made under torture was valid only if ratified when the torture was remote. But one made in the presence of the instruments was invalid, unless ratified later, even if the proceedings had got no further than the stripping of the accused.[31] Obviously, then, the Inquisitors themselves understood the weakness and the injustice of torture, but were not able to free themselves wholly from the methods of criminal procedure then in vogue.

Considering that no one was condemned, or even tortured, without the consent of the Bishop, and usually the advice of a numerous

[31] *Ibid.,* pp. 481-484.

and representative jury, the life or freedom of the accused did not depend, certainly, on one man's whim or logic. In Eymeric's time the summoning of the jury was fairly universal. He instructed his Inquisitors to convoke it. As Pegna explains, an Inquisitor could disregard the advice of the *periti,* but could not do so "rashly or lightly." The Inquisitor was a theologian, the *periti* were not; hence he must rely upon his own judgment in the end, and if he made an error, he could not put the responsibility on the jury, but must take the full blame. It was Eymeric's opinion that the Bishop and the Inquisitor should explain the whole process to the jury, "completely and perfectly," and not furnish merely a summary. Pegna calls this axiomatic; otherwise the *periti* could not give a sound opinion.[32]

Thus Eymeric went on making fine distinctions to great length. If his instructions were sometimes disregarded by judges less skillful or less ardent, that is true of any system of law, and should not be charged against the Inquisition alone. No ideal is ever fully realized; but the carefully trained and chosen priests of the Holy Office came nearer to the goal than the secular judges did. To most of the people of the Middle Ages, a faithful Inquisitor seemed to be a servant of God, the champion of order against anarchy, of reason against ignorance, of lawful human passion and clean marriage against oriental perversion, of truth divinely revealed against hypocrisy and slimy deceit, of legitimate public authority against the dark subversive ways of secret societies unwilling to face the light of day, of God against the devil, Christ against Antichrist. It goes without saying that the Manichees, Waldenses and other heretics did not share this opinion. But viewed objectively, there was something in it.

Perhaps no other instrument could have kept western culture from dissolving into the chaos of anarchy, in that turbulent decadent Fourteenth Century. The English and French had been fighting like heathens since the invasion of France by Edward III in 1345; and this so-called Hundred Years' War would end with bloody civil strife in both countries. "Free Companies" of *con-*

[32] *Ibid.,* pp. 630-632.

dottieri ravaged the Continent, living off the land, and driving the peasants to such desperation that they took arms, only to be butchered as *Jacquerie*. One of these companies under Bertrand de Guesclin stopped at Avignon on the way to Spain, where Pedro the Cruel, with English aid, was at war with his brother Henry of Trastamara, and insulted and plundered the Pope. Conditions in Italy were unspeakable. Pestilence, famine and civil war raged everywhere. Rome was a shambles during the absence of the nine Popes who lived at Avignon, her population reduced to 30,000, her beautiful churches and monasteries falling to ruins. The lack of discipline had brought about an unspeakable condition among the clergy there. It was no vindictive and emotional George Segarelli or Ubertino of Casale, but Saint Birgitta of Sweden who said of them, not long before her death in 1373, that they "break all the laws of the Church, wear short cassocks and swords, and a coat of mail under the cassock; shamelessly they embrace their mistresses and their children; the convents of nuns are houses of ill fame, countless people die without ever having been to confession or to Communion—the world swarms with serpents and Peter's fish dare not lift their heads for fear of their venom. Oh, Rome, Rome, I must speak of thee now as the prophet spoke of Jerusalem! The roses and lilies in thy garden are choked by thistles, thy walls are broken down, thy gates have no watchmen, thine altars are destroyed, thy sacred vessels are sold, and no smoke of sacrifice ascends from thy sanctuary. The vessels of the Church have been carried off to Babylon, the sword of the fear of God is thrown away, and in its stead there is a bottomless bag of money; all the words of the ten commandments have been gathered up into one, and that is: Bring hither the money! . . . Simony is committed openly, without shame, indulgences are an article of merchandise; like Judas they sell Christ; the priests have grown savage like wolves, and shaking like loose stones, like thieves they walk in darkness; they are unclean like pitch and defile all that comes near them . . . the devil is as sure of them as the whale of her young that she keeps alive in her belly . . . [33]

Avignon, where Eymeric was calmly composing his *Directorium*

[33] Jörgensen, *St. Catherine of Siena*, pp. 159-160. English translation.

Inquisitorum all this while, was outwardly more peaceful than Rome, but in other respects not much better. There is a terrible passage in the *Dialogue* of Saint Catherine of Siena that probably reflects her opinion of the lives of some of the clergy there. The sad fact was that French regalism had brought the Church to her most shameful and helpless state—helpless, because each Pope (with the exception of Blessed Urban V, who went back to Rome temporarily) was bound to the throne of France by ties of politics, interest or a lack of independence in his character, for which in fact he had been chosen; and the vicious system was perpetuated by the constant creation of French Cardinals, to ensure their majority in the Sacred College.

The situation was so discouraging, in 1370, that only a divinely founded Institution could have survived it at all. But it was not an Inquisition alone, good brother Eymeric, that could save the Bride of Christ, surrounded by false friends and servants, from the destruction that seemed to yawn at her feet. The impetus toward reform and regeneration, the striving toward first and holy things that has always risen up within the Catholic Church at the moment when her human elements seemed weakest and foulest, was already in motion; and it was beginning where it always began, not with political churchmen, no matter how worldly-wise, not with the greatest theologians (if they were nothing else) but with simple, humble loving souls who had the sincerity to take the words of Christ quite literally, and the courage to follow Him in His sufferings, even if the end was death. It was not Eymeric who was to save the Church, but Saint Catherine.

Eymeric was still at Avignon when that frail young woman in the habit of his own order arrived there with her friends, after a journey across the Alps, in June, 1376. He may even have been present in the great Gothic hall of the castle from which, as from a dungeon of gold, she sought to deliver the captive vicar of Christ. Gregory XI listened as her chaplain interpreted her burning Tuscan words. At the end he replied quietly that he would leave the whole matter in her hands, asking only that she remember the dignity of the Church.

The battle was not yet won, however. The lords of Florence

had no desire to make peace soon with the Papal States. The French Cardinals urged the Pope to stay where he was. The French Crown exerted all its pressure for the same end, and sent the Duke of Anjou, brother to the King, to win over Catherine; but it was the Saint who made a convert of him. Nor was the complacency of irresolute Pope Gregory any match for the spiritual flame that burned in the frail woman of Siena, who bore the stigmata of Christ's wounds on her body, and lived on the Blessed Sacrament alone. On one occasion she looked into his secret soul and reminded him of a vow he had made while a Cardinal, to restore the Chair of Peter to Rome if he became Pope. "Holiest and most blessed Father in Christ, sweet Jesus," she wrote him, "your unworthy and miserable daughter Catherine strengthens you in His precious blood and desires to see you delivered from all slavish fear. For the timorous soul has no strength to perform his good resolutions and holy desires, and therefore I have prayed to the sweet and good Jesus to take away from you all slavish fear, so that only holy fear may remain. The fire of love burns in you, so that you may not be able to hear the voices of the incarnate devils who, from what I learn, would frighten you and hinder your journey by saying that it will be your death. And I say to you in the name of Christ Crucified that you have no cause whatsoever for fear. Be of good courage and depart, trust in Christ Jesus; when you do that which is your duty, God will be with you, and none can be against you. Be a man, Father, arise . . . You ought to come to Rome, therefore come." [34]

The Inquisition began making inquiries about Catherine while she was in Avignon. People had begun to whisper (perhaps some of the evil-living persons whose very presence obviously sickened her) that she might, after all, be one of those false mystics who seem so holy without, but were full of heresy and all foulness within. One day three Inquisitors called upon her. One of them was a Franciscan archbishop; it is not clear whether Eymeric was one of the others or not. They asked her all sorts of questions about her ecstasies, her fasting, her beliefs. They found no heresy, of course, in her. It was one thing to criticise the lives of prelates,

[34] *Ibid.*

and even to admonish the Pope to his face, and quite another to deny the authority of the Church and of Christ's Vicar. Those who love to make early Protestants of such saints as Catherine of Siena and Joan of Arc forget this vital distinction.

Catherine herself, however, understood the difference between sin, which could be expiated and forgiven, and the tragedy of being cut off from the source of grace. "The Church is no other than Christ Himself," she said, "and it is she who gives us the Sacraments, and the Sacraments give us life." [35] She reproved the government of Florence in these words, "He who rebels against our Father, Christ on earth, is condemned to death, for that which we do to him, we do to Christ in Heaven. We honor Christ if we honor the Pope, we dishonor Christ if we dishonor the Pope . . . Well do I know that there are many who do not think they are offending God by so doing, but rather that they are doing Him a service by persecuting the Church and her servants, for they defend themselves by saying: 'They are so corrupt and work all manner of evil.' But I tell you that God wills and has so commanded that even if the priests and the pastors of the Church and Christ on earth were incarnate devils, it is seemly that we are obedient and subject to them, not for their sake, but for the sake of God, out of obedience to Him, for He wills that we should act thus . . ." This was the spirit also of Saint Francis, who had said, "I will fear, love and honor as my masters and will have recourse to the priests who live according to the laws of the Holy Roman Church and are consecrated by it, even though they persecute me, and will see no sin in them, for I see only the Son of God in them, and they are my masters."

Pope Gregory told Catherine to shut her door in the faces of the Inquisitors, if they bothered her again. But there was no need. The investigators of the Holy Office were her devoted friends after that first conversation. And at last came the day of her victory, when the Pope, stepping resolutely over the prostrate gray head of his aged father, Count de Beaufort, who had thrown himself across the threshold, left the palace at Avignon forever, and took the hard road that Catherine had pointed out to him.

[35] *Ibid.*, p. 200.

Eymeric went along in the Pope's entourage to Marseilles, where they took a ship for Genoa. There Gregory hesitated again, for he heard that Rome was in revolt, and the Florentines victorious over the papal troops in the north and east. But Catherine also had arrived in Genoa, having gone by way of Toulon; and a few words with her gave him courage to proceed to Corneto and thence to Ostia. Finally on January 17, 1377, he entered the Holy City, humble, unarmed, seated on a white mule, as his Master had ridden to Jerusalem. The Roman people danced for joy, and flowers fell about the returning exile.

Catherine was in Florence, saying prayers of gratitude; but Eymeric was probably somewhere in that long procession that filed through the neglected streets to Saint Peter's Square as the dusk fell, and eight hundred lamps began to glow.

As Catherine had promised, Gregory did not die from his journey or from the hands of murderous men. But when Rome resumed its rioting and seemed a hopeless Hell on earth, he made an unfortunate decision to return to Avignon. Then he died before he could get away.

The curse of the exile was ended, but not so the troubles of the Church. Eymeric was in Rome during the turbulent days when Urban VI was elected; but when Clement VII, the anti-pope, was chosen by the French Cardinals on Urban's angry refusal to return to Avignon, the Inquisitor, like many of his fellow countrymen, followed the Spanish Cardinal Pedro de Luna into the service of the anti-pope, who, as a Cardinal had ordered the frightful massacre at Cesena. Saint Catherine of Siena, on the other hand, with that direct perception of the truth about men and affairs that characterized her, took the part of the rightful pontiff, and went to Rome to help him, in 1378, about two years before her death. Clement VII meanwhile had gone to Avignon. There, in the course of time, Eymeric's friend and patron, Cardinal de Luna, himself became an anti-pope under the name of Benedict XIII.

The Great Schism of the West proved more injurious to the Church than even the exile at Avignon had been. Nothing so impaired the respect men owed the Papacy than the general feeling of uncertainty as to which of two or even three claimants was the real Vicar of Christ. If there had been an Innocent III in Rome in 1431, perhaps the execution of Saint Joan (a victim of the Inquisition not in its ordinary course, but by the intrusion of English political intrigue) might not have occurred. It was not until 1447 that the confusion and helplessness ended with the acknowledgment of Nicholas V by the whole Church.

Brother Eymeric meanwhile had not returned to Avignon, but had gone back to Spain, to the Dominican convent at Gerona, and his old work of hunting down the little foxes who destroyed the vines. We may infer that he put into practice, as thoroughly as possible, the principles he had laid down in his *Directorium,* and renewed his attack upon the works of Ramón Lull, which, six decades after the death of their author, were enjoying popularity even in high places. Eymeric made no secret of his conviction that Lull had been a most dangerous heretic, and of his intention to make the Lullists abjure their errors or face the consequences.

At this point some of the most powerful personages in Aragon declared themselves in favor of the Lullists, and the Inquisitor was met with a storm of opposition which would have stopped a less determined man. Don Pedro *el Ceremonioso* had already become a champion of Lull's memory in 1377, requesting the Pope to have the books in question examined, not in Rome, but in Barcelona, "for since they were Catalan, they would be better understood by Catalans than by men of some other nation."

Eymeric's old enemy, Bernard Ermengaudi, who had succeeded him as Grand Inquisitor of Aragon, announced on May 19, 1386, that three false propositions which Eymeric had imputed to Lull's *Philosophia amoris* were nowhere to be found in that work. The following year, King Juan I, who had once called Eymeric *"religiosum et dilectum nostrum fratrem"* became so exasperated over the attack on the Lullists that he now described him in an official document as "an obstinate lunatic, diabolical enemy of the faith, greased with the venom of infidelity, our mortal enemy and a poisonous man." [36]

[36] *Loco pertinax, endiablado enemigo de la fe, untado con ponzoña de infidelidad, mortal enemigo nuestro y hombre venenoso."*—Menendez y Pelayo, *op. cit.,* Vol. III, p. 276, note. See also page 278 for other particulars about Eymeric's controversy with the Lullists.

Ordered out of Aragon, the old Inquisitor (he was then 71) retreated with his foes crying "Liar!" after him, and retired to Barcelona, to intrench himself. There he was bombarded at long range from Valencia, where the *jurados* wrote to the Council of Barcelona in 1391 complaining of the insults he had inflicted upon certain Lullists of their community, and asking their sister community to join them in complaining to Rome about his *diversos y enormes crimenes*. The Councillors of Barcelona replied, July 8, that if Valencia wished to make a general accusation against Maestro Eymeric, the city of Barcelona would make "one arm and a single heart" with them; but not if the complaints were of individual cases. As for Lull's works, they were resolved to ask the Holy Father to commission some prelate of the province to examine them, with the help of theologians, and to declare with apostolic authority whether the condemnations of Eymeric were just or unjust.[37]

Whatever faults Eymeric may have had, no one ever accused him of lack of courage. Undismayed by the furious reaction to his assaults on the books and followers of Lull, he took on, in his old age, an even more formidable adversary. He tried to make a heretic of Saint Vincent Ferrer, a member, by the way, of his own order.

Vincent was made of that same unearthly fire that burned in Saint Catherine of Siena, and had much of the same irresistible power over men and events. He had been a student at Toulouse, amid the scenes of Bernard Gui's activities, when Eymeric was going to Rome with Pope Gregory in 1377. Two years later he was employed by Cardinal Pedro de Luna to try to gain the obedience of the King of Aragon to the anti-pope at Avignon, in whose cause Vincent then believed. In 1385 he began giving a series of sermons in the Cathedral at Valencia, preaching as no man of that time had ever preached before. In later life he walked over a great part of Western Europe, addressing huge crowds in Italy, France, Spain, the Low Countries, Germany, and even England and Ireland; and wherever he went he repaired some of the ravages of the Black Death, the Exile and the Schism. At one time he was followed by about 10,000 penitents. He cared for the plague-stricken

37 *Ibid.*, p. 278.

and the hungry. He performed astonishing miracles. Moslems and Jews were moved by his eloquence. He made thousands of converts among the Mohammedans of Granada. And not the least of his achievements, by any means, was the conversion of from 25,000 to 30,000 Jews.

The Jewish population of Spain had grown enormously. Bernaldez says that "when the Jewish books were burned at the time of Saint Vincent," [38] there were 100,000 families of that race in Castile alone. They were beginning to recover from the cruel onslaught that fell upon them after the Black Death, when, like the Jews all over Europe, they were accused of having caused the plague by poisoning the wells, and were put to the sword in spite of the strenuous efforts of Pope Clement VI, then at Avignon, to save them. Clement was not the best of Popes, but he followed the example, as he said, of Calixtus II, Eugenius III, Alexander III, Clement III, Celestine II, Innocent III, Gregory IX, Nicholas III, Honorius IV and Nicholas IV, in pointing out the absurdity of attributing such public misfortunes to the Jews. He explained that the plague had raged in countries where no Jews lived; and he ordered all prelates to proclaim in the churches that no Jews were to be beaten, wounded or slain, under pain of the Holy See's anathema.[39]

By 1385 they had regained their old prosperity and influence in all parts of Spain. There had always been some converts to Christianity among them, but the number was relatively small until Saint Vincent, by his preaching and his miracles, began to touch their hearts with pity for the sufferings of the Crucified Jew. In 1390 he played a part in a conversion that was destined to have momentous consequences, as we shall see, in Spanish history. He baptized the famous rabbi, Selemoh ha-Levi, who, as Señor Madariaga observes, was "known in all Spanish Jewry for his scholarship and talent," was "equally respected for his science and for his virtue," and was "no doubt upright and honest." [40] This has been the general verdict upon him, save from some of his more

[38] *Historia de los reyes católicos.*
[39] Lea, *The Inquisition of Spain,* I, p. 89 *et seq.*
[40] *Christopher Columbus,* p. 124.

bitter Jewish critics, who resented his conversion. He became just as illustrious in the Catholic Church as he had been in the synagogue, and taking the name of Don Pablo de Santa Maria (he is said to have seen Our Lady in a vision), he became in time Bishop of Burgos. Now, this good and sincere man, after his conversion, accused the Jews of applying Jacob's prophecy, "The sceptre shall not be taken away from Juda," to Spain, which they planned to control and make into a New Jerusalem; and he was responsible for legislation restricting the activities of Jews.

He was not a murderous fanatic. There was, however, such a man in Sevilla; and in 1391 this Jew-baiter, defying the orders of the Archbishop, the Chapter and the King, incited a mob to slaughter the Jews and plunder their rich houses. The pogroms spread from city to city. There were thousands of baptisms as the frightened Jews sought to keep their goods and their lives. Unfortunately too many of these conversions were different from the genuine ones resulting from the preaching of Saint Vincent and the example of Rabbi Paul, and were to have some terrible consequences.

Meanwhile Saint Vincent was continuing with his work. Like all the saints, he loved Christ better than he loved his own life; yet, like all the saints he had a strong individuality, unwarped by the touch of oriental quietism, and followed no pattern of thought save those imposed by divine revelation or reason. Once in a sermon at Valencia or elsewhere, he made the somewhat unconventional assertion that Judas had done penance, and might have been saved.

Eymeric was on his trail at once. One imagines the hoary Dominican, restless perhaps after too long an exile from the labors in which he was so expert, going about diligently to interview witnesses, to peer into the past life of the preacher, to finger lovingly his various forms of denunciation and delation, interrogation, condemnation and relaxation, carefully distilled from long experience as Grand Inquisitor for Aragon in the splendid days gone by. Perhaps he received exaggerated or distorted accounts of what had been said, perhaps he took evidence from the enemies of Vincent; at any rate, he lodged a formal charge that the Saint was teaching that Judas was saved.

Vincent was probably never in much danger. His old master, Cardinal Pedro de Luna was now the anti-pope Benedict XIII at Avignon, and when he heard of the matter, he had the papers sent to him, and tore them up.

This, in the last months of Brother Eymeric's life, must have been a sore trial to him. But he had seen a great deal of human frailty and perversity, and probably found ways to console himself as he prepared himself for the great Inquisition to which he presently went, on January 4, 1393.[41] He was buried in the Dominican church at Gerona.

The Catholic Church has not yet formally declared Judas to be in Hell; though, with certain words of her divine Master before her, she has certainly not asserted his presence in Heaven. She has asserted the presence of Saint Vincent there. The worst blows, however, to the reputation of Eymeric, both in his lifetime and in later years, fell upon it in consequence of his attacks upon the works of the Mallorcan mystic Ramón Lull. The best account in English of the career of that eccentric but lovable poet, who at the age of thirty left wife and children to wander about the world seeking the conversion of Jews and Mohammedans, because he had seen, or thought he had seen, several visions of Christ Crucified, who wrote some five hundred books, gave advice to Popes, studied in his old age at Paris, wore Franciscan robes, and was stoned to death by the Moslems to whom he preached at Bugia (though there is some conflict in the accounts of this, as of his alleged revelations and some of his journeys) is to be found in the biography of Professor Allison Peers, the skilled translator of *Blanquerna* and other works of Lull. Our concern here must be with that strange genius's connection with the Inquisition.

Almost immediately after the death of Ramón in 1315, the people of Mallorca and Catalonia began to venerate him as a martyr. Stories were heard of miracles through his intercession. In time there appeared a Mass and an Office composed in his memory. Fifty years after his death, his works were still popular in all the

[41] This is the date on his tombstone; see Pegna, *loc. cit.*

Latin countries. As far away as England Caxton would print one of his books. A vast number of quaint treatises dealing with alchemy, necromancy and sundry superstitions were falsely attributed to this prolific writer. Devout Catholics read him as they read the *Imitation*. On the other hand, many heretics took up his doctrines and changed them to suit themselves.

It was about 1366 when some of his books, with others erroneously attributed to him, fell under the inquisitorial eye of Brother Eymeric. From the works themselves, and from the characters of some of the people who distributed them, the Inquisitor became convinced that he was dealing with a most dangerous anti-Christian force, whose Manichean effects were already at work in all parts of Christendom. He brought the matter to the attention of Pope Gregory XI, who, in a bull, *Nuper dilecto,* instructed the Archbishop of Tarragona, in 1372, to collect Lull's writings, and if he found them erroneous as charged, to have them burned. The Archbishop, after looking into twenty of the works, reported that no errors had been found. Eymeric, "with great labor" as he tells us in the *Directorium,*[42] took the twenty tomes to Avignon and insisted on showing them to the Pope. Then, he says, the Holy Father had them submitted to twenty masters of theology, who returned a verdict quite at variance with that of the Archbishop. No less than 500 errors, of which Eymeric gives 100 examples, were found; and the Pope, after condemning the teachings of Lull in a Consistory, issued a Bull forbidding their dissemination, and warning the faithful against them.

Modern Lullists have gone so far as to accuse Eymeric of the deliberate forgery of this bull, since no copy could be found in the papal archives. Pope Paul IV, some two hundred years later, believed it authentic, for he confirmed it; and it may be argued on Eymeric's side that if he had forged the document, he would hardly have had the effrontery to include it in the *Directorium,* which must have been known at Avignon during the lifetime of Gregory.[43]

[42] Page 255.

[43] Professor Peers inclines to the view that the so-called bull of Gregory XI was forged by Eymeric, and cites the failure of later Lullists to find it. Yet, in favor

Whatever may yet come to light about the bull, the controversy over Lull's sanctity, which began shortly after his death, has continued to this day, with Franciscans and certain Jesuits inclining to regard him as a saint, and Dominicans sharing the suspicions of Eymeric. If such heretics as Giordano Bruno were influenced by him, so, on the other hand, was that rock of orthodoxy, Cardinal Ximenes, Inquisitor General of Spain, who established a professorship for the teaching of his works at the University of Alcalá; and Philip the Second had his books collected at the library of the Escorial. Obviously, then, the problem is a subtle one, and I do not presume to anticipate in any way the judgment of the Church.

Eymeric left no doubt on his opinion of Lull, whom he described as "a Catalan merchant . . . a layman, a necromancer, an unskilful fellow, who published so many books in the vernacular Catalan, though he was totally ignorant of grammar; whose doctrine . . . is believed to have been got from the Devil, since he did not get it from man, nor from human study, nor from God—for God is not a teacher of heresies or errors; though Raymond himself asserted in his books that he got it on a certain mountain from Christ, who (so he said) appeared to him crucified; who it is thought was the Devil, not Christ." [44]

Among the hundred errors he cited from the 500 he imputed to Lull were the following: (1) That God has many essences. (19) That the Holy Ghost is conceived of the Father and Son. (41) That through Christ, chiefly, was the world created from nothing. (47) That the Body of Christ on the cross was dead, in so far as the soul left it, and was not dead, in so far as the deity did not recede from it . . . Christ therefore remained alive and dead; he was dead according to the course of nature, but remained alive *supra cursus naturalem*. (50) The holy souls in Heaven see God face to face, but below cannot contemplate him without a medium. (This means, remarks Eymeric, that before the Ascension

of the alleged beatification of Lull by Pope Leo X, he argues that "similar cases of lost bulls of beatification and canonization are cited, and it is pointed out that the seventeenth century processes assumed beatification and were concerned with canonization only"—his "authority" for this, and the reported beatification, being Avinyó, *Historia del lulisme*, pp. 550-1. (*Op. cit.*, p. 386, n. 1.)

[44] *Directorium*, p. 255.

Christ could not be contemplated by or contemplate the Divine Essence immediately and easily.) (53) That the will of Mary is against justice, for she did not wish her son dead. (54) That the Pope is the Vicar of Saint Peter. (55) That in consequence of original sin, all the world was corrupted—vegetables, animals, everything that served man. (56) He who is in a state of sin, has no right to plants, animals, or any creature, since the rational soul is the form of the body, which takes nourishment from them. (65) That virtue is so good and in such great quantity that any man can have it by his will. (66) That there is no man who cannot multiply his love and will, as much as he chooses. (68) That any man can contemplate God as much as he wishes, and where and when he wishes. (69) That any man can have as much charity and hope as he wishes. (72) That he who does not do the good he can do, does not wish to please God. (74) That he who does not do all he can to convert all infidels, errs, and ought to fear God, and is without charity. (75) That God is so bent upon indulgence, that nothing can stop His indulgence save despair. (76) That God has such charity for His people that almost all the men in the world are saved, because if as many are damned as are saved, the mercy of Christ would be without great charity. (77) That without charity, we cannot have any virtue, as without eyes we cannot see. (91) Every one is obliged to be in religion or matrimony; any other states are in conflict with the final end for which man was made. (92) That in matrimony man is generated with sanctity; and that matrimony so binds, that no man ought to approach his wife, except for the sake of offspring. (97) That ignorant men, rustics, servants and so on do not know how to use their reason, and are brought to the articles of faith by faith, not reason; but learned and subtle men through reason rather than faith. (100) That God Himself taught all this to R. Lull, appeared to him crucified, etc.[45]

Eymeric listed separately the errors of Lull's followers, whom he accused of teaching:

That the Lullian doctrine excels all others, even that of Augustine, in goodness and truth.

[45] *Ibid.*, pp. 255 *et seq.*

That God has withheld true theology from the theologians of modern times because of their sins.

That all doctrines will be destroyed except Lullism, which will last forever.

"That in the time of Antichrist we theologians will apostatize from the Faith, and then the Lullists through the doctrine of Ramón will bring the Church back to the Catholic Faith."

That the Old Testament's doctrine is of God the Father; the New, of God the Son; Lull's, of the Holy Ghost.

That Lull's doctrine cannot be learned by study or through men, but only by a revelation of the Holy Spirit.

That, if revealed by the Holy Spirit, it can be learned in 30, 40, 50 and 60 hours.

That no one can understand the Lullist doctrines but the Lullists themselves.

That Pope Gregory XI, who prohibited the works of Lull, is vehemently suspected of heresy, while the sacred college and the twenty masters of Theology consulted by the Pope did not understand Lull's doctrine, and were deceived, and "erred *turpiter*." [46]

Even Lull's friends have admitted that some of his followers went to ridiculous lengths; so, for that matter, did some of Saint Francis'. As for Eymeric's charges against Ramón himself, a spirited defense has been made by Don Marcelino Menendez y Pelayo:

"Of most of the propositions imputed to him, it is hardly necessary to take notice. Some are mere cavils of Eymeric, who was blinded by hatred; others are not in the Lullian writings, and belonged to Raymond of Tarrega, with whom some have confounded him. Certain phrases, which seem of pantheistic or quietistic flavor, have to be interpreted benignly with an eye to the rest of the system, and to be considered exaggerations and improprieties of language, to be excused in the lively imagination of Lull and of other mystics . . . The ardor of Lull was audacious, dangerous if you will, but not heretical." [47]

---

[46] *Directorium,* p. 260.
[47] *Historia de los heterodoxos españoles, segunda edicion refundida,* Madrid, 1917, *tomo* III, p. 272.

Modern investigators, says Don Marcelino, no longer look upon Lull as a mere visionary, a mere inventor of logical formulas, "but as a profound and original thinker, who sought the unity of knowledge and wished to identify Logic and Metaphysic, founding a sort of *rational realism;* as a true encyclopedist; as a keen observer of nature, although his alchemistic claims are false and doubtful; as an illustrious poet and novelist, unrivaled among the Catalan cultivators of the didactic and symbolic form, and finally, as a text and model of language in his own native tongue. The Mallorcan people go on venerating him as a martyr of the Catholic faith; the Church has approved this immemorial cult, and almost all the ancient accusations against the Lullian orthodoxy have been dispersed." [48]

How then explain the peculiar animus with which Eymeric and some of his Dominican successors attacked the opinions and works of Ramón Lull? Eymeric was no fool, as any one who takes the trouble to read his *Directorium* will have to agree; he was a man accustomed to weighing evidence carefully, and to making fine and just distinctions. It is to be noticed, too, that the attack on his honor and veracity came from the enraged Lullists whom he sought to prosecute, and arose out of the Lullian controversy. The accusation that he forged the bull of Gregory XI rests only upon the assertion of the Lullists that they could not find the original, not on any evidence of the deed alleged. It may be argued that among the thousands of authentic bulls (formal letters) issued by various Popes, many have been lost for shorter or longer periods; some have been discovered after centuries.

Again, it may be said for Eymeric that he was himself to some extent deceived. Believing honestly but mistakenly that certain works of black magic and heresy, attributed to Lull even by some of his own less judicious followers, had been written by him, he approached the authentic Lullian works in a spirit of understandable suspicion, which led him to exaggerate anything that seemed to savor of unorthodoxy. It is easier now to see Ramón in a right perspective than it was in that chaotic Fourteenth Cen-

[48] *Ibid.,* pp. 257-8. Would it not be more exact to say that the Church has *permitted* the local cult?

tury, when so many vicious enemies of society went about in clerical garb, sowing errors under the pretence of saving the world.

Finally, it is apparent as one reads the formidable list drawn up by the Inquisitor, that if they *had* been Ramón's opinions, many would have deserved to be challenged, that the thing that Eymeric conceived to be Lullism should have been opposed. Eymeric was not attacking a personal enemy; he was the champion of divine revelation and of common sense. He was defending the essential goodness of everything God had made; the right even of a sinner to eat and keep life in his body; the obvious truth that virtue is one thing, and the ability to reason another; the Church's view that marriage exists for mutual comfort and pleasure as well as for offspring; the right of a woman to remain a spinster, or of man to live as a bachelor, without being considered an enemy of God; the right of the poor and the rustic to be considered rational human beings; the necessity of having every alleged revelation proved, before submitting the faithful to the danger of being deceived by wolves in sheep's clothing. He thought he was attacking a man who challenged all these verities, and he was prepared to fight to the end, even in the face of an enraged public opinion, to destroy what he considered wicked nonsense. And it was wicked nonsense. Eymeric's mistake seems to have been in suspecting a man who never seriously taught it.

Again, as in all historical matters, one must remember the circumstances. Segarelli and Dulcinus had preached their anarchy in Franciscan robes during the lifetime of Lull. Only a decade after his death, the Franciscan fanatics, in their strife with John XXII, had invoked the heresy of the omnipotent state, whose consequences to the world are now evident enough. Some of them had gone so far as to say that the Pope derived his spiritual powers from the Emperor, and they called upon Ludwig the Bavarian and other potentates to go to Rome and chastise the Vicar of Christ. Did not Lull, in his *Blanquerna,* have Ramón the Fool (a self-portrait) go to the Papal Court to give instruction by an allegory, saying that he had been sent there *by the Emperor* to practise his profession? And who could prove that Lull had had a revelation from God? All the most pernicious religious quacks made the same sort of claim. Who could prove that he had died a martyr's death? Where were the witnesses? What was the exact date? Why should a married man leave a good wife, if he were not infected with Manicheism—especially when some of his writings were found to have a Kabbalistic tinge? And that itch to regulate the whole world—almost all the heresiarchs had it.

Eymeric (let us be fair to him) saw plainly the superficial and disquieting resemblance of Ramón Lull to the *Fraticelli* and the *Apostolici;* what he failed to see was that in all essentials they differed. The heretics rejected this or that Catholic dogma; but Lull accepted all the teachings of the Church without reservation; and if he sometimes unintentionally distorted them, he wrote always with a willingness to submit to correction by Holy Mother Church, if in anything he erred. He had an overwhelming and apparently a continual awareness of the divinity and the humanity of Christ, as most heretics did not; and he had a tender devotion to the Mother of Christ, as most heretics did not. He exposed the heretic Segarelli. He fought valiantly, particularly in the latter part of his life, against the errors of the Averroists. Indeed, the chief faults of Lull's teaching arose from his ardent desire to combat their destructive fallacies. To the Averroist, a thing could be true in faith and false in reason; theology and philosophy were thus divorced. To Lull it was so plain that truth must be one and consistent with itself that in his zeal to demonstrate this he went toward (but not *to*) the error opposite the one of Averroës. If he sometimes gave the impression of confusing faith and reason, of identifying theology with philosophy, he also said that philosophy was the *handmaid* of theology. Eager though he was to prove by reason all that could be proved, he acknowledged its limitations. And if his revelations and martyrdom rest upon rather vague and conflicting accounts, some obviously of later date, the Lullists continue to hope for miracles to confirm them.

One thing is made clear by this controversy: the tremendous intellectual breadth of the Catholic Church. She did not approve of hunting dissenters, as the modern liberal imagines, merely for the pleasure of persecuting them. She distinguished between those who were not in good faith, and those who were; and although the latter, especially if eccentric in any way, were sometimes in danger from overzealous or fanatical inspection, they usually had nothing to fear, and were allowed to write and to talk as they pleased—as indeed Lull was during a long life. The Inquisition did not suppress the intellectual energy of the Middle Ages; on the contrary, it stimulated it, while it kept it sane.

V

Torquemada

FRAY TOMÁS DE TORQUEMADA was born at or near Valladolid, in Old Castle, in 1420. It was less than half a century after the return of Gregory XI to Rome, three years after the end of the Great Western Schism, five after Agincourt; a generation after Eymeric's last assault on the works of Lull, the conversion of Paul of Burgos, and the massacres of the Spanish Jews.

The Torquemadas were at that time a distinguished family. According to the fifteenth century chronicler Pulgar, himself a *Converso* and a contemporary, they were partly, at least, of Jewish descent; this was denied by the Sixteenth century chronicler Zurita.[1] However that may be, little Tomás had an uncle John who had joined the Dominican Order, excelled in literature, philosophy and administration, and about the time our hero was born, was attracting attention at Rome. Eleven years later he was made Master of the Palace. As a theologian at the critical Council of Basle, he made an eloquent defense, against bitter political opposition, of the rights of the Vicar of Christ, thus helping to end many scandals and miseries of the age, and to restore to the Holy See its just and necessary preeminence. Again at the Council of Ferrara, Torquemada rendered such services to the Pope and to the whole Church that Eugenius IV, in gratitude, bestowed on him the title of Defender of the Faith, and in 1439 made him a Cardinal.

Jewish or not, this prelate was one of the great Catholics of his

[1] Pulgar, *Crónica de los reyes católicos*; Zurita, *Anales de la corona de Aragon*, XX, cap. 49.

time, and one of the most respected members of the Sacred College. He was tireless in his charities. He founded the Confraternity of the Annunciation to provide dowries for poor girls who otherwise in those times could not have married; and he helped to build the chapel at Santa Maria Sopre Minerva, where a painting may still be seen of him, presenting three of the daughters of the poor to Our Blessed Lady. A great Thomist, he was admittedly the most learned Cardinal of his time. His *Summa* against the enemies of Church (1450) the most important work of the later Middle Ages on the papal power, influenced Catholic scholarship down to the eighteenth century. Something of the man's character, and his alertness to the dangers that would soon beset Christendom, may be gathered from the preface of this work:

"If ever it was incumbent on Catholic doctors, as soldiers of Christ, to protect the Church with powerful weapons, lest many, led astray by simplicity or error, or craft or deception, should forsake her fold, that duty devolves upon them now. For, in these troubled times, some pestilent men, puffed up with ambition, have arisen, and with diabolical craft and deceit have striven to disseminate false doctrines regarding the spiritual as well as the temporal power. With these they have assaulted the whole Church, inflicting grievous wounds upon her, and proceeding to rend her unity, to tarnish the splendor of her glory, to destroy the order established by God, and shamefully to obscure her beauty, they have undertaken to crush the primacy of the Apostolic See, and maim the supreme authority conferred on it by God; they have so poisoned the whole body of the Church that hardly any part of her seems to be free from stains and wounds. The sacrilegious accusations of these godless men against the Church and the Holy See are shamefully published everywhere. Thus not only is evangelical truth attacked, but the way is prepared for divisions and errors, dangers to souls, dissensions between princes and nations; and it is evident to all that the assaults of these persons are aimed not only at the portion of the Church, but at the very foundations of the Christian religion. Catholic scholars should hasten to oppose these antagonists with the invincible weapons of the Faith." [2]

[2] Von Pastor, *History of the Popes*, English trans., II, 8.

With such an uncle young Tomás was likely to be a marked man in any Order. Apparently he made the most of his opportunities, studied, taught, prayed, as he made his way humbly and noiselessly, in his black and white robes, through the unpublicized world of cloister, sacristy, confessional and classroom, until at last he became Prior of the Dominican convent at Segovia. He was then about thirty-five, spare and vigorous, with a little border of hair around the smooth dome of his tonsured head; and if we can depend upon a likeness supposed to be his in a famous painting in the *Prado,* he had a fine intellectual brow, well-set intelligent eyes, a hooked nose that seems to lend support to Pulgar's statement about his ancestry, and a rather long heavy jaw—the whole face suggesting alertness, determination and energy. For twenty years this priest quietly presided over an exemplary religious community, and was known in the city and the country round about as a good and holy man.

He was about fifty-four years old when he first began to attract attention in the great world, outside his own Order. He was then in the prime of his vigor, energetic and fearless, a strict disciplinarian, but respected by all his subordinates, not only because he was deemed just, but because he was even stricter with himself than with others. A Carmelite could hardly have been less self-indulgent. He never ate meat, slept on a bare board, and would wear nothing finer next his skin than the rough cloth of his habit. He was the sort of man one might expect to find wearing a hairshirt. History is silent on that point; but if Torquemada did subdue his flesh after the manner of Saint Francis, Saint Teresa, Saint Thomas More and many other ascetics, he would not be the man to say anything about it. The chroniclers of his time used none of the epithets by which later historians described him. Rather, they mentioned his incorruptible honesty, his efficiency as an executive, and the confidence he inspired in great persons accustomed to judging human nature. He loved books, solitude, beautiful buildings—architecture, in fact, was one of his chief enjoyments—and like a good monk, saw everything in its relation to God, *sub specie aeternitatis.*

Living so many years in such a city as Segovia must have had no small influence in forming his character and ideas. Much blood had been spilled throughout the centuries on the narrow streets between the lofty aqueduct of Trajan—"el puente del diablo"—and the grim Alcázar that thrusts itself against the sky, like a ship's prow, out of the solid rock ridge on which the whole town clusters. There, in the summer resort of Emperors, early Christian martyrs had been racked; there a warrior bishop had died at the head of his people, defending their homes against the invading Saracens. Nor were its days of sudden death mere history. For all Castile, since Torquemada's youth, had been a land of hatred and anarchy, of wars and rumors of wars. The death of the complacent King Juan II, in 1454, had left the sceptre of Saint Fernando in the incompetent hands of his son, Don Enrique *el Impotente,* who had surrounded himself with Moors and Jews, whose blasphemies against the Christian faith echoed through his corrupt court. The degenerate King gave away his royal patrimony to favorites. When his wife, after seven years of marriage, bore a daughter, it was said openly that the father was His Majesty's best friend, Don Beltran de la Cueva; and this accusation was flung in the face of Enrique by his rebellious nobles. The successor of Don Beltran as royal favorite was Don Juan Pacheco, Marqués of Villena, descendant of Ruy Capon, a Jew much joked about in Spain (the only capon, the wags would say, ever known to have such numerous offspring). Pacheco ruled the realm, not for the benefit of the people, but for that of his own family and friends. He became enormously wealthy. His orthodoxy was suspect, and his enemies professed to believe that he had attained power by the practice of the black arts. When the King's young half brother, Alfonso, suddenly died, Pacheco was suspected (perhaps unjustly) of having had him poisoned; and there is no doubt that he set on foot a plot to seize Alfonso's sister, Doña Isabel, fearing that if she succeeded to the throne, he would lose the vast possessions given to him by Enrique.

Isabel happened to be a woman of genius; one of the most splendid in all history. She had health, courage, brains, beauty and an invincible faith that if she served God as she ought, He would help her to gain her father's throne and restore peace to a land

ridden by highwaymen, cutthroats, degenerates, usurers, tax-gatherers, charlatans and scoundrels of a thousand varieties. At seventeen, in defiance of Enrique's command and all the machinations
of the Marqués of Villena, she followed the advice of the Archbishop of Toledo, the warlike Carrillo, and secretly arranged to
marry young Ferdinand of Aragon.

Isabel was often in Segovia, where the Bishop was Don Juan
Ariás Dávila, of a famous Jewish-Catholic family, and the royal
governor another *Converso,* Andres de Cabrera. She was there
when Enrique died in December, 1474, and it was in the power
of Cabrera to say whether or not, by a bold stroke, she should be
proclaimed Queen of Castile before the partisans of *La Beltraneja*
could act. Cabrera was bound to Isabel's cause by the influence,
no doubt, of his wife (Beatriz de Bobodilla, the Princess's girlhood
friend) and even more by the fact that Pacheco had betrayed his
friendship and sought to kill him. Probably, too, he was captivated,
as many men were, by the queenly character of Isabel, who had
refused the crown offered by Archbishop Carrillo in Enrique's
lifetime, because she would not strive against the lawful sovereign,
and only a year ago had spurned the suggestion of some bigots of
her own faction in Valladolid that she gain power by condoning
a massacre of the *Conversos.* At a critical moment the Catholic
Jew governor decided for her, and on Saint Lucy's day she rode
on a white palfrey, with Cabrera on one side of her and the Archbishop on the other, to a platform on the *Plaza Mayor,* where the
great crown of San Fernando was placed upon her fair auburn
hair, and the Governor knelt to give her the keys of the Alcázar,
where the treasure of Castile was stored.

Surely Fray Tómas de Torquemada, then prior of Santa Cruz
convent, must have been a witness of that historic scene, must have
heard the shouts of *"viva la reina!* Castile, Castile for the Queen
Lady Isabel!"—must have heard the joyous clangor of all the bells
in the city, and the booming of lombards from the ancient walls.
Likely enough he was one of the many notables of the city who
advanced to kiss the hand of the new Queen and to pledge fealty
to her. Perhaps on that day he looked upon her for the first time,

and saw in her, as others did, the only hope for Christianity and civilization in Spain.

Isabel was then twenty-three, shapely and vigorous (a great horsewoman), with fair skin and blue eyes, flecked with green and gold. From her earliest days, even amid the corruptions of the court of *El Impotente,* she had kept an integrity and innocence which made her irresistible to the good and terrifying to the wicked. Fearing nothing but God, she had passed miraculously, as it seemed, through many dangers; she was like one set apart and anointed for a great mission. Only such, in fact, could even hope to face the enormous task that lay ahead. Portugal was about to declare war against her on behalf of *la Beltraneja,* niece of the fat Alfonso V. There was no army in Castile worthy of the name. Robber barons and marauders fought private wars, preyed on the poor, looted and burned at will. Feuds, racial and personal, raged in several of the larger cities. Money was scarce, but famine and pestilence were everywhere. The Moslems still held rich Granada in the south, and might at any time, with reinforcements from Africa, carry fire and sword, as in the eighth century, over the whole peninsula. The times cried out for some strong man of genius, a San Fernando, to bring back peace and order. What could a woman do? Yet there was something in this woman that made men believe in her.

Either at this time, or somewhat later, Fray Tomás de Torquemada became confessor of this child of destiny. The office was none of his seeking; he had no desire to take upon his shoulders the spiritual responsibilities of kings. But he already had a considerable reputation in Segovia as a wise and understanding director of souls. Among his penitents were Hernán Nuñez Arnalt and his wife Doña María Dávila. Nuñez Arnalt became a secretary to Queen Isabel, his wife one of her ladies in waiting. Knowing that Their Majesties were looking for a good confessor, Doña Maria recommended the Prior of Santa Cruz. He declined at first to accept the office. The Queen insisted, and he accepted. Isabel usually had her way.

The story told by later historians of the Inquisition that Fray Tomás took this opportunity to suggest to his royal penitents the establishment of an Inquisition in Castile, seems to be legendary. That he must have had influence in their councils is obvious. They both formed a high opinion, never to be revised, of his character and judgment, and tried to show their gratitude in the usual ways. In the course of time, as the two greatest Sees in Spain fell vacant, they offered first to have him made Archbishop of Toledo, later Archbishop of Sevilla. If Fray Tomás had been an ambitious man, he could undoubtedly have become a Cardinal, like his famous uncle, and might even have aspired to be Pope. But he preferred always to remain a simple monk.

Now for a time he dropped out of the limelight of history, as the Queen rode westward to help her husband in the war against the invading Portuguese. After King Fernando's decisive victory at Toro, she galloped about the countryside, holding court wherever she happened to be, hearing complaints against murderers and thieves and other criminals, and ordering them shot or beheaded, if found guilty, with no more delay than might be necessary to make their confessions. Evidently this fair young woman, who had time, with all her military and judicial activities, to bear five children in the course of some sixteen years, who learned Latin laboriously that she might teach them, who heard Mass and read her breviary daily like any nun, never so much as flickered one of her auburn eyelashes as she rode away on her white horse, after saying crisply, in effect, "Off with his head!" Stolen goods were restored, criminals feared to shed blood, decent people slept soundly once more in their beds. In Sevilla, a notorious centre of crime, she had malefactors executed in such numbers that the aged Archbishop finally pleaded with her not to let justice forget mercy. She desisted, but not without compelling two powerful nobles to put an end to their private war, and unite in the service of their country.

About that time Fray Tomás of Torquemada was discharging a very agreeable obligation. His penitent Hernán Nuñez Arnalt had died, leaving a will which provided, among other things, for the building of a new Dominican monastery in Ávila; and he had made Fray Tomás his executor. Torquemada was there in 1479, supervising the beginnings of one of the loveliest architectural monuments in all of Europe—the Dominican convent that he named for his great namesake of Aquin.

In the meantime Fernando and Isabel had come to some momentous decisions. They wanted some assurance that the peace and prosperity they had won so dearly would be permanent. They had restored the medieval ideal of kingship, as representing all the people, and supreme over the great nobles who, unless restrained by the crown, had tended to struggle against one another and to oppress the lower classes. In Spain this ideal was united to a very workable system of representative government. The cities and towns sent to the Cortes elected delegates who opposed the King if he attempted anything against the *fueros* which set forth the inalienable rights of man—rights upon which the Catholic Church had always insisted. Without the consent of the Cortes, for example, the King could not lay his hand upon public funds. On the other hand, he had far more scope in administrative matters than the modern constitutional monarch has: the right of life and death, for example, over all his subjects, but always with the understanding that if he did not respect their *fueros* they had a right to rebel. The system had worked well under strong kings, or under weak kings with strong and just advisers. Isabel and Fernando meant to perpetuate it. The first step must be to make certain that Christian Spain would not fall again under the heel of an alien invader.

In short, the Moslem power, which had gradually been driven beyond the mountains of Granada by successive waves of reconquest throughout the centuries, must be expelled or assimilated. This meant war, long and costly. Its inevitability seemed clear when Muley Abou'l Hassan, after making a three-year truce with them in 1478, raided Murcia with 4000 horse and 30,000 foot, and slew all the inhabitants of Ciefa, men, women and children. "Total War" is not a modern discovery. It was practiced, at a somewhat slower tempo, by the Mohammedans of the Middle Ages. With such neighbors to the south, the Castilians were bound to have to fight sooner or later, whether they wished to or not.

It is axiomatic that in time of war a country must have a unity of will and purpose which did not yet exist in Spain. The old kingdoms still retained their independent sovereignty—Isabel was Queen of Castile and Leon, and took good care that her husband should be king there only by courtesy, while he ruled his ancestral kingdoms of Aragon, Catalonia and Valencia. True, this remarkable couple were so compatible and so reasonable, that in all important matters, as one of their chroniclers has it, "they acted as one person;" hence there was a virtual if not legal unity of government in the Christian kingdoms.

It was becoming increasingly evident to them, however, and to such thoughtful Spanish Christians as Torquemada, that something would have to be done about the Jewish Problem before they could undertake the final war of liberation. Not the religious problem of the Jews of the synagogue, for their right to freedom of worship was acknowledged; not the racial conflict of modern times, for the intelligent Catholic Spaniard did not indulge in the stupid unchristian theory that Jews as human beings were essentially different from or inferior to other children of Adam. The peculiar difficulty confronting Fernando and Isabel arose from the presence of a large and powerful class of Jewish Christians. On every side the young Queen heard that these *Conversos,* as they were called, were insincere Christians, most of them, and could not be depended upon in time of war.

The problem was far more complicated than it has seemed to those modern historians who have made such facile use of the word "bigotry" to explain all. There was something more here than a question of the oppression of a minority by a majority. There was an age-long conflict between powerful opponents, a conflict described in its beginnings by Saint Paul and Saint John, and foretold by Christ himself; and Spain had become the battleground. Now, conflict has a way of accentuating qualities useful in conflict, and repressing others, and it was so in this case. It was fairly obvious that Jews had sought to build, in Spain, as elsewhere, a new Jerusalem; consciously or unconsciously, they had tended to work together to this end, offering too, such resistance to assimilation as one might expect in a people once chosen and set apart. Their remarkable success, and even their occasional failures, had produced in them a certain hardness, a certain pride. The Catholics, on their side, undoubtedly took on certain militant, sometimes even fanatical and ferocious characteristics not found in Catholics of other nations. For more than seven centuries the Christians of the peninsula, generation after generation, had breathed the atmosphere of war, war that they felt in their souls to be not only just, but holy; and this was bound to beget in them also a hardness and pride, all the more offensive because inconsistent with the teachings of Christ and the Church. In fighting against Moslem barbarians, who made slaves of prisoners if they did not care to butcher them, the Christians tended to adopt similar methods. They had, moreover, a powerful inward assurance of being right, which no Moslem or any one else (except an orthodox Jew of the synagogue, living up to the Law of Moses in good faith, in ignorance of the revelation of Christ) could have had. This assurance, unless accompanied by humility, can itself beget pride, even in those who have the truth. Here, then, the struggle of Christ's Church against the world took on a peculiar color and intensity.

The struggle could end only in one of three ways: (1) the destruction of Christianity and the triumph of a Jewish, semi-oriental, anti-Christian culture; (2) the conversion of the Jews to the Catholic Faith, and the elimination of the racial problem by marriage and assimilation; (3) the complete suppression, if not total destruction, of the Jewish power by a triumphant and militant Christianity.

The outline of these three stages, in the order named, may be discerned in Spanish history. In the light of the truth of Christian revelation, the second was of course the most desirable solution of a conflict which had no real foundation in ideas: for the law of Moses and the Law of Christ were, and are, essentially one. This was the goal for which thoughtful and sincere Catholics strove; yet even these men would doubtless have agreed that if they *must* choose between (1) and (3), it must be (3). The Jews would admit no solution but (1).

Events seemed for several centuries to move toward this first solution. Under the Visigoths the Jews had become numerous and flourishing; they were not persecuted until it was discovered that they were conspiring with the Arabs in Africa to overthrow the

Gothic monarchy. Finally, at the beginning of the eighth century, they did send an invitation to the Mohammedan Berbers, through the Jews of Africa, to cross the straits and take Spain. The conquest of the whole peninsula, and the almost complete suppression of Christianity (fatally weakened by Aryanism) resulted; and although there were Jews in the Spanish army, as in the African, it must be obvious that the Jews at heart were generally on the side of the invaders. Wherever the Berbers went, Jews opened the gates to them, and were made governors of all the principal cities as a reward. This was an historic fact not soon to be forgotten by the generations of crusaders who slowly fought their way back into the lands of their ancestors.

Under the Mohammedans the Jews attained a high state of culture and prosperity. They grew rich on silks, slaves and usury. They excelled in medicine, and in Aristotelian studies. Nor were they persecuted at first by the advancing Christians. Saint Fernando, on taking Córdoba from the Saracens, turned over four mosques to the large Jewish population, to convert into synagogues, and gave them one of the most delightful parts of the city for their homes, on two conditions: that they refrain from reviling the Christian religion, and from proselytizing among Christians. The Jews made both promises, and kept neither. Yet for a long time they were undisturbed and continued to flourish, partly because they were useful to many of the kings. Their population, in Castile alone, must have been from four to five millions [3] at the close of the thirteenth century.

So powerful had they grown by the fourteenth century that in many respects they were above and beyond the law. The laws against blasphemy, for example, could not be enforced against them. They could encourage heresy, and, in defense could claim the freedom of worship granted to the Jews. Business, property and even government passed into their hands. The Kings, in return for loans, would "farm out" to them the right to impose and collect

[3] Dr. Cecil Roth and others have disputed this estimate, made in my *Isabella of Spain*, 1930, p. 197; but I still believe it to be reasonable. As Lea points out, each male adult Jew was taxed three gold *maravedis* per year, and in 1284 the total tax paid was 2,561,855 *maravedis*. Allowing for the women, the children, and the youths under 21, must there not have been *at least* four million Jews in Castile?

public taxes on a generous commission basis. A great deal of bitterness against Pedro the Cruel arose from the fact that he gave his Jewish friends complete control of his government; a circumstance that led his enemies to call him a Jewish changeling, and contributed to his denunciation by a Pope as "a fautor of Jews and Moors, a propagator of infidelity, and a slayer of Christians."

Unhappily the popular hatred against the Spanish Jews was not wholly without cause. They were disliked not for practising the things that Moses taught, but for doing the things he had forbidden. They had profited hugely on the sale of fellow-beings as slaves, and practised usury as a matter of course, and flagrantly. As Lea notes, they demanded forty percent interest at Cuenca during the famine of 1326, when farmers needed money to buy wheat for sowing. They were much given to proselytising, even by a sort of compulsion; thus they would force Christian servants to be circumcised,[4] and urged their debtors, sometimes, to abjure Christ. Again, Moses had condemned blasphemers to death. Yet it was a custom of many Jews to blaspheme the Prophet for whom Moses had warned them to prepare; they made mockery and travesty of the ceremonies of the Christian religion; they jibed at priests and nuns. Moses had said, "Neither let there be found among you . . . any wizard, nor charmer, nor any one that consulteth pythonic spirits, nor fortune tellers, or that seeketh the truth from the dead. For the Lord abhorreth all these things. . . ." Yet the Spanish Jews, by contamination no doubt from the superstitious Mohammedans, were often found busying themselves for financial profit in what the people called *hechicerias* (literally, "doings")—witchcraft, black magic, astrology, alchemy, the selling of love potions, the use of charms to bless the marriage bed, or (at the instance of a revengeful rival) to render the young husband impotent—for which purpose the *genitalia* of a rooster were sometimes insinuated under a nuptial couch, or cabalistic horrors scrawled under a window.[5] There was a widespread fear, shared by

---

[4] Menendez y Pelayo, *op. cit.,* III, p. 390 *et seq.*

[5] See Menendez y Pelayo, *op. cit.,* III, p. 348 *et seq.,* for an interesting account of all this.

some holy persons, of the power of witches and wizards to "bind" with spells and charms.

Queen Isabel despised all such beliefs. When one of her ladies, the Countess Haro, complained that a young relative was *ligata* by the demon, through the malefic art of a jealous rival, the Queen summoned Fray Diego de Deza, a great Dominican theologian (a man of Jewish descent, later Inquisitor General and patron of Columbus) and asked him if it was possible for the devil to have any power over matrimony, which is a spiritual union.

"Excellentissima domina," replied the future Archbishop, according to Clemencin, who tells the tale, *"hoc sic se habet."* He went on to explain that Saint Thomas, and other doctors of the Church, said it was possible.

"I hear you, Master," said the Queen, "but I still ask you, whether it is against the Catholic Faith not to believe this."

Fray Diego admitted that it was not of faith, but repeated that learned and holy doctors held it and asserted it.

Isabel replied that if the Church did not teach it, she would not believe it, no matter what doctors held it. "These divisions," she added with her usual positiveness, "come from human incompatibility rather than from the power of demons." [6]

Although the Church did not teach that demons had power to divide or unite men and women in matrimony, she did not hesitate to throw the full weight of her influence on the scale against all impostors who did teach it, or who pretended either to bind or unbind the natural powers with the aid of demons; and like our father Moses, she sternly forbade spiritualism, black magic, attempts of any sort to establish contact with evil powers, and all manner of superstition. Unfortunately for the Spanish Jews, many of them had forgotten the ancient teaching.

What hurt them most in the estimation of Christians was the general belief that behind the mysterious cohesion and unity of conduct and purpose observed among them there existed a central control, in the inner circles perhaps of a modernized Sanhedrin,

[6] Menendez y Pelayo quotes the whole of this curious conversation from the appendix of Clemencin's *Elogio de la Catolica*, pp. 569 and 570; see *op. cit.*, III, p. 385, n. 1.

which directed a conspiracy to build up a Jewish State within the state. Was this an illusion born of fear, envy, jealousy? So the Jews have replied. Yet the illusion, if such it was, has been persistent. Delegates from all the Jewish communities in southern France had held a meeting in 1215 under a leader who added to his name of Levi the title of *Nasi,* or Prince, which in ancient times had belonged to the president of Sanhedrin, even to that infamous and wily Annas who had demanded the blood of Christ. And whether or not the Spanish Jews had any such leadership, the Christians had no doubt they were planning to rule Spain, enslave the Christians, and establish a New Jerusalem in the West.

This conviction, whether true or false, was a result of the widespread conversions that followed the sickening massacres of 1391. How could the Christians think otherwise, when they saw one of the most illustrious Jewish rabbis, Selemoh ha-Levi, long respected by Jews and Christians alike for his high character and profound learning, becoming a Christian, a Thomist philosopher, and a Bishop, and finally publishing two dialogues in which he categorically declared that the Jews were bent upon ruling Spain? It was this Jewish Bishop of Burgos, also, who drew up the so-called Ordinance of Doña Catalina, which restricted the activities, professions, and so on, of Jews and Moors—though another Jewish convert, Diego Árias Dávila allowed the Jews to evade it, especially as regarded the profitable farming of taxes. Still another Jew, Fray Alonso de Espina, confessor to Henry IV and Rector of the University of Salamanca, wrote and published in 1459 his *Fortalitium Fidei,* one of the most bitterly anti-Jewish documents in history. This opus was more violent against the *Conversos* than against the Jews of the synagogue, and suggested that if an Inquisition were established in Castile, large numbers of them would be found to be only pretending Christians, engaged in judaizing and in undermining the Faith they professed.

It has been the custom of Jewish apologists to dismiss all such instances with an explanation which we can understand, and have some sympathy for, but cannot accept. In this view Selemoh ha-Levi, and all such, were turncoats and renegades; they became

Christians in time of persecution through fear, and tried to win the favor of their new associates by confirming their darkest prejudices.

This theory undoubtedly has some evidence to support it. It does not explain away, however, the undeniable sincerity of numerous Jewish conversions in times when Christians, not Jews, were being persecuted. Saint Peter and Saint Paul did not improve their worldly state when they went forth to preach in poverty what was certain to win for them an ignominious death. Some of the notable Jewish converts of our day have become Catholics at a great cost in popularity and material advantages. As for Selemoh ha-Levi, the theory of hypocrisy robs his career and his strong character of all their consistency and righteousness, and makes no sense of him. He was converted before the massacres of 1391. He must have lived through other persecutions of his people, and must have suffered, like every Jew, from unjust and uncharitable contempt, without giving up his ancestral religion. Yet he was an honest man, and when he saw the light of truth, he followed it, even when it led him, like Moses, Isaias, Jeremias, to denounce the sins of his own people, to call upon them to give up the golden calf of usury and luxury and turn back to the God of Abraham, of Isaac and of Jacob, to the Father of Christ. For this, naturally, he got little thanks from men resolved not to see what he saw.

There is no other reasonable explanation for the attitude of such honest convert Jews as Pablo de Santa Maria toward those Jews who, as pretending Christians, made a mockery of her sacraments, while they grew rich and powerful under her protection, and like their ancestors of old, sat down to eat and drink and rose up to play. The wholesale conversions seemed to have given to this opportunist type of Jew a chance to eat his cake and have it too. He could enjoy all the advantages of going to Mass on Sunday, and going to the Synagogue on Saturday. His children were barred from no profitable and honorable occupations. They could marry, thanks to his money, into noble impoverished families, and succeed to the proudest titles in Castile. They could become priests, even bishops. There was Andres Gomalz, parish priest of San Martin de Talavera, who, according to his own confession, celebrated Mass from 1472 to 1486 without believing in it, or having the proper intention; and heard confessions without ever granting absolution. There was Fray Garcia de Tapate, prior of the great Jeronymite monastery of Toledo, who, as he elevated the Host at Mass, used to mutter, "Get up, little Peter, and let the people look at you," and would turn his back on the penitents in his confessional, instead of giving them absolution.[7]

This situation could not go on indefinitely without an explosion; and unfortunately there were many explosions of the worst possible sort. The mob, seeing the government of Enrique *el Impotente* unwilling to do anything to curb the *Conversos,* and virtually handing over to them the conduct of both State and Church, took matters into their own hands. In one city after another, just before Queen Isabel came to the throne, the *Conversos* were put to the sword and their houses burned.

The series of massacres began at Toledo in the summer of 1467. The canons of the Cathedral had sold to certain Jews the privilege of taxing the bread of the nearby town of Maqueda. An influential Christian ordered the Jews beaten out of town—a move highly popular with the already overtaxed and harassed people. In retaliation the *Conversos* organized, and one of their leaders, Fernando de la Torre, a hot-headed man of wealth, was foolish enough to boast that he had 4,000 fighting men well armed, six times as many as the Old Christians had; and on July 21 he led his army against the Cathedral, while the Christians were assembled at Mass. The armed *Conversos* burst in, crying "Kill them! This is no church, but only a congregation of vile men." The Christian men drew swords, and defended themselves in a gory fray before the high altar. Reinforcements appeared from the nearby towns, made a counter-offensive in the luxurious section where the *Conversos* lived, hanged Fernando de la Torre, and then butchered New Christians indiscriminately.

Six years later, in Córdoba, a famous statue of the Blessed Virgin carried in solemn procession, on the second Sunday of Lent, was showered with a bucketful of foul liquid from a window in the house of a rich *Conversos*. Lea tells us, on his own authority, that

---

[7] Lea gives these and other examples of the insincerity of the *Conversos: The Inquisition of Spain.* See also Bernaldez, *Historia,* cap. 43.

it was "an accident." The Jewish historian Graetz is more honest; he says that it was "either accident or design," and that a girl threw on the statue "what was unclean." [8]

The Christians were not in a mood to make inquiries or distinctions. Swords were drawn, and a massacre followed. Don Alonso de Aguilar, who had married a daughter of the Marqués of Villena, and is said, also, to have been in need of ready money, defended the New Christians. A veritable state of war ensued for four years. Massacres followed in Montoro, Adamur, La Rambla, Ubeda, Jaen and other places. At last there were a terrific pogrom in Segovia, on May 16, 1474.

This final horror, in the city where Torquemada lived and Isabel made her temporary capital, was the result of a feud between two *Conversos*. The Marqués of Villena, to pay off his grudge against the Governor, Cabrera, decided to attack him with an armed force under pretext of an uprising against the *Conversos*. Early Sunday morning, the cavalry of the Marqués rode into the city, crying, "Death to the *Conversos!*"

Cabrera was warned of the plot at the last minute by Cardinal Borgia (later Pope Alexander VI) who, as a legate for Pope Sixtus IV, was then at Guadalajara. He saved the *Conversos* from annihilation, but some of their most beautiful houses were burned, and when Isabel and Fernando returned to the city a few days later, the streets were still foul with traces of carnage and arson. They praised the governor highly for his defense of the New Christians.

Now, in the face of all this, it makes little sense to accuse such a woman, as some have done, of establishing the Spanish Inquisition through racial prejudice or sheer cruelty, or, as others have done less honestly, to make it appear as if the Queen who faced down Fray Diego de Deza and other theologians, and on occasion spoke her mind to the Pope himself, was led into the affair by subservience to "ghostly advisers." The fact was, that during these bloody years, she came to the conclusion that no ordinary expedient could restore civil peace and tranquillity in Spain. For the sake of the *Conversos* themselves, if for no other reason, it was necessary to substitute some form of workable judicial procedure for the

[8] *History of the Jews,* Vol. IV, p. 304.

crude administrations of mob "justice." The existing civil courts could not accomplish this, precisely because so many of the judges and lawyers were *Conversos*. As for the Church courts, the same was true; many priests, and even bishops, were of Jewish descent, and the orthodoxy of some was so suspect that nothing was to be looked for in that direction. Isabel was led inevitably, not only by pressure of public opinion, but by logic itself, to reach for the only weapon within her grasp—an Inquisition like that of the Middle Ages, in which the judges would be Dominican monks, carefully chosen and beyond the reach of intimidation or bribery.

Was it Fray Tomás de Torquemada who first suggested this course to her? There is no proof of this. The real father of the Spanish Inquisition was the great Cardinal Pedro Gonzales de Mendoza, future patron of Columbus. It was he who set up the first Castilian Inquisition by asking Pope Sixtus IV to name four delegates to work in conjunction with the bishops to stamp out the heresy of the *Conversos*.

This effort proved futile. The rich *Conversos* arranged to have themselves called to Rome on appeal, obtained delays, found various means of having the cases dropped. Something else had to be done, if the rule of Isabel and Fernando was not to end, like that of Enrique *el Impotente,* in another "time of pride, heresy, blasphemy, avarice, rapine, wars and feuds and factions, thieves and foot-pads, gamesters, pimps, murderers, public tables for rent where the names of Our Lord and Our Lady were blasphemed, renegades, slaughterings and all manner of wickedness," as Bernaldez reported it.[9]

The Bishop of Cadiz, commissioned by Queen Isabel to investigate the situation at Seville, reported to her, when she went to that city in 1478, that nearly all the *Conversos* were secretly practising Judaism. About the same time the Inquisitor of Sicily, Fray Felipe de Barberis, who happened to be in Spain on business of his order, explained to her the monastic Inquisition as it had existed under Gui and Eymeric. Fray Alonso de Ojeda, another Dominican, reported the failure of his strenuous efforts to bring the *Conversos*

[9] *Op. cit.*

to a sincere practice of the Christian faith, and urged stronger measures.

Torquemada must have been consulted at this point and probably gave the same advice. It was he that the King and Queen commissioned with Cardinal Mendoza, to write a petition to be sent to Rome, asking the Pope for the necessary authority. This document was read and approved by a *Junta* of nobles, lay and clerical, before it was despatched.

On November 1, 1478, Pope Sixtus IV wrote a Bull which makes plain the sort of picture that must have been painted for him by the representatives of the Spanish monarchs at Rome.

"The genuine devotion and sound faith manifested in your reverence for us and the Roman Church," he wrote, "require that as far as we can in the sight of God, we grant your requests, particularly those which concern the exaltation of the Catholic Faith and the salvation of souls. From your letter recently shown us, we learn that in various cities, sections and regions of the Spanish Kingdoms, many of those who of their own accord were born anew in Christ in the sacred waters of baptism, while continuing to comport themselves externally as Christians, yet have secretly adopted or returned to the religious observances and customs of the Jews, and are living according to the principles and ordinances of Judaical superstition and falsehood, thus falling away from the true orthodox faith, its worship, and belief in its doctrines. They have not feared, nor do they now fear, to incur the censures and penalties pronounced against the followers of heretical perversity under the constitutions of Pope Boniface VIII, our predecessor of happy memory; and not only do they themselves persist in their blindness, but they also infect with their blindness those born of them, or having communication with them, and their numbers increase not a little. And because of their continued crimes, they weary our forbearance, as is piously believed, and that of the ecclesiastical prelates who are expected to look into such matters, by their wars, by slaughter, and by other evident injuries to men, endured by God, in despite of the aforesaid Faith, to the peril of souls, and the scandal of many. For this reason you have caused humble supplications to be addressed to us, that so pernicious a sect be totally uprooted in the said Kingdoms . . .

"Rejoicing in God over your praiseworthy zeal for the safety of souls, and hoping that you will not only drive out this falsehood from your realms, but that, also, in our times, you will reduce to your rule the Kingdom of Granada and those adjacent places where infidels live, and through the divine mercy will convert the infidels to the true faith, so that what your predecessors, on account of various obstacles, were denied, may be accomplished by you, and your glory be crowned with that eternal beatitude which is the reward of a vow well kept, we therefore, wishing to grant your petitions and to apply to these things the suitable remedies, are desirous of granting your supplications and permitting three—or at least two—bishops or archbishops, or other men of good reputation who are secular priests or religious of the mendicant or non-mendicant orders, men above forty years of age, of good conscience and praiseworthy life, masters or bachelors in theology, either doctors in canon law or licentiates carefully examined, God-fearing men, whom you may cause to be selected in various cities and dioceses of the said Kingdoms, to take action straightway concerning those accused of crimes, and those who conceal or aid and abet them, under the usual jurisdiction and authority that law and custom allow to Ordinaries and Inquisitors of heretical depravity." [10]

Fernando and Isabel, armed though they were with the tremendous authorities and responsibilities conferred by this Bull, did not hasten to brandish it over the heads of the *Conversos,* and to light the vast and lonely horizons of Castile with bonfires; as they would have done, had they been the bigots they have been accused of being. On the contrary, they decided to consider the matter further, and put the document away for nearly two years. They were influenced in this by the counsels of Cardinal Mendoza, who reminded them that if many of the *Conversos* were ignorant of the truths of the Catholic Faith, it might be because they had

[10] For the complete Latin text of this Bull, see the *Boletin de la real academia de la historia,* Vol. IX, p. 172; also, with related documents, in Vol. XV, p. 453 *et seq.*

not been taught them by those whose business it was to do so. The Cardinal prepared a catechism for all the parishes of his own diocese.

The results, after several months, were discouraging. Even after the prosperous and worldly-wise *Conversos* were given good reasons why Christ was the Savior of the world, and why His Church of which they were members must be obeyed in His stead, they mocked His name and that of the Blessed Virgin; and it was reported to the King and Queen that some of the priests of Jewish descent were "on the point of preaching the Law of Moses from Catholic pulpits"—meaning Judaism without Christ.

Toward the end of the second year of futile catechizing, all Christendom was thrown into a panic by the ruthless victories of the Grand Turk, Mohammed II, who, angered by his failure to storm Rhodes, sent his fleet westward, ravaged the coast of Apulia, and on August 11, 1480, took the city of Otranto in the Kingdom of Naples. Nearly half the civil population of 22,000 were butchered in cold blood, while the Archbishop and all the priests were slaughtered after the most brutal tortures.

The reaction in Spain when the news of these outrages arrived, sometime in September, probably had something to do with the decision of King Fernando and Queen Isabel to put into effect, without further delay, the powers granted to them by Sixtus. On the twenty-sixth, at Medina del Campo, they published a decree making the Inquisition effective, and appointing as members of the first tribunal in Castile, Cardinal Mendoza, Fray Tomás de Torquemada, and two other Dominicans, Fray Miguel Morillo and Fray Juan de San Martin.

From what ensued, it would appear that the directing head of the new organization was the Cardinal, while Torquemada acted as a consulting expert; and it is quite possible that he had beside him, for reference, a copy of Eymeric's *Directorium,* borrowed from some Dominican convent in Aragon or Languedoc. Morillo and San Martin were to be the active Inquisitors, and as such gave their first attention to the almost Jewish city of Sevilla, where they went late in October to take evidence. On the second of January, 1481, they published an edict of grace, calling upon all

Christians who had been guilty of Judaizing, blasphemy, apostasy, or other offenses against the faith, to come before the tribunal, abjure their errors, and be reconciled to Holy Church. Two other edicts followed. The third warned all good Christians to avoid associating with the Judaizers, and denounced the secret meetings which it was said the latter were holding, in conspiracy against the Faith.

The powerful *Conversos* of Sevilla, related by marriage to rich Jews and to noble Christians, could not believe that young Queen Isabel meant to burn some of them, if necessary. When Morillo and San Martin began to show that they were in earnest, by summoning suspects and witnesses for examination, these millionaires decided they could not tolerate an Inquisition; even as the *Cathari* of Languedoc had decided. A group of them met to consider what should be done. Could anything be more eloquent of the extent to which Judaism had bored within the ranks of Catholicism than the fact that this fateful meeting was held in the Catholic Church of San Salvador? Among the crypto-Jews present were Catholic priests, priors of monasteries, three of the Twenty-Four who ruled the city, the *alcaide* of Triana fortress, the Dean of the Cathedral chapter and many other persons of note. A millionaire rabbi, Diego de Susan, demanded armed rebellion. Leaders were appointed, some to drill troops, some to buy arms. The Inquisitors were to be slaughtered and the King and Queen informed that no Inquisition would be tolerated in Sevilla.

The seriousness of this situation, with the Turks on the sea, and war with the Moors of the south imminent, can be imagined. Fortunately for the new-found unity of Spain the conspiracy was revealed by a daughter of Diego de Susan to her Christian lover, who informed the Inquisitors. Several of the leading men of Sevilla were arrested. Arms for a hundred were found in the house of the Dean of the Cathedral. The evidence was submitted to a jury of lawyers, *viri boni et periti,* and as a result of their recommendations, the first *auto de fe* in Castile was held February 6, with Mass at the Cathedral, followed by a sermon by Fray Alonso de Ojeda.

Considering that in any country in the world at that time, a conspiracy to take arms against the sovereign would have meant death for high treason for all concerned, some of the *Conversos* implicated got off very lightly. Those who had confessed were given the usual penances and reconciled to the Church. And so the *auto de fe* ended with solemn music; for an *auto* was literally an "act of faith," and was purely a religious ceremony.

Outside the church, six of the chief conspirators, who had not been let off with mere penance, were handed over to the civil authorities, who proceeded to burn them outside the walls of the city. Some days later, Diego de Susan and two others were burned. According to Bernaldez, who was in Sevilla at the time, the rabbi died as a Christian.

There was no longer any doubt in the minds of the secret Jews that the Queen was as earnest about this affair as she had been about the murders and lootings she had punished. Panic seized them, and they fled in all directions, some having recourse to Rome. At one *auto*, 700 abjured and were reconciled.

Meanwhile the plague was raging in Andalusia. In Sevilla alone, 15,000 died of it that summer. The *Conversos* begged the Inquisitors to let them leave the city until the epidemic was over, and the permission was granted. There was a courtesy, peculiarly Spanish, in this indulgence under the circumstances. Some of the fugitives, of course, never returned. Others met at Rome, and raised the clamor of righteous indignation and injured innocence at which the Jews, in their long unhappy history, had learned to be so skilful.

During the summer another edict of grace, this time for two months, was published, and in all Castile, 17,000 confessed and were absolved—1,500 of them at one *auto* alone.

Pope Sixtus, meanwhile, had come to the conclusion that some, at least, of the complaints he was receiving from the Christian Jews were well founded, and that the new Inquisitors in Spain had gone far beyond what he had authorized. He was in a difficult position, under strong pressure, and aware that there was truth on both sides: that some of the *Conversos,* as the sovereigns complained, were undoubtedly lying when they told him they had been good Christians; and that Morillo and San Martin, in their zeal, had arrested some good Christians of Jewish descent, and treated them harshly and unjustly. His Holiness had instructed them to proceed in cooperation with the Bishops, as the medieval inquisitors had done, but this they had failed to do, nor had they observed the canon law in other particulars. When Isabel and Fernando, toward the end of 1481, asked permission to extend the Inquisition to Aragon, Sixtus refused, and on January 29, 1482, he wrote them a vigorous letter complaining that, although he had never doubted their sincerity in asking for the Inquisition, their ambassador at Rome had given a vague, confused and incomplete explanation of the situation in Spain, which had caused him to issue documents at variance with the traditions established by his predecessors. Many of the Spanish Jews, professing themselves to be "Christians and true Catholics," had fled to the Holy See, "the refuge of all the oppressed everywhere," and had appealed to him "with much shedding of tears". Some of the Cardinals advocated the removal of Morillo and San Martin from office. Sixtus said he did not wish to embarrass the sovereigns by publicly condemning their appointments; but he would remove the two Inquisitors if in future they should "conduct themselves otherwise than with zeal for the faith and the salvation of souls, or less justly than they ought." He demanded the assurance of the Spanish sovereigns that they would obey him in all this, "as Catholic Kings ought", so that henceforth they would deserve to be "commended before God and men." [11]

In the meantime the Moors had begun the long threatened war by storming lofty Zahara, under cover of a storm, the night after Christmas, 1481; and Isabel and Fernando were in for ten years of exhausting combat. More than ever was it necessary to be sure of the loyalty of all their subjects. Sixtus IV sympathized with them in this. On the other hand, he was father of all the faithful, of whatever race, and not merely of Spaniards.

How little "racism," in the modern sense, entered into the situation that produced and perpetuated the Spanish Inquisition is indicated by a controversy between the Queen and the Pope, the same year, over the appointment of a bishop for the vacant see of

[11] There is a fuller quotation from this bull in my *Isabella of Spain*, New York edition, pp. 224-6. The complete Latin text is in the *Boletin*, Vol. XV, p. 459.

Cuenca. Sixtus, whose great fault was nepotism, proposed to appoint one of his nephews—not the resolute Giuliano, who became Pope Julius II, nor reckless Pietro, whose excesses bore him to an early grave, but Raffaello Sansoni, Cardinal of San Giorgio. Queen Isabel had already promised the place to her chaplain, Alonso of Burgos, and she insisted that no one else should have it. She represented that her ancestors had been allowed to nominate bishops in Castile, since the circumstances of the Moorish crusade made it necessary to have Spaniards worthy of trust in the frontier sees. Sixtus, mindful of the rights of the Holy See, and of the great evils that had resulted from the naming of prelates by kings (particularly in France, but also in other countries) would not accept her nomination. She threatened to urge the princes of Christendom to convoke a General Council against him. When Sixtus sent a special legate to Spain to discuss the matter with her, she refused to see him. Finally Cardinal Mendoza intervened, and brought about an understanding, whereby Sixtus, for the sake of peace, named Isabel's candidate to the see. It was the beginning of a bad custom, even though Isabel and some of her descendants named very good bishops; the thing was essentially wrong, and however deplorable the nepotism involved, the Franciscan Pope was insisting on a right now generally recognized. Popes nowadays are free not only from the trammels of nepotism, but from the interference of rulers in making appointments to spiritual offices.

The thing to notice here, however, is that Isabel's candidate was a man of Jewish descent. At the very moment when she was establishing the Inquisition to punish the secret Jews for judaizing, she was insisting, even at the risk of a new schism in Christendom, on placing the mitre on the head of a son of Jewish converts. Moreover, then and later, her best secretaries, her chief men of state, a large part of her entourage and many of her personal friends, were of Jewish descent. Clearly, then, there was no question of race in her mind.

Sixtus had yielded in the matter of the see of Cuenca; but he insisted upon having his way where the Inquisition was concerned. In February, 1482, he appointed eight Inquisitors for Castile and Leon, who, he said, had been recommended to him "for their purity of life, love and zeal for religion, gentleness of manners, extensive learning and other virtues." [12] They were all Dominicans: Pedro de Ocaña, Pedro Murillo, Juan de Santo Domingo, Juan del Espiritu Santo, Rodrigo de Sagarra, Bernardo de Santa María, and Tomás de Torquemada; besides the Dominican Provincial, Alonso de San Cebrian, who had nominated all the rest in accordance with the custom of the medieval Inquisition. The Pope again censured Morillo and San Martin for their indiscreet and unjust conduct in Sevilla, and the Spanish ambassador for not making the circumstances clear to him. He commanded the new Inquisitors to proceed "prudently and carefully, according to canon law and tradition." He bade them, "in remission of their sins and in the love of God," to lay aside all fear and to accept the dangerous office "in a spirit of fortitude," because of the urgency of the business, and "in hope of eternal reward . . . that the inner root of this perversity may be torn up through your care and solicitude, and the vineyards of the Lord, after the little foxes have been driven off, may bear abundant fruit." [13]

Henceforth, said the Pope, he would make the appointments of the Spanish Inquisitors himself, and he reserved the right to himself and his successors to revoke them. This done, he sent King Fernando, April 17, 1482, permission to extend the Inquisition to Aragon, but withdrew it in October, probably as new throngs arrived in Rome with complaints of unjust persecution and the unwarranted confiscation of their estates.

The rich *Conversos* apparently represented to Sixtus that the chief purpose of Fernando and Isabel in setting up the Inquisition had been to have a pretext for plundering them, to finance their war against the Moors. Fernando wrote a bitter letter to the Pope, protesting against the letters of immunity given at Rome to some of the men and women condemned in Spain, and declaring that he would not honor them.[14] The Queen wrote in

---

[12] *Boletin*, XV, p. 462.

[13] *Ibid.*

[14] Bergenroth, in the introduction of the first volume of his *Calendar of State Papers*, has mistranslated this letter of King Fernando. See *Isabella of Spain*, p. 496, note 14 to Ch. XIX. Lea gives the complete text of the letter, in Latin, in the appendix of his *Inquisition of Spain*, Vol. I.

a more conciliatory tone, it would seem, in September, and again in December, 1482; so at least we infer from the reply of Sixtus.

This letter of the Pope, dated February 23, 1483, has been curiously distorted. Prescott informs us that Sixtus was "quieting the scruples of Isabella respecting the appropriation of the confiscated property!" [15] The *Jewish Encyclopedia* has the Pope hinting that her majesty had been urged to excessive rigor "by ambition and greed for earthly possessions, rather than by zeal for the faith and the true fear of God." What Sixtus really said was just the opposite.

"Your letter is full of piety, and singular devotion to God," ← he wrote. "We rejoice exceedingly, daughter very dear to our heart, that Your Highness has employed so much care and diligence in the matters we so eagerly desire. It is most gratifying to us that you should conform to our desire, in punishing the offenses against the divine Majesty with such care and devotion. Indeed, very dear daughter, we know that your person is distinguished by many royal virtues, through the divine munificence, but we have commended none more than your devotion to God and your enduring love for the orthodox Faith." And lest she fear that he might believe that in punishing "those faithless men who, pretending to the name of Christians, blaspheme and crucify Christ with judaical treachery," she was motivated more "by ambition and by greed for temporal goods than by zeal for the faith and for Catholic truth, or by the fear of God, let her be assured," added Sixtus, "that we have had no such suspicion. For if there are not lacking those who, to cover up their own crimes, indulge in much whispering, yet nothing from that source can persuade us of any evil on your part, or that of our very dear son above-mentioned, your illustrious consort. Not every spirit do we believe. If we lend our ears to the complaints of others, we do not necessarily lend our mind." As for the Queen's request for a Court of Appeals in Spain, instead of in Rome, the Pope would discuss the matter with the Cardinals, "and according to their advice, so far as we may be able before God, we shall endeavor to grant your will. Meanwhile, very dear daughter, be of good

[15] *History of the Reign of Ferdinand and Isabella*, I, 313.

spirit, and cease not to pursue this pious work, so pleasing to God and to us, with your usual devotion and diligence; and be assured that nothing will be denied to Your Highness that can honorably be granted by us."

After this diplomatic preamble, however, the Pope went on to make it clear that while he did not blame the King and Queen *personally,* he was not all convinced by their letters that the complaints of the secret Jews of the injustice of the Inquisitors at Sevilla were feigned or without foundation. "Since we behold, not without wonder, that which proceeds, not from your intention nor that of our above-mentioned beloved son, but from your officials, who having put aside the fear of God, do not shrink from laying the scythe to an unseemly harvest, from breaking our provisions and the apostolic mandates . . . without being hindered or retarded, as is obvious, by any regard for censures— this, since it is offensive to us, and foreign to your custom and station, and the respect due to us and to the apostolic Chair and your own equity, we have caused to be written to Your Serenity. We urge and demand, therefore, that you carefully avoid censures of this kind, to be feared by any of the faithful whomsoever, nor suffer so evident an injury to be inflicted upon us and upon this Holy See; and so let it be your care lest the liberty and apostolic right which your illustrious progenitors, to their great glory, were zealous to defend and to increase, may not appear to be wronged or diminished in the time of Your Highness. For thus the Lord, in whose power are Kings themselves, will direct your desire, the favor of the apostolic see aiding you; He will cause your posterity and your affairs to flourish; and all things will happen to Your Highness, walking in the right way, according to your wish." [16]

Moses himself could not have delivered a more tactful, and at the same time sternly austere warning than this. The great Queen's enemies remembered it years later, when her posterity and her affairs were not flourishing; and Jews, even in modern times, have attributed the misfortunes of her children to God's judgment on her severity toward their ancestors.

The Pope, meanwhile, was discussing the situation with the

[16] *Boletin,* Vol. V, p. 468.

Cardinals; and he decided to try the Queen's suggestion that he appoint a judge of appeal who should reside in Spain and be free from the influence of the *Conversos'* friends in Rome. Sixtus named the elderly Archbishop of Sevilla, Iñigo Manrique, appointed him directly, instead of permitting the sovereigns to do so, and commanded him, under holy obedience, to accept the difficult office. At the same time he removed from office, over the heads of the King and Queen, the Inquisitor Christopher de Calves, of Valencia, who, he said, had acted "impiously and imprudently."

The Archbishop was learned and highly respected, but he was quite old, and no doubt would have encountered pressure from the powerful King and Queen if he had shown any inclination toward excessive indulgence. The *Conversos* complained to the Pope that his court was so severe that they did not dare to appeal to it.

On August 2, 1483, Sixtus finished writing a bull ten pages long *"ad futuram rei memoriam,"* in which he reviewed the history of the Spanish Inquisition, as a matter of record, and professed himself entirely displeased with the court of appeals at Sevilla. Cases before the Archbishop and his deputies, he said, had been put off under pretence that the Archbishop himself would attend to them, while the officers of the King and Queen showed open contempt for his authority. The rigor of the Inquisitors at Sevilla "exceeded the moderation of law." Some of the accused were prevented from placing their grievances before the court of appeals. Men and women of Jewish descent, who had returned from Rome with Papal letters of pardon, were afraid to present them, having heard that their effigies had been burned in their absence by the Inquisitors. Hereafter, ordered the Pope, the Archbishop must proceed not by himself only (a pretext for delay) but through his ordinaries and the Inquisitors, in expediting the hearing of appealed cases. All those who had been prevented from appeal or presenting papal letters must have their cases reopened, heard, and settled according to justice, with all speed. "And meanwhile, because the shame of public correction has led the erring into such a wretched state of despair that they choose rather to die with their sin than to live in disgrace, we have resolved," wrote Sixtus, "that such persons must be relieved, and the sheep who are lost must be led through the clemency of the Apostolic See to the fold of the true Shepherd, Our Lord Jesus Christ." Complete freedom of appeal must therefore be granted to all persons, and all penitents, whether judaizers or other heretics, must be received, absolved, and admitted to penance "secretly and circumspectly." Even the convicted, when absolved and penanced, must be completely reinstated in their former positions, and unmolested in any way. The *Conversos* whose appeals were then pending in Rome must not be persecuted under any pretext, but "must be treated and considered as true Catholics."

Sixtus concluded with a solemn warning:

"Though human nature is in all things surpassed by the divine, it is mercy alone that makes us like unto God . . . and therefore we ask and exhort the said King and Queen, in the heart of our Lord Jesus Christ, that imitating Him, whose way is always to pity and to spare, they should wish to spare their citizens of Sevilla and the citizens of that diocese who recognize their error and implore mercy, so that if henceforth these wish to live, as they promise, according to the true and orthodox Faith, they may obtain indulgence from their majesties, just as they receive it from God . . . and that they may remain, abide, live and pass safely and securely, night and day, with their goods and their families, as freely as they could before they were summoned on account of the crimes of heresy and apostasy." Finally, the Pope threatened any who opposed his wishes with the indignation of God and the most severe censures and penalties of the Church.[17]

On the strength of a brief he issued eleven days later, modern anti-Catholic historians have accused Sixtus of insincerity, of "revoking" this merciful bull of August 2 and allowing the severity of the Spanish sovereigns to take its course. But the text of the brief shows plainly that Sixtus did not "revoke" or "recall" the bull; he merely suspended its operation until he could consider some new objections which had been raised—doubtless by the Spanish ambassador, who, it is safe to infer from what happened on

[17] For Latin text, see *Boletin*, XV, pp. 477-487. Llorente's text is defective.

many similar occasions, probably made the direst threats against
the aged and ailing Pontiff in his final efforts to obtain *carte
blanche* for his master and mistress.[18] The Bull, however, was
despatched, and remained in force. It was received by the Bishop
Évora and published by him January 7, 1484—later he cited it in
censuring the Inquisitors of his diocese for undue severity. The next
two Popes, Innocent VIII and Alexander VI, followed the same
principles in dealing with the Spanish Inquisition. If anything
further is needed to refute Lea's denial that "the papacy sought
to mitigate the severity of the Spanish Inquisition," it will be
found in an instruction issued by Torquemada himself, at the
end of 1483, when Sixtus was dead: "Since in the time of Pope
Sixtus IV of good memory, there emanated from the Roman
court certain orders and bulls and excessive rules for penitence
against equity to the detriment of the Inquisition and its ministers,
Their Highnesses command that letters and provisions be read
which together are general for all the realm, by which is prevented and can justly be prevented the execution of the said
orders and bulls, if any persons ask for them and desire to use
them, until the Pope may be consulted and informed of the truth
by command of their Highnesses; for it is not to be presumed
that the intention of the Holy Father would be to cause any
hindrance to the affairs of the holy Catholic faith; but the said
provisions of their Highnesses shall not be published until it is
seen whether Pope Innocent VIII, newly elected, will concede
certain bulls and mandates in place of those which have been sent
from his court, to the detriment of the Holy Inquisition."[19] Thus
Torquemada contributed to the beginnings of that Caesaropapism
which at certain times would be highly injurious to Christendom,

---

[18] The misrepresentations of the brief of August 13 by Llorente, Lea, and Bergenroth are discussed in *Isabella of Spain,* p. 268. Graetz is equally unfair in saying that Sixtus "recalled" the bull of August 2, "saying that it had been issued
with too great haste." Graetz (*History of the Jews*) has some violent and unwarranted strictures on Sixtus, making him, among other things, "infamous as a
monster of depravity, sensuality and unscrupulousness"—all on the authority of
the Pope's enemy Infessura, whom no reliable historian takes seriously.

[19] Lea publishes these instructions of Torquemada, in Spanish, in the appendix
of his *Inquisition of Spain,* Volume I, but he does not correct his text to accord
with them.

even if it served Spanish interests. Carried a little further, beyond the line of obedience, it would be the spirit of Henry VIII.

Torquemada! There was a man who might be able to do what all the other Inquisitors had failed to do: please the King and Queen and the Pope at the same time. He understood the situation in Spain, and the need of drastic remedies; he was heartily in favor of the new strongly centralized monarchy, for having lived in Segovia, he had seen the tragic results of anarchy; and he was tactful enough, while daring to forbid the publication of a papal bull in Spain, to leave a loophole which would save his obedience to the Holy Father at Rome until the Ambassador there had had an opportunity to drop a few acid words about a General Council or a possible schism at the Vatican. A quiet, forceful and skilful man, Torquemada, and Isabel and Fernando, sometime in 1483, conceived the idea of centralizing all the powers of the Inquisition, and putting him at the head of it—under their own direction, of course. Cardinal Mendoza agreed with them that the Holy Office needed unity of organization, under one head. Every one knew that there had been dissension between the diocesan delegates, on the one hand, and Torquemada and Antonio de Palavicini, on the other. Now all was to be remedied. The situation was explained in Rome, and one of the last acts of Pope Sixtus IV, in October, 1483, was to appoint Fray Tomás Inquisitor General for Castile and Leon. Fernando and Isabel at the same time made him, *ex officio,* a member of their royal Council.

In spite of all the legends which have pictured Torquemada as only waiting for the moment when he could begin to burn Jews wholesale, to his heart's desire, and regale his nostrils with the sweet aroma of roasting Protestants, he was not concerned, professionally, with either of those classes; he never persecuted Jews as Jews, and of course there were no Protestants, at least under that name. His whole endeavor was to make all Catholics be loyal Catholics. Nor was he desirous of accepting even this responsibility. It is generally agreed that the man never wanted to be Inquisitor General; had nothing of megalomania about him, and would much rather have gone on, as a simple monk, building Gothic cloisters where other monks after him could study and meditate, and serve God. Other Inquisitors after him became Archbishops and Cardinals, and confidential ministers of Kings; Torquemada resolutely refused every high honor offered him, to the very end. Even Lea admits that his selection "justified the wisdom of the sovereigns." [20]

What then of the cruelty for which his name has become almost a synonym? Had it lain dormant in him all those years in the monastery until, at the age of 63, he found himself forced into a position of great power that drew the monster out in him?

Before these questions can be fairly considered, we must remember that Torquemada was a man of his time, not ours, and that the best and wisest men in Spain did not consider the Inquisition an instrument of cruel oppression but an instrument of reform, which substituted a judicial punishment of the guilty for indiscriminate mob butchery of guilty and innocent alike. Being an Inquisitor, then, or favoring the Inquisition, was not necessarily, in itself, an evidence of a cruel nature.

The question then resolves itself into this: Did Torquemada, as Inquisitor General, show himself more cruel than other men who believed they were doing their duty to God and society in the inquisitorial courts?

He began his regime by doing away with all the worst abuses of Morillo and San Martin. Then he planned, and patiently put into execution, an elaborate system of jurisprudence that was far in advance, on the whole, of any in Europe. He improved the prisons, the prison food, the procedure and other conditions, until it became notorious in Spain that men lodged in the civil jails for various crimes would sometimes pretend to be heretics that they might be transferred to the well-lighted and well-ventilated houses in which the prisoners of the Holy Office were usually kept, and be judged by Dominicans rather than civil officers. There were exceptions to this, of course; and as time went on there were instances of cruelty, of persecution, of the intrusion of political animosity and personal vengeance; not because of Torquemada's rules, however, but in spite of them. If we turn from the texts corrupted by Llorente to authentic ones of Torquemada's *Ordenanzas* of 1484, which be-

[20] *Op. cit.*, Vol. I, p. 174.

came the cornerstone of the Spanish Inquisition, it begins to be more clear why they have been called, by serious Spanish scholars (Saldaña, for example), "a monument of penal science and humanitarianism." They were approved by the *Cortes* of Tarazona, and by a great *Junta* at Sevilla in October, 1484. Public opinion was on their side.

As Torquemada reorganized the Holy Office, it was a joint court representing both the Church and the Civil power. At the head of the system was the Supreme Council, known in Spain as the *Suprema,* which occupied a place only second in dignity and authority to the Royal Council of Castile. Its members, entitled to be addressed like princes, as "Your Highness," were special delegates of the Holy See in ecclesiastical matters, and of the Kings in civil ones. They were the court of last resort, from whose decision no appeal could be taken, even to the Pope himself—this by a special concession at Rome, which Leo X made binding under pain of excommunication. Only bishops, archbishops and cardinals were beyond the jurisdiction of this powerful *Consulta.* Torquemada planned its membership and balance with the greatest care, to ensure its efficiency, independence, and immunity from the usual sources of political corruption. There were to be five members, two of whom must belong also to the Royal Council of Castile. There must be one Dominican, and one from each of the other orders in rotation. Almost invariably the choice fell upon distinguished and able men, famous judges, theologians, professors. Attached to the council were a fiscal or prosecutor, who must be a *letrado;* an advocate, two secretaries, an *alguacil mayor* (usually a post of honor given to some person of note); a notary, and various subordinate officials, all of whom must be of good character and reputation, and of known loyalty.

The Inquisitor General, or as he came to be known, the *Inquisidor Supremo,* was a member of the Council, and had only one vote, as such, in its debates and deliberations, except on administrative and economic matters, in which he ruled supreme. But on the question whether a certain appeal of an accused person from a local court, for example, should be granted, he had no more influence than any other member of the Council.

The salaries of the Grand Inquisitors were very modest. The *Inquisidor Supremo* received 2,816 *reales* per year; the other members of the Council 1,810 apiece; though they were allowed also to dispose of certain ecclesiastical prebends, annuities and other funds to defray their personal expenses.

This Council was a sort of Supreme Court of the Inquisition, with certain executive functions added. It handled all appeals from the local Tribunals. It received and dealt with complaints against local judges or other officials. It passed laws on matters not foreseen in the *Instrucciones* or *Ordenanzas* of Torquemada. It sent *Visitadores* or inspectors to look into the affairs of the local courts, and to punish any corruption, excess or inefficiency. Most important of all, perhaps, its approval had to be obtained before any person could even be arrested, or have sentence passed upon him, in any part of Spain. Here was a check upon fanaticism or overzealousness that did not exist in the earlier Inquisition.

The lower or local Tribunals, as organized by Torquemada, consisted each of two judges (who must be learned men) and a theologian. These functionaries were obliged to work six hours a day (except on *fiestas*) and commenced their duties each morning by attending Mass. They must wear ecclesiastical robes. They must never be absent from the city on days when court was in session. They were forbidden, under the strictest censures, to accept "presents" of any sort, beyond their salaries, which were not excessive. A judge, for example, got 2,941 *reales* per annum, and half as much again for his expenses. He was entitled to the social status of *Señoria*. Each court had also two *consultores,* who must be theologians, three or four jurists to examine the processes; a certain number of *calificadores* (usually eight) who must be "more than forty-five years old, and either theologians or masters of canon law, of good repute," to examine writings which were denounced as heretical or immoral; two *notarios del secreto,* whose authorization was required for secret proceedings; notaries to investigate the ancestry of the accused, to ascertain whether or not they had "clean blood" (an offensive term which certainly smells strongly of the racist heresy); notaries to take charge of confiscated goods, some for the Crown, some for the share alloted to the Holy Office for its expenses; court messengers, to go from one tribunal to another; *proveedores,* whose business it was to provide food for the prisoners; physicians, surgeons and barbers, who must attend the prisoners without charge; chaplains, to minister to the spiritual needs of the *reos,* and four honest and reputable persons to assist the chaplains, without pay, in visiting prisoners, teaching them, consoling them, and so on.

The *familiares* or constables of the Spanish Inquisition made arrests, acted as jailers, and on state occasions attended the Inquisitors. They did not go about in armed squads, as in medieval France and Italy, but looked very much like ordinary citizens, carrying only the arms any one was allowed by common law to have; and these they must not use at night. In general they went armed only when making arrests. They must be decent men of good reputation, with no Jewish ancestry. They could use crosses and the various insignia of the Inquisition only on the feasts of Saint Dominic, Saint Peter Martyr (the Inquisitor assassinated by the Manichees) and *Corpus Christi;* at *autos de fe* and when royal personages were received. Most of them belonged to the Confraternity of Saint Peter Martyr, which met in Dominican convents, usually, and had sundry pious purposes: visiting prisoners, consoling them, and doing other acts of charity for them.

The Inquisitors generally went about, like other priests, in religious habit, unarmed. Torquemada at one time had a bodyguard, of which propaganda history has made much capital. We have Lea's word for it that he went about with 250 armed familiars of the Holy Office, and 50 cavalrymen besides; moreover, in his constant fear of assassination he kept on his desk the horn of a unicorn, supposed to be potent in discovering and neutralizing poisons. Lea swallowed this whole from the corrupt and dishonest pages of Llorente, who in turn borrowed it from the fanciful Paramo; but when we go back to the fifteenth century for contemporary evidence, we find nothing, except the probability that Queen Isabel, alarmed by threats and possibly even attempts of the secret Jews against the life of her Inquisitor, insisted upon assigning a bodyguard to him. As for Torquemada, one gathers from all accounts that he was a man who could not be bribed or intimidated by any efforts of the highly astute and persistent people he was investigating; it seems a reasonable inference, then, that he was a fearless man, who would have been glad to die for the cause of Christ.

As for procedure, he adopted the general forensic practice of his time, and improved greatly upon it. Court was opened with great solemnity and all possible publicity, with all the people and clergy at High Mass to hear the reading of the edict of grace, usually for forty days. Under Torquemada there were generally a second and a third edict; and all who came forward and confessed were absolved and given their penances secretly. Only after the third period of grace did the Inquisitors proceed against the unrepentant. They could begin by general inquisition, investigating rumors, "clamorous insinuations" and so on, or by special inquisition of particular errors or persons holding them.

Like Moses and Pope Gregory IX, Torquemada insisted that two witnesses of good repute and apparent sincerity must depose against a person, before a *pesquisa,* or secret preliminary investigation, could be set in motion. The complaints had to be in writing, and signed (later on, under oath before a notary). No anonymous complaints were accepted. False accusations were severely punished. One of Torquemada's courts imposed the death sentence on some Jews who had denounced certain *Conversos,* in a spirit of revenge, for offenses of which they were proved to be innocent.

A person denounced by two witnesses was then investigated, usually without his knowledge: his past, his reputation, his ancestry, his business affairs, his associates. If *indicios* were found against him that were "clear, certain, and specific" (all three were necessary) a process was begun, and he was either summoned before a court, or, if his flight seemed likely, arrested. He could be kept in prison only (1) if five witnesses, with satisfactory proofs, testified against him; (2) with the agreement of the Bishop, the Inquisitors and the fiscal, after the *calificadores* had decided that the statements involved were heretical; (3) by a decree of the Bishop, under certain conditions. In any case, the approval of the Supreme Council had to be had before a man could be imprisoned. Finally, two doctors examined him, as to his mental condition.

The prisoner must have a hearing within three days after his arrest. He appeared before the judges, swore to tell the truth, was informed of the charge against him and the grounds for it, and urged to confess and be reconciled. If he refused, he had another hearing after ten days. A third session was granted if he was still obstinate. After that the *interrogatorio* began.

Torquemada's instructions were that in this *interrogatorio,* the Inquisitors were to be "cautious, circumspect and charitable," and seek nothing but the truth. They must seek to learn all about his education, upbringing, occupations, friendships, and so on. If he had been corrupted by teachers, books, or a certain place of learning, that must be taken into account as extenuating. Even the crime of heresy was excused in those deceived by a priest of reputed knowledge or virtue, or brought up in error by parents, or deluded by *maestros* or prelates of heretical views, before these latter were canonically condemned, or the teachers removed from office. During the *interrogatorio,* there must be present in the room, as defenders of the accused, two ecclesiastical persons, not members of the court. After four days his statement was read to him. He could make any corrections he desired, and have as many hearings as he requested.

The *interrogatorio* concluded, the *Fiscal* presented his proofs to the Inquisitors, and asked for judgment according to the law. The accusation, from beginning to end, was then read again to the accused (so we would call him—they called him the *reo,* or criminal), with a pause after each article for his reply, while the notary wrote down what he said.

The accused was allowed counsel, and later on, by the reform of Valdés, the Holy Office had to pay the cost, if the defendant was poor. If he named none, the Court appointed a learned man of good reputation, who took an oath to defend him with zeal, loyalty, impartiality and good faith. This attorney for the defense had access to the minutes of the trial, could rebut the accusations of the Fiscal, disqualify witnesses, ask for new information or hearings, and had full access to the accused, who also could see copies of the processes,—though the names of witnesses were withheld from him, as in the earlier Inquisition, and for the same reason. He could, however, mention all his enemies, and all who had a motive to injure him, and this must be taken into consideration by the Inquisitors. Many of the interminable delays with which historians have taxed the Spanish Inquisition, were in fact, the result of this privilege. If the machinery was sometimes ponderous and slow-moving, it was because the conscientious Thomists who planned it were anxious to have justice done.

Torture, unhappily, was used. It was taken over with all the rest of the legal *impedimenta* of the time. Yet it is surely ironic that Torquemada should have been made into a veritable symbol of it, when it was one of his great achievements to limit and mitigate its use. He made clear that it was not to be used as a means of *punishment,* but to obtain absolute proof of what was already established beyond reasonable doubt; that is to say, there must already be proof *semiplena* against the accused; he must have contradicted himself in serious matters, his bad faith must be evident, or there must be an overwhelming preponderance of witnesses against him. Nor could the instruments of torture be used without a decree of the *fiscal* and the *consultores,* the approval of the bishop of the diocese, and the *visa* of the Supreme Council.

If all these citizens of good repute agreed that the accused should be subjected to torture, he was examined by physicians to make sure that his physical condition would permit. A doctor must be present when the torture was applied, and at his command it must be stopped.

The method that Torquemada substituted for the more barbarous ones of the Renaissance was known as "the water cure." The *reo,* if he refused to clarify the contradictions in his testimony, or was strongly suspected of withholding important information, was stretched naked and tied with cords upon a very forbidding-looking *escalera,* or ladder. His nostrils were stopped, his jaws held apart by an iron prong, and a piece of linen placed loosely over his mouth. Into this cloth water was slowly poured, carrying it into the throat. This gave him the fear, and some of the sensations, of suffocation, without allowing him to suffocate. If he squirmed, the cords hurt his wrists and ankles. If he proved very stubborn, one of the *familiares* might give them an extra twist or two. This must have been a very painful and harrowing experience. Yet it seldom did lasting harm, and it often obtained confessions. On the other hand, it sometimes made the innocent confess. Torquemada assumed that the Inquisitors would seek to avoid injustice in this connection by checking the confessions with known facts. Probably the torture was no more dangerous or disagreeable, all things considered, than certain modern police methods: such as keeping a man awake under a strong light, and having him questioned by relays of detectives for an indefinite number of hours. At least it was an advance over the cruder expedients of the fourteenth century.

Such was the machinery with which Torquemada proposed to purge the restored Spanish Catholic State of its disloyal elements. He proceeded to apply it with all necessary vigor. He organized tribunals at Sevilla, Córdoba, Jean and Ciudad Real, where the judaizers were most active. He convoked a general synod of all the Inquisitors at Sevilla, in the presence of the King and Queen, to impress upon them the principles he had already incorporated in his *Ordenanzas*. Several of the instructions issued by this Synod— in particular those numbered 3, 8, 10, 23 and 24—are intended to enforce the merciful requirements of the Bull of Pope Sixtus IV, dated August 2, 1483, the bull that modern propagandists ask us to believe the Pope wrote, but never despatched. In December, 1483, Torquemada issued some additional instructions. In one of them he made it clear that the confiscations of the property of convicted Judaizers were to be used toward the expenses of the war against the Moors, and to help defray the expense of the Inquisition itself. In another he cautioned Inquisitors to be merciful to persons who had been sick, or had other good excuses for appearing after the expiration of a term of grace.

The next step, after things were running smoothly in Castile, was to organize the new Inquisition in Aragon. This proved to be no easy task. Not only were the Aragonese themselves exceedingly quick to resent any encroachment on their ancient *fueros,* but the nation was controlled by a Jewish plutocracy even more powerful, perhaps, than that of Castile; and all the wealth, influence and ingenuity of this group were bound to be pitted against the elderly Dominican monk who went among them to announce that he intended to punish the disloyal *Conversos* who were their instruments, and to confiscate their property. The Governor of Aragon was a *Converso*. Most of the judges and lawyers, most of the members of the Cortes, were *Conversos*. The King's government was made up largely of *Conversos*—for example, his Chief Treasurer, Sancho de Paternoy (a "Catholic" who had a seat in the synagogue of Saragossa); his treasurer, Gabriel Sanchez; his vice-chancellor, Alfonso de la Caballeria; and many of his secretaries. The fury of propaganda stirred up against Torquemada as he approached may be imagined.

Undaunted by all this, the Prior of Santa Cruz himself arranged for the edict of grace, and for the first *auto de fe,* held at Saragossa. There were no executions afterwards; at the *auto* itself four persons who abjured their errors were penanced, fined, and reconciled.

Torquemada then appointed two very able men as Inquisitors for Aragon: Fray Gaspar Juglar, a Dominican, and Master Pedro Arbues of Épila, a member of the Order of Canons Regular, attached to the metropolitan church at Saragossa. The appointment was virtually a death-sentence for both of them. However, they proceeded to do their unwelcome duty, while Torquemada returned to his labors in Castile.

The Jews also went to work. They launched a great campaign for "democracy." Skilfully appealing to the *fueros,* as dear to the Aragonese as the *Magna Carta* to an Englishman, or the *Declaration of Independence* to an American, they organized a huge mass meeting; they had resolutions passed in the *Cortes,* and they sent two monks to Córdoba to ask the King and Queen to call off the Inquisitors. Also, "they offered large sums of money," says Zurita, "and promised on that account to perform a certain designated service, if the confiscations were taken off; and they especially tried to influence the Queen, saying that she was the one who most favored the General Inquisition." [21]

When Isabel spurned the bribe, the Jews and secret Jews decided

[21] *Anales, lib.* XX, cap. 65.

to have the Inquisitors murdered. Some Jewish millionaires met at the home of Luis de Santangel, one of a powerful family of money-lenders, lawyers and tax-gatherers, and arranged, through Juan de la Badia, to hire a gang of cutthroats to attend to the affair for 10,000 reales. Vidau Durango and some other French Jews were imported for the purpose.

Father Juglar presently fell ill and died, poisoned, it was said, by *rosquillas,* or sweet-cakes, given him by some *Conversos.* Some un-successful attempts were then made to dispose of Father Peter Arbues. Finally, one midnight, when he was kneeling at prayer before the Blessed Sacrament, saying his Matins, the gangsters stole through the dark nave and stabbed him in the back. When some priests came running in with lanterns, he was still saying the office, and particularly invoking Our Lady. He died twenty-four hours later, "glorifying Our Lord," says Zurita, "till his soul left him."

The great investigator Lea follows Zurita's account, but not as accurately as might be desired. "He lay for twenty-four hours, repeating, we are told, pious ejaculations. . . His blood, which stained the flagstones of the cathedral, after drying for two weeks, suddenly liquified, so that crowds came to dip in it cloths and scapulars, and had to be forcibly driven off when he was buried on the spot where he fell: when the conspirators were interrogated by the inquisitors, their mouths became black and their tongues were so parched that they were unable to speak until water was given them. . ." [22] So Lea continues in sarcastic vein.

Notice how this impartial scholar changes the text of his author-ity, Zurita, who says plainly that Peter Arbues was buried, not two weeks later, but "the following Saturday" (*el sabado siguiente*). A mighty throng was present, adds the Aragonese chronicler, and as the body was laid in the sepulchre, some of the blood that had fallen profusely on the flagstones and had dried there, suddenly became liquid and bubbled up, and "Juan de Anchias and Antic de Bages and other notaries who were present testified to the fact with public acts." [23]

Of the fact that eye-witnesses of some intelligence and good

[22] *The Inquisition of Spain,* Vol. I, p. 252.
[23] *Anales, loc. cit.*

character made affidavits (presumably under oath, as such documents generally are) setting forth what they had seen, Lea says nothing. The Catholic Church, however, after her usual careful investigations, was convinced of the miraculous nature of certain events concerning the dead priest, and in the course of time (1867) raised him to her altars as Saint Peter Arbues. The King and Queen meanwhile caused to be erected on the spot where he fell a beautiful statue, inscribed, "Happy Saragossa! Rejoice that here is buried one who is the glory of martyrs." Thousands still pray at his tomb, close to the spot where Saint James the Greater is said to have first preached the gospel of Christ in Spain.

Naturally the King and Queen spared no pains to have the conspirators hunted down and punished. All the ringleaders were executed, except Juan de la Badia, who committed suicide by swallowing glass in prison. A massacre of the *Conversos* by the enraged mob, the day after the murder of the saint, was averted, happily, by the presence of mind of the Archbishop of Saragossa.

Saint Peter was a mild, studious man, who had undertaken his office unwillingly, as a sacred duty. There is no evidence that he ever sentenced any one to death. According to a document of doubtful authenticity,[24] he preached the sermon at the second *auto* in Saragossa, June 3, 1484. There were no other *autos* until after his murder in September, 1485.

Both in Aragon and Castile, however, the saint's death put an end to all opposition and gave Torquemada a free hand to carry on until the power of the Jewish State within the State was broken. In 1485, at the most critical moment of the war of independence, he discovered and frustrated a plot of the Jews and *Conversos* of Toledo to seize that important strategic city during the *Corpus Christi* procession, and murder all the leading Christians.[25] In 1488 he issued some new instructions, further reforming the procedure of the Inquisitors.

How many deaths in all was he responsible for during the whole

[24] *Memoria de diversos autos,* in Lea, *op. cit.,* Vol. I, Appendix. Lea considers it authentic, although he admits the handwriting is of the seventeenth or eighteenth century.

[25] *Boletin de la real academia de la historia,* Vol. XI, pp. 292-3; see also Lea, *The Inquisition of Spain,* Vol. I, p. 168.

of his career? The monstrous figures accepted by generations of Protestant Englishmen have of course been drastically revised. Wherever actual records of the Inquisition have come to light, they have refuted the swollen figures of Llorente, who set in motion the legend of "bloody Torquemada." Pulgar, secretary to Queen Isabel (himself of Jewish descent), says that in her whole reign 2,000 persons were put to death by the State, after the Inquisition had handed them over as impenitent, relaxed or pertinacious.[26] This number included those convicted not only of heresy, judaizing, blasphemy and other offenses directly religious, but bigamy, sodomy and certain other crimes, which in Spain were dealt with by the Inquisition instead of the civil courts. This figure is now generally accepted, even by anti-Catholic historians. If it is correct, Torquemada was responsible for perhaps half or more—let us say, at a hazard, between 1,000 and 1,500. Bernaldez, who was chaplain to his successor, wrote that from 1481 to 1488, seven hundred persons from all parts of Andalusia were burned in Sevilla; while 5,000 were sentenced to "perpetual" imprisonment, though five years later they were released and ordered to wear *sanbenitos.* Among those burned, according to the *Cura de los Palacios,* were three priests, three or four friars, and a doctor of divinity called Savariego, "a great preacher and a great falsifier and heretical impostor, for he refused to come on Good Friday to preach the Passion, and stuffed himself with meat." [27]

One of the few local Tribunals for which accurate statistics have been found is that of Barcelona. The court was established by Torquemada in 1488. In the ten years following there were thirty-one *autos de fe.* Ten persons from the city or the country round about were strangled and then burned, thirteen were burned alive, fifteen were burned dead, 430 were burned in effigy, 116 were given penances, with prison sentences; and 304 were reconciled after voluntary confessions.

An analysis of these figures will give some idea of how severe Torquemada's Inquisition was in practice. Here we have 888 accusations. Of the persons accused, 430 escaped, leaving only the

[26] *Cronica de los reyes católicos.*
[27] *Historia de los reyes católicos.*

poor satisfaction of burning their images; and 15 were dead. There remained in the hands of the Inquisitors 443 persons. Of these, 304 were released without punishment, and told to go and sin no more. Of the remaining 139 (less than a third), the vast majority, 116, were sentenced to terms in prison, whose durations are not stated. Twenty-three were executed, ten of them with the privilege (considered an act of mercy) of being strangled before being burned. Of those accused and arrested, the Inquisitors turned over about five percent to the State for execution. One prisoner out of twenty was put to death in the Barcelona district.

If we may accept the estimate that in Torquemada's entire regime 100,000 prisoners passed before his Tribunals, and if we take Pulgar's estimate of 2,000 executions for the reign of Queen Isabel, including the early days of Morillo and San Martin and the later administrations of Deza, the percentage becomes even more favorable to the Inquisitor General. Hardly more than one percent of all the prisoners in Spain, during Torquemada's term of office, could have been executed.

If we compare these figures with those of Bernard Gui in thirteenth century France, we find the percentage of executions considerably less, both in Spain as a whole, and in the Barcelona district. The conclusion forces itself upon us that Torquemada made the Inquisition decidedly more merciful.

A good idea of his procedure may be had from the extant portion of the testimony in one of his most famous cases, the one concerning the *Santa Nino* of La Guardia; but as I have given an extended account of this *cause célèbre* in a previous work,[28] and have no desire to dwell further on so disagreeable a subject, I will say here only what is necessary: that the arrest of a *Converso* with a consecrated Host on his person (he admitted that it had been stolen from a Catholic Church) led to the arrest of five other New Christians and two ignorant Jews, all of whom confessed to having participated in a rite of black magic, wherein another host was used, and in a peculiarly revolting murder intended to insult Christ and bring about the madness and ruin of all Christians—all this under the leadership of a wizard named Tazarte.

[28] *Isabella of Spain*, Ch. XXV.

On November 16, 1491, in the presence of a vast crowd from Avila and other places, the two Jews and six *Conversos* were relaxed to the secular arm, and burned, all confirming their confessions at the stake. The *Conversos* also were reconciled to the Church, and were strangled before being burned.

Jewish writers have sought to prove that Torquemada or his subordinates "framed" this group of victims, to complete the work of discrediting and suppressing the Spanish Jews, with a view to their expulsion. I have great sympathy with the motives which inspire such defenses as those of Dr. Isidor Loeb[29] and Dr. Cecil Roth,[30] and in so far as the ritual murder accusation was involved in this case, I wish to take my stand with them in repudiating and condemning this cruel charge from which the Jews have suffered in so many lands and ages. I do not believe that Jews, as a racial group or a religious community, ever practised such an iniquity— it stands to reason, from what we know of human nature, that the thing cannot be true as a general proposition. It does not follow, however, that individual Jews, or groups of Jews, have never committed bloody and superstitious crimes.

Some of the Jewish arguments against the guilt of the men executed at Ávila in 1491 have considerable force. They allege that it cannot be proved that any *corpus delicti* was established; that there were discrepancies in the statements of the prisoners; that there is some confusion even as to the name of the boy supposed to have been slain, and no definite proof of his real identity. One of the witnesses contradicted himself as to the date of the crime.

On the other hand, the dossier of Yucé Franco, discovered in 1886,[31] is only one of several. The others are still missing, and may yet resolve some of these difficulties and discrepancies. Meanwhile certain facts still militate against the "judicial murder" theory. The process of Yucé has about it an air of reality; of something that happened. The fact that it remained hidden for four

---

[29] In the *Revue des Études Juives*, Vols. 15, 18, 19 and 20.

[30] *Dublin Review*, Oct., 1932.

[31] P. Fidel Fita published the full text of Yucé's process in the *Boletín de la real academia de la historia*, Vol. XI, pp. 7-160. Six of the prisoners were named Franco.

centuries destroys the hypothesis that it was manufactured for propaganda purposes, to get rid of the Jews. There are discrepancies in all human testimony. Torquemada himself appointed the judges for this trial. Two lawyers were assigned as counsel for Yucé, and when he asked for a third, by name, the request was granted. One of his counsel made a spirited and able defense. When the evidence was all in, it was submitted to two different juries of educated men—first, to seven of the most distinguished professors at the University of Salamanca, and later to five of the leading citizens of Ávila. All twelve found the accused guilty, and recommended the death sentence. It is a sad commentary upon the good faith of Dr. Lea that in his two accounts of this case,[32] he makes no mention of the two juries, and changes a very important and material date to support his claim that the confessions were only the desperate imaginings of the torture chamber. Finally, some of the most scholarly and fair-minded historians in Spain [33] have concluded, after examining such evidence as is extant, that the accused were guilty.

Now, it is not impossible that the final verdict of history may support the Jewish position about all this. Then again it may not. We are asked to believe meanwhile that three Dominican Inquisitors, well taught in the philosophy, science and theology of their time, and twelve other educated Catholic gentlemen all conspired to burn eight innocent Jews, or were led by ignorance, bigotry and superstition to accomplish that iniquity,[34] rather than to believe that untutored Jews conspired to commit a murder, involving superstition. Which, after all, is the more probable? With this question I leave the matter to future historians, who may have more complete evidence on which to base a conclusion.

The King and Queen praised Torquemada for his conduct of the

---

[32] In his *Inquisition of Spain*, Vol. I, pp. 133-4, Lea refers the reader to his longer study in *Chapters from the Religious History of Spain*. Compare this study of twenty pages with the process of Yucé. Note the change of a vital date (p. 452); *cf.* my *op. cit.*, Ch. XXV, note 10.

[33] Menendez y Pelayo, *op. cit.*, V. La Fuente, *Las sociedades secretas;* the Espasa *Encyclopedia,* article "Tribunal," etc.

[34] This was the charitable supposition of Dr. Cecil Roth in his controversy with me in the *Dublin Review.*

case;[35] and at the same time sent an edict to Ávila (after a Jew had been cruelly stoned to death by the angry mob) forbidding injury to the Jews, under pain of capital punishment. Meanwhile undoubtedly they were considering the expulsion of the Jews from Spain; for on the last day of March, 1492, they signed their names at Granada to the fatal document, commanding that all should accept baptism or leave the country. They explained that as long as the Jews remained as a center of dissent and intrigue, drawing the *Conversos* away from the Church, the root cause of all the evils they had been trying to destroy would remain. If it was just to dissolve a college for "some serious or detestable crime," how much more so to expel "those who pervert the good and honest life of cities and towns"? Here was the severity of Moses, turned against his own. Very few Jews accepted baptism. Most of them sold their goods for a pittance, and left on the date finally set, August 2, 1492, the day before Columbus set sail from Palos. Not more than 160,000 departed—these are the figures of Bernaldez, now generally accepted by Jews and Christians. Some went as far as the Balkans, some found refuge with the Pope in Rome (the Jews there tried to exclude them, because a pestilence had broken out among them; but Alexander VI insisted on admitting them); some went to Africa, to suffer theft, rape and butchery at the hands of the Moors. Their sufferings, which I have described more fully elsewhere,[36] moved every Christian who saw them, said Bernaldez, to tears. Many straggled back to Spain and were baptized. "A hundred of them came here to this place of los Palacios," he wrote, "and I baptized them, including some rabbis," whose eyes, he added, were opened at last to the meaning of the prophecies of Isaias.[37]

This uprooting of the Spanish Jews from the land where their ancestors had dwelt for centuries was not without consequences for Spain. They were not, however, the consequences so glibly related in so many textbooks: "the expulsion of the Jews caused the economic decline of Spain," and so on. The going of 160,000 persons who had sold their immovable property at a loss could

---

[35] *Boletin*, XXIII, p. 427.
[36] In my *Isabella of Spain*, Chapter XXV.
[37] *Historia*, etc., *cap.* CX.

not have ruined so large a nation; and the fact remains that the Spanish Empire attained its greatest limits and material and intellectual power in the century after the Expulsion. The number of Jews who remained in the country as *Conversos* was far greater than that of the exiles; and these baptized Jews possessed great wealth, which remained in the country with the shrewd minds of its possessors. Some of the greatest Spanish Catholics undoubtedly derived from them: perhaps they gave the Spanish genius its energy and direction. On the other hand, many remained Jews or unbelievers at heart. In the following centuries their descendants were in communication with Jews scattered all over Europe, building up new commercial empires, especially in the Low Countries and in England, and quietly kept the anti-Spanish and anti-Catholic forces of the world informed as to naval, military, and commercial happenings in the peninsula. Thus the Jews, in the long run, took their revenge on the country that had cast them out. In this sense only can it be said truthfully that the exodus led to the decline of Spain.

Torquemada undoubtedly had something to do with all this. Perhaps he has been assigned more than his share of the responsibility for the Expulsion. Llorente's tale of his rushing to the sovereigns to hold a crucifix before them and to beg them not to sell Christ, like Judas, when the Jews offered them a bribe, has no foundation in contemporary evidence. It is not even certain that it was he who suggested that Fernando and Isabel expel the Jews. They had other trusted advisers. But there is no evidence, either, that he opposed the suggestion, and the probability is that he was wholly in favor of it, considering it necessary to complete his work. It was now certain, thanks to the Inquisition and the Expulsion, that Spain would remain Catholic, and militantly Catholic, during her discovery and colonization of the Western World; and thus the spiritual health of all Latin America was assured. Nevertheless it is impossible to justify the attempt to coerce the Jews into accepting baptism; and one must admire the fortitude of men and women willing to suffer so much for what they believed, however mistakenly, to be true. Finally, the resentment set up or confirmed in Jewish minds must have kept many sincere souls from examining the claims of the Catholic Church. The consequences of the expulsion were to be enduring and world wide. If God has often punished the Jews from turning away from Him, He has also punished those who treated them unjustly.

It is to be inferred that Torquemada, looking back on his labors, perhaps not seeing the Jewish point of view at all, was very well pleased when at last the sovereigns allowed him to lay down the burden he had carried for a turbulent decade, and to retire to the beautiful monastery he had built at Ávila. There, in 1497, the remains of the only son of Fernando and Isabel were laid in an exquisite tomb; and there within a few months, the body of Fray Tomás of Torquemada himself was laid. It was 1498, the year of Savonarola's death in Florence. The great Inquisitor had been seventy-two at the time of the expulsion of the Jews; he was seventy-eight when he died.

Post-mortem appraisals of his character depended upon the point of view of the appraiser. To the Jewish historian Graetz he was "a priest whose heart was closed to every sentiment of mercy, whose lips breathed only death and destruction, and who united the savagery of the hyena with the venom of the snake." [38] To the Spanish Catholics, almost to a man, he was a gentle student who had left the cloister to perform a disagreeable but necessary task, in a spirit of justice tempered with mercy, and always with skill and prudence; a great lawgiver; the man who, next to the King and Queen and perhaps Columbus, contributed most to the greatness of Spain's *siglo de oro,* in the next age. To some he was more than that; he was a saint. When his tomb was opened for the removal of his remains, those present reported that a singularly sweet and agreeable odor came from it. People began to pray at his tomb. He has not, however, been canonized.

Torquemada left the Inquisition so strongly established and so generally respected and approved by the Spanish people, that it was to remain in operation for more than three hundred years after his death.

[38] *History of the Jews,* IV, 348.

VI

Cardinal Ximenes

AN interesting book could be written on the influence of the Sacrament of Penance upon the course of history. The kings who contributed most to the greatness of Spain, surely, were careful in their choice of those who directed their consciences; for on the words of such men depended not only the monarch's salvation, but the destiny of his people. Even so wretched a king as Enrique *el Impotente* had holy men to advise him, however indifferently he followed their precepts. Queen Isabel *la católica* of course was most particular. She had chosen Fray Hernando de Talavera because he had shown complete disregard for her royal dignity and her personal feelings at their first interview, insisting that she kneel beside him like any other penitent. "This is the confessor I have been looking for," she said; and she confessed to Talavera for several years.

In 1492, on conquering Granada, she was desirous of showing her gratitude to him; and she insisted (much against the good old man's inclinations) on having the Pope make him Archbishop of the recovered see in the south. After he went there, she used to write him long letters, asking his advice about matters of conscience; and she would accept his counsel and reproof as humbly as if she were a scullery maid. In one letter she apologized for some compliance with the French custom of allowing ladies and gentlemen to dine together, and for yielding somewhat in her opposition to bull-fighting, an amusement that Talavera disliked even more than she did. Once the Archbishop noted that she had received the French ambassadors in a somewhat more sumptuous gown than seemed necessary for a Christian ruler; and Isabel replied, in her own defense, that it was really an old dress, made of simple silk, with only three gold bands on it—indeed, she had worn it before in the presence of the same diplomats.

Now she required a new confessor, and she wanted some one who, like Talavera, would hold before her soul nothing less than the stern justice of God. As usual, she turned for advice to her old friend and counsellor, *El gran cardenal.*

As usual, Don Pedro Gonzalez de Mendoza knew the very man Her Majesty was looking for. There was a Franciscan monk in the little monastery of Salceda, who was learned and intelligent, humble, discreet, fearless and incorruptible, loyal to the death. Such must have been the character that His Eminence gave to Fray Francisco Ximenes de Cisneros. But the Queen was not the one to accept a confessor without seeing him. The Cardinal must summon him to Valladolid, where the court then was, and arrange for her to meet him, as if by accident.

Presently there appeared in the palace at Valladolid a strange figure, at which men turned to look as it glided noiselessly by on sandaled feet. Not that a man in a Franciscan robe was a novelty in those days. Penitents often put on brown robes more or less resembling those of Saint Francis; beggars and impostors sometimes made use of them; and Christopher Columbus, who had recently disappeared from Palos into the void of the western ocean, had been seen about the Castilian court for years in just such garments. But there was something different about this Franciscan. He did not have the appearance of seeking any one or anything; he had found what he wanted, he had arrived. His old patched robe hung loosely about his gaunt limbs, as if draped upon a skeleton. Well along in his fifties (he was then 56, to be exact), he must have had a fringe of graying hair about his tonsured skull. His face was so lean and so pale, and his whole aspect so unearthly, that even Peter Martyr of Anghera, who had the curiosity and some of the cynicism of a modern journalist, turned to stare after him, and jotted down that he looked like one of the early hermit fathers, just emerging from his retreat in the woods. There hovered about Ximenes the composure of one who has completely cast off the shams and desires of this world. It was not the quiet of death and inaction; it was rather the serenity of a man who has found something more alive than life. He spoke very little, and in monosyllables. Some said that he was supposed to be learned, but did not talk, look, or act like a theologian. His eyes, though deep-set and sometimes piercing, were always watering. He had rather thick lips, the upper one protruding a little. When he smiled, his teeth showed, tightly packed: and the eye-teeth were so prominent that the courtiers began calling him The Elephant.

Gonzalo Ximenes de Cisneros (for that was originally his name) was born in Torrelaguna, a little place near Madrid, in the diocese of Toledo, in 1436. His father, Alfonso, had a small government position, probably as collector of the *alcabala* tax. Biographers have noticed that the family was reduced in circumstances, but of very ancient nobility; on what authority does not appear. The fact is, nothing is known about the ancestors of Ximenes. If they were tax collectors under John II and Enrique IV, it is not at all beyond the bounds of possibility that some of them may have been Jews, though no Spanish historian, to my knowledge, has offered this suggestion.

Ximenes studied at Salamanca University, then one of the great intellectual centres of Europe and then took some courses at the *Studium Generale* maintained at Alcalá de Henares under the patronage of the Primate of Spain, the fiery Archbishop Alfonso Carillo—warrior, reformer, patron of education and builder of the beautiful palace that commemorates him. As this period young Ximenes appears to have been ambitious, perhaps somewhat worldly; at any rate, his great desideratum was to find himself a comfortable and lucrative benefice, where he could lead a studious life in peace. To this end he set forth to seek his fortune in Rome, crossing the Pyrenees and traveling by the land route through France. On the way he was robbed twice, and reached Aix-en-Provence completely destitute. Being one of those men, however, for whom things usually turned out well, he had the good fortune to run across a fellow-student at Alcalá, named Brunet, who was going to Rome himself, and paid his expenses. This was in 1460. Ximenes remained in the Holy City for more than five years, studying, and practicing as a lawyer in the consistorial courts. Unfortunately nothing else is known of this formative period of his life.

Possibly he found Rome at that time congenial for ambitious young Spaniards; for on the Chair of Saint Peter sat a Spanish Pope, Callixtus III (Alfonso Borgia), who had owed his first benefice to his support of the Spanish Anti-Pope Benedict XIII. Thus out of the Great Schism, among other consequences, arose the house of Borgia, with all that the name came to imply, both good and ill, for Christendom. In Callixtus III, the founder of this ecclesiastical dynasty, the contrasting qualities of later extremes could be noted in embryo. He was obliged to spend most of his pontificate in leading an heroic struggle against the advancing hordes of Islam. It was in his time that the sentence of the Inquisition against Saint Joan of Arc was reversed, and her innocence proclaimed. The great fault of this vigorous Pope, with his hooked nose and fighting jaw, was nepotism; and he died leaving a very large amount of money. What were his relations, if any, with young Gonzalo de Ximenes from his native Spain? History is silent here; but Ximenes was not wholly unsuccessful at the Roman Court, for when he decided to leave, in 1465, on learning of the death of this father, he took with him, as a pledge of future preferment, a prized *letra expectiva*.

This was an appointment, by papal authority, to the next benefice vacant in Spain, in any diocese Ximenes might specify. Naturally he chose Toledo, which included his birthplace. Perhaps he had a widowed mother whom he expected to help. We know that he had two younger brothers, Juan and Bernardín. Possibly the death of his father had left Ximenes with a responsibility for the whole family. At any rate, he returned to Spain, doubtless with many youthful hopes, and waited for some priest with a suitable benefice to die.

In 1473 the archpriest of Uzeda went to his reward. His benefice was not a very large one, but it suited Ximenes. It was near home, near the people he loved; it would serve. Armed with his *letra expectiva* from Rome, he moved in.

In a very short time he heard from the Archbishop of Toledo.

Most likely Don Alfonso de Carillo summoned him to Alcalá to give an account of himself. Most likely Ximenes, with his habitual calmness and decisiveness, laid his *letra expectiva* before His Grace, with every hope that he would then be welcomed into the archdiocese. It happened, however, that the ruddy warrior-archbishop, who had commanded the rebels at the bloody field of Olmedo, had a friend of his own to whom he had promised this particular living; moreover, he had a peculiar aversion to communications from Rome, and in particular to *letras expectivas*. He informed Ximenes that the papal letter was of no validity in that diocese, and ordered him to take himself out of Uzeda without further delay.

It was a case of Greek meeting Greek, diamond upon diamond. There was something in Ximenes that made it impossible, apparently, for him to give way when he felt convinced that he was right. He refused to budge. The Archbishop had him arrested and locked up in a strong stone tower. He sent word that he could be released at any time, if he would renounce his benefice. Ximenes replied that he never would renounce it.

Meanwhile great events were happening. Henry the Impotent died in 1473, Isabel was crowned, and the King of Portugal took arms to defend the counterclaim of his niece, La Beltraneja. Archbishop Carillo, who had once vainly attempted to persuade Isabel to accept the crown in Henry's lifetime, now broke with her and went over to the side of the Portuguese; according to Pulgar, the secretary and chronicler of Isabel, "some imputed his discontent to pride, some to greed, but we believe that it was chiefly envy of the Cardinal of Spain, because of the honor paid him by the King and Queen." When the conflicting forces met for a bloody decision at Toro in March 1476, the Archbishop was in the saddle again, a coat of mail under his rochet, fighting valiantly on the losing side, while his rival, the future Cardinal, plucked down the Portuguese standard and helped with his strong right arm to drive the invaders in headlong flight from Castile.

With all this, the Archbishop did not forget his prisoner at Uzeda, and every now and then he would send to ask Ximenes whether he had changed his mind about the benefice. Finally he had the young man taken to the fortress at Santorcaz, where priests who needed discipline for one reason or another in his archidiocese were incarcerated.

Ximenes never wavered. It was the old Archbishop who finally decided that he was dealing with an adversary who would remain in prison for life rather than surrender, and that the benefice in question was not worth the trouble. He voluntarily released Ximenes after something more than six years of imprisonment.

Left in possession of the field, so to speak, and free to take his *arciprestazgo,* Ximenes discovered that he no longer wanted it. During those six years or more, he had doubtless done a great deal of solid praying and thinking, and had come to certain conclusions. He had discovered the practical truth of what the author of the Imitation made the title of his first chapter: "Of the Necessity of Following Christ and Despising All the Vanities of the World." Perhaps he read the famous book in his cell; very likely he read, too, some of the works of Ramón Lull, whose main thesis was much the same. When he came forth into the world, perhaps a little dazed, a little surprised that Carillo had given way, a little uncertain as to his future course, he soon made up his mind that he wanted nothing more to do with this Archbishop, and exchanged his benefice at Uzeda for a chaplaincy in another diocese, at the cathedral of Sigüenza.

The Bishop of Sigüenza was Don Pedro Gonzales de Mendoza, who had been chancellor to Enrique IV and now occupied the same post under Queen Isabel. He had just been appointed Archbishop of Sevilla, or was about to be appointed, when Ximenes appeared. How the two future archbishops of Toledo became acquainted is not clear; but it is certain that Mendoza soon discovered that the newcomer was no ordinary man, and made him his vicar general. Ximenes meanwhile continued studying theology, and found a Jew to teach him Hebrew and Aramaic, so that he could read the revealed Word of God in the original. He said that he would give all his knowledge of other subjects to be able to explain one passage in Holy Scripture.

Three or four years as vicar general brought to full vigor the disgust for the world that he had conceived in his prison cells at

Uzeda and Santorcaz; and in 1484 he informed his benefactor that he wished to renounce all hope of eccelesiastical advancement, and to leave the world altogether. He applied for admission to the Observantine branch of the Franciscan order, and was received into the monastery of *San Juan de los Reyes* at Toledo, giving up even his baptismal name of Gonzalo, to take that of the founder of the order. After his year's novitiate he was sent to the Franciscan convent of Santa María de Castañar, which, as the name implies, was in the midst of a great forest of chestnut trees. The community was small and poor; it seemed to be just what Ximenes wanted.

He never did anything by halves, and when he undertook to follow in the footsteps of the Poor Man of Assisi, he meant to do just that. He ate barely enough of the poorest kind of food to keep body and soul together. He slept on a bare board. When he travelled, he went on foot, as Saint Francis had walked along the hot roads of Italy, as Our Lord had walked the hard roads of Palestine. He ministered to the poor round about; he heard confessions of people who went to the little monastery looking for help.

Presently he discovered, to his dismay, that he had acquired a reputation throughout the district as a director of souls. Demands upon his time became more frequent, and no doubt there were many of the usual suggestions that so capable a man should be preaching in a large place, or should be a bishop—anything but the contemplative that Ximenes wished to be, speaking alone with' God in the little hut he had made himself in the chestnut woods near the monastery. They were coming after him soon—he must have sensed it—to put him in some position of trust, where the last remnants of human pride, vanity and greed that he had striven to quench from his heart would be fanned by the sickening breath of flattery and hypocrisy. Ximenes begged his superiors to send him to a more obscure and poverty-stricken convent at Salceda, and they did so.

There he was, leading the ideal Franciscan life as perfectly as he could, in 1492, when the great world that he despised and had almost forgotten, was shaken by one of those convulsions that change the direction of events and determine the courses of empires and men for hundreds of years. In a single fateful year (1) America was discovered; (2) Spain was freed at last from the Mohammedan peril in the south, and left free to walk the high and dangerous road to world power, free to colonize and Christianize vast portions of the globe, free to engage also in an unchristian struggle with France for the political dominance of Italy and of Europe; and (3) the Spanish Sephardim Jews were scattered to the four winds— to Africa, to Portugal, to the Balkans, to Turkey, to England, to France, to Germany—to begin anew their struggle against the Christian revelation and all that had come in their minds to represent it. In that vast reshuffling and realignment of forces, destined to reverberate about this planet and down the secret labyrinths of centuries, the Queen of Castile, who had just expelled the Jews, made her Jewish confessor Archbishop of Granada. She needed, therefore, a new director for her conscience; and invisible hands reached into the solitude at Salceda to pluck forth Ximenes and set him, all reluctant, among the courtiers at Valladolid, where he found himself one day walking in a corridor beside that gentleman of gentlemen, that truest of all aristocrats, Cardinal Mendoza.

Soon a lady appeared, and the Cardinal presented his Franciscan visitor to the Queen of Castile. Isabel, at forty-one, was beginning to show the strain of the tremendous labors and anxieties that had brought her to the climax of her glory; yet she was still a handsome woman with fair skin, whose blue eyes looked straight through a person, with something like the wisdom of the serpent and the innocence of the dove, and saw at once all she needed to know. Her quick and accurate judgment of men had been one of the elements of her success; it usually took her only a few minutes to find out whether a visitor was a great man or a charlatan. It is not recorded what pleasant remarks she let fall to Ximenes, or just what artless questions she asked, with a quick little glance to see how his face changed expression; but it is said that Ximenes, like Columbus before him, met her with simple and fearless dignity, and that she was so pleased that after a short conversation she told him why he was there: he was to be her confessor.

Ximenes asked to be excused. He was not fitted for any such responsibility. God had made him a simple monk, who knew only to stay in his monastery and pray; he understood nothing of the ways of great folk, and could not imagine himself living in a court. Perhaps the Cardinal at this point suggested that God, who had placed him in the forest, now called him to another duty in the court. Ximenes was sure that God wanted him to live in solitude and prayer. All this probably convinced Isabel that he was just the man she wanted for her confessor, and would have. The Cardinal spoke of holy obedience. Ximenes finally agreed, on condition that he be allowed to continue his residence in the convent at Salceda, and to answer the Queen's summons when she had need of him. It was so determined, and Ximenes went back to his silvan retreat.

Whether he knew it or not, however, the contemplative life would never more be his; he was to be henceforth a man of action. For a while he went to the Court when sent for, heard Her Majesty's confession, gave her absolution and advice, and returned to Salceda. He still travelled on foot, accompanied by another Franciscan. Once he and his companion slept in a barn on some stacks of corn. In the morning the other friar woke Ximenes to tell him of a marvelous dream he had had: he had seen him arrayed in purple and crowned as Archbishop of Toledo.

"Sleep on, brother, sleep on," said Ximenes. "Dreams are only dreams."

This was the second prediction of the sort. A prison companion had once told of dreaming that he saw Ximenes as Archbishop of Toledo, and Ximenes, looking about his cell, had remarked, "My beginnings don't seem to promise such an ending."

Yet (whether these traditional anecdotes are authentic, or were invented afterwards) such an ending certainly awaited him. He had been the Queen's confessor three years when his old benefactor, Cardinal Mendoza, died in the See of Toledo. The problem of choosing his successor occasioned one of the rare differences between King Fernando and Queen Isabel. Fernando had proved himself in the Moorish war one of the great generals of his age, and he was now beginning to demonstrate that he was worthy of the high and in some respects unenviable praise bestowed upon him by Machiavelli, as a statesman more than a match for such contemporaries as Charles VIII and Henry VII; but he was no saint, and had stained with infidelity the great love that bound him and his queen. He now had the effrontery to propose that his illegitimate son, the Archbishop of Zaragoza, be nominated for the primate See of Castile. Queen Isabel naturally refused even to consider such an idea. She proposed her confessor, Fray Francisco Ximenes de Cisneros—tradition says at the instance of Cardinal Mendoza on his death bed. Her ambassador at Rome asked Pope Alexander VI for the appointment.

She had said nothing of this to Ximenes, knowing, doubtless, what his reaction would be. She did not mention it even on Good Friday, 1495, when he appeared at the palace early in the morning to hear her confession. Presently his gaunt form was seen going forth again to where his companion, Fray Francisco Ruiz, was waiting for him; and the two set forth on the road to Ocaña, where they were going to stop at a Franciscan monastery. After a while they heard the beat of hoofs, and were overtaken by messengers from the Queen, commanding them to return at once to the palace.

Ximenes cheerfully faced about and walked back. The Queen was waiting for him, holding a paper which had just come by courier from Rome. She placed it in his hands. Unrolling it, he began to read:

"To our beloved son, Fray Francisco Ximenes de Cisneros, Archbishop-elect of Toledo."

Ximenes handed back the parchment, saying: "This doesn't belong to me," and unceremoniously left the room. When the Queen sent for him, he had left the palace. Her noble emissaries finally overtook him walking rapidly along the dusty road to Ocaña. According to one of the numerous stories, not very well documented but widely accepted as consistent with what men knew of the later Ximenes, one of the great lords of Castile knelt before him and said, "If you consent to be archbishop, I kiss the hand of an archbishop. If you refuse, I kiss the hand of a saint."

Ximenes refused, and it does not appear whether his hand was kissed or not; but there is no doubt that he continued to reject the high honor until Isabel asked Pope Alexander VI to send him a special brief, commanding him, by virtue of holy obedience, to accept. It was now evident even to him that God had laid this heavy penance on his shoulders. He was consecrated, and sat dourly on the chair of his old persecutor, Archbishop Carillo.

Though now master of the huge revenues of the See of Toledo, he made no change at all in his way of life. He gave his riches to the poor, he ate the same coarse food, he went about in such a shabby state that people began saying it was a scandal for an archbishop to make such an exhibition of himself. The Queen, who understood the psychological effect of splendor upon the public, and on state occasions put on gorgeous robes which in her heart she despised, wrote again to the Pope, asking him to instruct him in what he owed the dignity of his office. Toward the end of 1496, according to Gomez,[1] Ximenes received a letter from the Roman Curia, reminding him that the holy universal Church, the city of God on earth, was for all men and all ranks; and while it was wrong to seek the badges of honor too earnestly, it was also wrong to reject them too contemptuously, for each state of life had its own conditions, which were pleasing to God. Prelates should avoid excessive display and arrogance on the one hand, and on the other any false or excessive humility that would weaken their authority.

From then on Ximenes wore the rich robes of his office, and occupied the sumptuous chamber in the palace at Alcalá. Under the magnificent bed, however, he kept a little board pallet, which he drew out at night and slept upon. He used to mend his own clothes till they were a mass of patches. There is a story that an ardent young Franciscan who had admired his austerity concluded that he had succumbed to the seductions of wealth and power. One Sunday, when Ximenes sang the High Mass in vestments of silk and cloth of gold, this monk preached before him on the vain pride of ecclesiastics who betrayed the doctrine of Christ. After Mass he sent for the young preacher to visit him in the sacristy; and there, without a word he began taking off his vestments. Under the beautiful chasuble, under the immaculate alb, was the old patched Franciscan robe. This too the Archbishop laid aside for a moment, revealing a hair shirt next to his skin. Then, putting

[1] Alvaro Gómez de Castro: *De rebus gestis a Francisco Ximenio Cisnerio, Archiepiscopo Toletano,* Alcalá, 1569.

back the robe of sackcloth, he smiled indulgently and walked away
without a word.

Ximenes was born to rule. From 1495 on, while continuing to
guide the Queen's conscience, he began to play the same dominant
role on an international stage that he had played in spite of himself, wherever he had been, whether in the lonely cell at Uzeda, or
as superior of the convent at Salceda. There is space here for only
a hint of his many and vast achievements. At Granada, where
Archbishop Talavera seemed to be converting the conquered Moors
too slowly, Ximenes was sent by the Queen to expedite the process;
and although he brought about 4,000 conversions, he behaved with
a severity which it is safe to say would have seemed shocking to
Saint Francis, and was the cause of an insurrection that might have
had fatal consequences if Talavera had not gone before the Moors,
who loved and trusted him, and asked them to lay down their
arms. The forcing of baptism upon some of the Moors was an
error for which no one can offer a defense of Ximenes on Christian
principles; at Granada, surely, he revealed in himself the opportunist statesman rather than the priest. On his return to Alcalá,
he had the pleasure, in 1500, of laying the corner stone of his University, which he then proceeded to build up into a worthy rival
of Salamanca, by getting the best possible teachers from all parts
of the world; and it was there that he had printed, after infinite
labor by Christian and Jewish scholars, and the combing of the
whole world for manuscripts, the first great Polyglot Bible (the
so-called Complutensian), with texts of the Old Testament in
Hebrew, Greek and Latin, and of the New in Greek and Latin.
All this he did at his own expense. In 1509, when he was seventy-
three years old, he organized a crusading army and fleet, with the
King's permission, and conquered the Mohammedan kingdom of
Oran, in north Africa, a thriving centre of trade with the Levant,
as well as a pirate's nest whence the lean black ships of the Moslems
put forth by night to prey on Christian shipping, and now and then
to slay and burn along the coasts of Spain. It was Ximenes who
laid the foundation of Spain's African empire.

On more than one occasion he saved from destruction the peace
and unity of Spain, which Fernando and Isabel had wrought, by

such tremendous labors, out of the chaos they took over from Henry the Fourth. He was the Queen's confessor until her death, in 1504; and as one of the executors of her will he was in a position to exert a wise and sane influence when ambitious men, long restrained by her firm prudence, began to grasp again for power. The only son of Isabel and Fernando having died, the crown of Castile was placed upon the bewildered head of their daughter, Juana *la loca,* who was already half-mad with jealousy over the philandering of her husband Philip the Fair, son of the Hapsburg Emperor Maximilian. Foreseeing the probable incapacity of Juana, her mother had tactfully arranged in her will that if her daughter "for any reason" should be "unwilling or unable" to rule, King Fernando should act as regent until the majority of their grandson Charles, first-born of Juana and Philip—this by virtue of "the magnanimity and illustrious qualities of the King my Lord, as well as his large experience and the great profit that will redound to the state from his wise and benevolent rule." Fernando was a great ruler, a worthy consort for such a Queen; but he found matters far more difficult when she was not beside him. Castile and Aragon were still independent kingdoms, jealous of their sovereignty; and the Castilians had never had as much love as respect for the lord of Aragon.

Hardly had the great Queen been laid in her tomb at Granada when a faction of intriguing nobles began to unravel her life's work by pitting her son-in-law against her widower. The leaders of this movement were the Marqués of Villena (son of Don Juan Pacheco, who had virtually ruled the kingdom under Henry the Impotent); the Duke of Najara; and Don Juan Manuel, who had been ambassador of Isabel and Fernando at the Emperor's court, but on hearing of the Queen's death, had hastened to Flanders to gain the favor of young Philip and to widen the breach between him and his father-in-law. A new division of Spain, even another civil war, seemed imminent as Philip prepared to go there to put himself at the head of the Castilian party. King Fernando countered by making a shrewd treaty with Louis XII, whereby he arranged to marry young Germaine de Foix, with the implied threat that her offspring, if any, might cheat Philip of Aragon, Naples and Sicily.

When Philip arrived in Spain, however, Ximenes was waiting quietly for an opportunity to carry out the wishes of his dead Queen. First of all he arranged for a meeting between Philip and Fernando, in a little hermitage. Philip appeared there with his new favorite, Manuel. As the monarchs greeted one another, the Archbishop took the courtier by the arm, saying:

"Their Majesties wish to speak alone. Let us go outside, and I will guard the door."

Before Manuel could recover from his surprise, Ximenes had led him away, and then, returning, locked the door and took his seat beside the two kings. The result was a treaty signed by both June 27, 1506. It was not entirely satisfactory, for Fernando, following a Machiavellian practice of the age, secretly denounced it as imposed upon him by force, and therefore not binding on his conscience. Ximenes, however, had gained time for further plans.

Feeling was so intense in those weeks that some of the nobles who opposed King Fernando went to greet him with armor under their courtly raiment. The old warrior was not taken in. "My dear Garcilasso, how stout you have grown lately!" he cried affably, as he clapped a hand on the shoulder of his Roman envoy of other days, and felt the steel under the silk and velvet.

Ximenes was keeping watch over everything, and praying for peace. Nothing seemed to disturb his serenity, but his keen eye was looking for some opportunity to win over Philip, and separate him from Manuel.

One day, when there was a bull-fight, the Archbishop was walking across an open space when suddenly there appeared, glowering upon him, a ferocious bull, released either by accident or by some foul device of an enemy. People scampered for shelter. Ximenes, in his flaming robes of scarlet, stood imperturbable, watching to see what the beast would do. Finally there came some of the guards of King Philip, who diverted the bull's attention until he could be captured. When Philip congratulated Ximenes on his narrow escape, the Archbishop remarked,

"There is never any need for alarm when the King's guards are near."

It had not escaped his notice that Don Juan Manuel had already begun to take advantage of Philip's vanity and other weaknesses, as the elder Marqúes of Villena had thrived on the frailties of Henry the Fourth. The King had already removed Queen Isabel's friend, Cabrera, Marqúes of Moya, from the governorship of Segovia, and conferred the office on his favorite—besides making him inspector of finance, and giving him reason to hope for the governorship of Burgos.

Ximenes was waiting for the upstart to overreach himself. And this at last he did. It was bad enough that Castile should be full of acquisitive gentlemen from Flanders waiting for the plums that the royal favorite dropped into their hands; it was bad enough that the situation had produced a revolt in Andalusia; but when Manuel violated the last will and testament of Queen Isabel by secretly signing a contract to farm out to a friend the revenues of the silk manufactures of Granada (which the Queen had left to her husband) he made a fatal mistake. Some one discovered the contract in a desk and took it to Ximenes. The Archbishop showed it to King Philip. Then he angrily tore it to pieces. This was the beginning of the end of Manuel.

In a sense it was also the beginning of the end of Philip. Within three months that debonair adulterer, though increasingly distrustful of Don Juan Manuel, had given him at last the desired governorship of Burgos. In gratitude for this, the favorite invited the King to a banquet. As usual, Philip ate and drank too much; afterwards he rode horseback and played a long time at tennis. When overheated and tired, he stopped and drank a jug of cold water. Before night he had a fever, and a few days later he was dead. He was twenty-eight years old.

Nothing but the strong wisdom and prudence of Ximenes saved the country from civil war and anarchy. King Fernando had started for Italy. Queen Juana, who was pregnant, began to display tendencies that even the Archbishop could no longer control. She insisted that her husband was still alive, she traveled about with his corpse, going only at night, escorted by an eery procession of torchbearers (for she said it was not becoming for a young widow to let the sun shine upon her); and once she slept in a field with the cold remains of Philip. A pitiful spectacle, this Spanish Ophelia; and no one in Spain knew what to do but weep and pray. Ximenes sent for King Fernando. The latter refused to return; some said because he was waiting to time his arrival, others that he was distrustful of the *Gran Capitan,* Gonsalvo de Córdoba, his viceroy at Naples, and wanted to clip his wings. So Ximenes ruled the kingdom, while Queen Juana sat in a darkened room, her chin in her hands, hating all women, and loving nothing but music and Philip.

The Archbishop had to handle the grandees very carefully. If he had openly declared for King Fernando, the Castilians might have revolted at once, and the cause of the absent monarch would have been lost. Ximenes, however, acting as one of several regents, postponed the issue while he gained the friendship, one after another, of the King's enemies, commencing with the Marqués of Villena.

When at last Fernando arrived, in July 1507, he brought with him from Rome a Cardinal's hat as a reward for his faithful minister, and at the same time had him appointed Inquisitor General for Castile. He had never liked the man, but he realized what he owed to him.

As Inquisitor, Ximenes rendered many inestimable services to the Church. If he had saved the monarchy and the national unity, it is not too much to say that he also kept Spain a Catholic nation, at a time more critical than even he imagined. His first contribution to this was a reorganization of the Holy Office itself. After the death of Torquemada, that institution had begun to manifest the usual symptoms that follow the passing of a dominant personality. The second Inquisitor General was decidedly inferior in talent. He was Fray Diego de Deza, Columbus's patron, now archbishop of Sevilla—a man of great general learning and a specialist in theology, in whom Fernando and Isabel rightly reposed a great deal of confidence. He lacked, however, the keen insight into human nature, and the ability to direct it, that both Torquemada and Ximenes possessed in a marked degree. He was completely taken in, for example, by one of the worst of the Spanish Inquisitors, Diego Rodriguez de Lucero.

Lucero had many of the characteristics that have been erroneously imputed to Torquemada. He was a stern, irascible individual, with a fanatical hatred of all Jews, apparently without any exceptions; he particularly despised the *Conversos,* and there is little doubt that if he had the management of the Church Catholic, he would have excluded from it all the blood-brothers of Jesus Christ. Looking balefully about the scene from which all the most loyal and heroic Jews had been expunged, he saw many Catholics of Jewish descent, some of whom, despite the Inquisition, were not Christians in good faith, and some of whom were even in secret conspiracy to destroy Christianity if possible. Into his dark and narrow heart there came the notion that one of these dissemblers was Archbishop Talavera of Granada. He persuaded the Inquisitor General that the Archbishop was a secret heretic. There was probably some personal difference, or conflict of temperaments, between Deza and Talavera. Both of Jewish descent, they had differed on many matters; Talavera had been skeptical about Columbus, for example, while Deza had been enthusiastic from the first. However this may be, Lucero won the approval of Deza by bringing before him many witnesses (probably bribed, according to Peter Martyr), who gave such alarming reports that the venerable Archbishop was formally accused of judaizing (1) because he had opposed the establishment of the Inquisition a quarter of a century before, and (2) because he was of Jewish descent.

Never before in the history of the Inquisition had an Archbishop been denounced. The Medieval Tribunal claimed no jurisdiction over bishops; only the Pope could discipline or correct them, and this only in matters of faith. The Spanish Inquisition, closely allied as it was to a restored monarchy with a tendency to caesaropapism, was impatient of the old canonical restraints. Deza did not dare step over them where a fellow-Archbishop was concerned; he therefore appealed to the primate of Spain for cooperation. Ximenes with his usual prudence reported the whole affair to Pope Julius II, to whom it must have been no little embarrassment. The evidence alleged by Lucero and Deza looked so formidable, however, that even the great reputation of Talavera for true Christian piety and charity did not seem to justify an acquittal without examination. Julius therefore took the case out of the hands of the Spanish Inquisitors, and ordered an investigation by his legate, the Bishop of Bertinoro, and a special commission.

Of Llorente's typical howler that Lucero, before proceeding against Talavera, first consulted and obtained the approval of the Queen who had made all her confessions to the good old man for a dozen years or more (and who thus becomes an ingrate as well as a bigot), it is necessary only to observe that Isabel had been in her grave for more than a year when the nonsense was first broached. Otherwise it is safe to assume that the charges would have died then and there. But Lady Isabel was in her tomb, and Lucero saw to it that the hearings proceeded. Fortunately the papal legate was not taken in by him. He treated the old Archbishop (Talavera was then eighty, and the business was a sad trial to him) with all consideration, and in the end gave him a triumphant acquittal. He sent to Rome the accusations against the Jewish relatives of the accused, many of whom Lucero had had arrested; and the Pope exonerated them all. Within a few months (May, 1507) Talavera was dead.

The injustice of Lucero was his own undoing. Some of those accused of judaizing in Andalusia conceived the clever idea of making false accusations against so many of their friends and relatives that there would be too many for the jails to hold or the Holy Office to prosecute; thus a general amnesty would be declared, all would go free, and the Inquisition would be discredited. Lucero's fanaticism led him to swallow the bait. He drew up denunciations against huge numbers of the most reputable citizens of southern Spain—lords and ladies, old and young, priests, nuns and lay people. Doubtless his imagination enlarged all he had heard into a repetition of the Susan plot of 1480, with all Spain and the Church in deadly peril. Thus no doubt he represented the situation to Deza; and the Archbishop again believed him.

Ximenes had been watching all this with a disapproving eye. He was not yet connected with the Inquisition, but he was primate of Spain; and he felt it his duty to suggest that King Fernando write the Pope, asking to have Deza removed from office. Zurita was unkind enough to suggest, in the following century, that Ximenes wanted the office for himself; this is possible, though hardly consistent with his customary attitude. At all events, the King was reluctant to follow the advice, for Deza was his friend and confessor, and postponed doing anything until after the arrival of Philip in Spain, when the powers of Deza as Inquisitor General were suspended, and committed for the time being to the royal council.

After Philip's death, Deza reassumed his office, and Lucero renewed the *pesquizas* of the Andalusians who had been denounced for judaizing. As a result, the citizens of Córdoba took arms in rebellion against the fanatical Inquisitor, who fled for his life, while the buildings of the Holy Office were seized by the crowd, and the prisoners were released by the Marqués of Priego. The revolt began to spread through Andalusia. Fernando at last agreed that Deza must be removed, and that the logical man to succeed him was the Primate of Spain.

Ximenes began with characteristic zeal, tempered by tact and quiet prudence, to reform the Holy Office. One of the first and most praiseworthy acts of his administration was to order the arrest of Lucero, who was incarcerated at Burgos. A thorough investigation of the Córdoba affair was made; and to avoid suspicion of local Castilian prejudices and feuds, a commission, chiefly composed of Aragonese, was appointed to review the sentences of Lucero. In 1508 they were all set aside, and his witnesses declared unworthy of credit. Lucero was released after a year in prison, on the theory apparently that he had erred through fault of temperament and not of deliberate intention; though it seems evident that his dealing with witnesses was dishonest. Ximenes removed several other Inquisitors from office. On learning that an assistant jailer of the Inquisition at Toledo had had scandalous relations with female prisoners, he asked the Supreme Council to decree a sentence of death for any such abuse. He had special parishes organized in some places for Jewish converts, to protect them from unjust suspicion on account of customs they naturally retained after baptism.

Statistics on the number of condemned during the regime of Ximenes are lacking; Llorente's figures, as usual, are fantastically swollen, and based generally upon the computing of probabilities from scanty evidence.

Indirectly, of course, his reorganization of the Holy Office had a beneficial effect upon the whole Spanish Church. But in a more direct sense it may be said, without exaggeration, that this Grand Inquisitor was the true father of the Reformation in Spain.

The word Reformation is used here in its correct sense. Heretical movements never reformed the Christian Church. All of them professed their intention to do so; but invariably their effect was to confuse and destroy Christian doctrine—to dissolve Christ, in the phrase of Saint John the Evangelist—without removing the human frailties complained of. From time to time, of course, there was need of reform in a world of men. The Catholic Church invariably accomplished the necessary corrections; sometimes slowly, in the face of stupendous obstacles. Never in all her history was she reformed by people who left her ranks, refused obedience to the Vicar of Christ, and cried out against the sins of others in the spirit of the Pharisee who thanked God that he was not like the rest of men. She was reformed by men who began, like the Publican, with themselves, saying, "Lord, have mercy upon me, a sinner" —such men as Saint Benedict, Saint Francis, Saint Dominic, Saint Ignatius Loyola; men who quietly influenced a small group of similar persons, until they set in motion a force so firmly and sanely founded on grace that it permeated the whole Mystical Body, and accomplished the divine cleansing process.

As a result of a series of calamities already mentioned, the Catholic Church in the fifteenth century was in need of one of her periodic housecleanings. Men who loved her saw this even more clearly than those who hated her. In other words, the best Catholics have always disliked bad priests, political prelates, aberrations, superstitions, and all such abominations in every age, quite as heartily as any heretic could. But they have seen no point in trying to cure a headache by cutting off the head.

There certainly was some need of reform in the Spanish kingdoms, and Catholics, even in the heydey of the Inquisition, were free to say so. A member of the Church could be burned for saying that the Pope was not the vicar of Christ (unless he recanted); but he could say with impunity (even if untruthfully) that the Pope was a scoundrel. Osuña, in his *Abecedario,* which profoundly influenced the spiritual development of Saint Teresa, made no secret of his opinion of bad bishops. Somewhat later a Dominican master of Theology, Fray Pablo de Leon, wrote in the vulgar tongue, under the very eyes of the Holy Office, an indictment of clerical corruption as vigorous as anything said on that subject by Luther. In his *Guide to Heaven,* a book of devotion that any young girl could read without interference from the Inquisitors, he inveighed against prelates and pastors who "never see their sheep, but put robbers over them as supervisors . . . who absolve no one except for money, nor dispense without being paid for it . . . who hold on to bread like usurers, and the dearest that is sold in the land is theirs . . . and the Church today has no greater wolves or enemies or tyrants or robbers than the ones who are shepherds of souls and have the largest incomes. . . . All the Church, on account of our sins, is full either of those who served or were favored in Rome, or of Bishops or sons or relatives or nephews, or those who enter by request as sons of grandees, or enter through money or something that is worth money—and through a miracle one gets in through learning or virtuous life. And so, as money puts them in the Church, they never look for anything but money, or have any purpose except to increase their income . . . for that is what they care for, and not for souls. . . . Oh Lord God! How many benefices there are today in the Church that do not have prelates or pastors any more . . . but only mercenary idiots, who do not know how to read, and do not know what a Sacrament is, and they give absolution for everything. . . . From Rome comes all evil . . . in Rome is the abysm of these ills and other similar ones. . . . Such men rule the Church of God; such men command her. . . ." [2]

There is exaggeration here, and no recognition of the less noticeable but numerous priests who led virtuous undramatic lives; but

[2] Señor Menendez y Pelayo (*op. cit.,* t. II, lib. I, p. 26, 1880 edition) quotes this from de Castro, *Historía de los protestantes españoles,* Cadiz, 1861.

the passage reflects the indignation of good Catholics over abuses which needed correction, and its publication shows that the Inquisition was concerned not with the suppression of truth, but only with that of dogmatic falsehood.

When Ximenes had completed the conquest of himself, he was called upon to correct irregularities in the lives of other priests; and he began, logically, with his own order. In 1494, at the request of Fernando and Isabel, Pope Alexander issued a bull (confirmed by Julius II) commanding a reform of all orders in the Spanish realms, and naming Ximenes as the reformer. It was no easy or desirable task, but the great Franciscan went about it with courage and thoroughness. He visited the monasteries one by one, burned up charters of privileges illegally granted, and cut off many incomes and inheritances, which he diverted to hospitals and other works of mercy. He compelled friars to put away soft garments and resume the rough and coarse ones called for by their rules; he cloistered nuns wherever he could; he insisted on complete observance of monastic discipline, including presence at choir and other duties.

The Dominicans, Augustinians and Carmelites did not resist. It was his own community that gave him one of the great battles of his life. After the death of Saint Francis, as we have seen, that order passed through a hectic period, at the end of which, when peace had been restored through the efforts of Saint John Capistrano, there still remained two divisions, the Conventuals, who took the easier road for human nature to follow as regarded property and other matters, and the Observantines, who sought to follow the ideal of Saint Francis in all its rigor. Ximenes himself, a member by choice of the latter group, put all Franciscans in Spain under the direction of the Commissary General, and then proceeded to reform them. The Conventuals were furious; many of them, in fact, were good men sincerely convinced that their modified rule was better than the original one. The dispute reached such a stage of acrimony that an Italian Franciscan General went to Spain purposely to put an end to the reform, spoke insultingly to Queen Isabel in his anger, and evoked from her a memorable rebuke, while Gonzalo de Cetina, secretary for Aragon, threatened to hang the distinguished visitor with the cord of his habit. Such strong representations were made at the Vatican that Alexander VI, in 1496, ordered the housecleaning suspended, but the following year, being better informed, he allowed it to go on. Ximenes carried on the war to victory. He had the satisfaction of learning that a thousand bad monks had given up the struggle in Castile, and had migrated to Morocco, where they might live as they pleased —some of them taking along women with whom they had given scandal. The Church and Spain were much better, of course, for their departure; and although Ximenes never completed his task with the secular clergy, he had carried the movement so far that when he died the boast was made, with justice, that the Spanish monks were noted beyond all those of Christendom for temperance, chastity, and virtuous living in general. In the course of time, the improved state of the monasteries had its effect upon the secular priesthood. It was probably the reform of Ximenes, therefore that saved Spain from succumbing, after his death, to Protestantism. Unlike his English contemporaries, he proved that monks could be brought back to discipline without cutting off their heads, destroying their works of mercy and handing over their lands to usurers.

Every heretical movement had two important elements: (1) a protest, usually exaggerated but with more or less foundation in fact, against abuses arising from the weaknesses of human nature in the Church; and (2) a conspiracy, often cloaked by some sort of secret society, to pervert the teachings of Christ and the Church, under pretext of reform. Ximenes had forestalled the first of these conditions in Spain. He also did a great deal to expose and prevent the second. It was while he was Inquisitor General, for example, that the sect known as the *Alumbrados* or Illuminates was first discovered in the Peninsula.

Nothing in history is without cause and without effect. The *Alumbrados* were a link in the chain of causality connecting the Manichees of the Middle Ages with modern anti-Christian movements; the Inquisition of Toulouse with the French Revolution and the Bolshevik Revolution.

The name *Iluminado* first appeared in Spain when a report was sent to Cardinal Ximenes concerning the activities of one Fray Antonio de Pastrana, who had begun to preach a revelation which he said came to him directly from God, called himself *Illuminatus,* and went about the countryside with certain holy women, on whom he had been instructed, by the inner voice he followed, to beget prophets. The Inquisition clapped him into prison, and scattered his sect.

Obviously he was a spiritual descendant of those Fourteenth Century impostors Segarelli and Dulcinus. It was no new cure that he dispensed. Nor was Illuminism but a distortion of Christian mysticism, any more than it was a perversion of Judaism. True, it made its way into the Christian Church under the guise of various heresies, as it deceived many of the scattered children of Moses under the covers of the Talmud; but in reality it was quite different in origin. The Law of Moses and the Law of Christ came from God, from the source of being, of good, of light, of growth; when free to do so they always produced orderly and beautiful living. And both of them were opposed, from very early times, by a totally different spirit, the spirit that denies, that hates life, that causes confusion and chaos. This dark spirit enthroned itself in the East, even before the Incarnation; and there, shielded by a singularly pure and austere code of morality, it evolved systems of thought which took on the appearances of religions, but were in reality elaborate forms of atheism. Is not the Nirvana of the Buddhists, the goal of all their strivings through countless reincarnations, nothing but the death and annihilation of the individual conscience, the extinction of human personality in an All which is but a step from Nothing? Buddhism, the child of pantheistic Brahminism, is atheism in disguise; and granting all that may be said for Buddha's good intentions, the sincere and self-sacrificing lives of many of his followers, and the truth of many of their teachings, the system itself contained the seeds of intellectual and spiritual degeneration. Out of it came a pseudo-mysticism based upon such conceptions as these: life is not worth living, personality is a burden and a curse, marriage is a bed of hot coals leading to the propagation of an evil, all labor and effort are useless, the family and other forms of society therefore become pointless, anarchy thus follows logically, and man can do no better than escape from the penalties of Karma and the chains of human desire into a cold and selfless (but actually selfish) absorption into Nirvana. Pure contemplation, to these mystics, meant that the soul lost its individuality and annihilated itself as it sank into the infinite essence, until at last it arrived at a state of perfection which was also a state of moral irresponsibility. Then, obviously, to such a soul, there could be no sin.

These ideas underwent many fantastic transmutations as they traveled from the dying East to invade the living West. But the dangerous correlary that to the pure all things are pure, that nothing a perfect soul may do in the ecstasy of contemplation can be sinful, persisted in the teachings of several heresies. It was taught by the early Gnostics, by Plotinus, by the Priscillians in Galicia, by the thirteenth century Albigenses of Southern France, by the fourteenth century Beghards or Beguins in Catalonia and Leon. And now the hoary superstition of the Buddhist *bhikkus* (beggars) which isolated the human soul from human society, from moral good (through breaking down the distinction between good and evil) and from God Himself, was reappearing under the mask of "Illuminism." In exposing and punishing the *Alumbrados,* then, Ximenes was merely resuming in Castile the battle that Eymeric had waged, more than a century before, in Aragon and Catalonia.

He was eighty years old when King Fernando died in 1516. Queen Juana was less fit than ever to reign. Her son Charles was in Flanders, where he had been brought up, and was not yet seventeen. All the old intrigues which had divided and weakened Spain in the past began to stir behind the scenes. Nobles were reaching again for power. Catholic Jews of slight orthodoxy saw a fresh opportunity to deal a blow at the Inquisition, which had fallen so heavily upon them or upon their ancestors. They offered Charles V 800,000 ducats if he would make certain "reforms" in the procedure of the Holy Office.

The young king was tempted to accept. What did the Inquisition mean to him? He had been in Spain very little, and was more of a Fleming than a Spaniard, both in looks and in training. Why not do as the *Conversos* suggested, and allow, among other things, publication of the names of witnesses and delators?

Ximenes, who knew that the Holy Office had been the corner-stone of the resurrected Spain, the fulcrum not only of political unity and power, but of spiritual reform, wrote a memorable letter to Charles:

"Most high and mighty Catholic King, most gracious lord: The Catholic sovereigns, as your Majesty is aware, have bestowed so much care upon the Holy Tribunal of the Inquisition, and examined its laws and institutions with so much prudence, wisdom and conscientiousness, that modifications of it are not needed, but would rather be harmful than otherwise. At the present moment such changes would fill me the more with sorrow, as they would assuredly tend to increase the defiance shown to the Inquisition by the Catalonians and the Pope. The pecuniary embarrassment of your Majesty is, I confess, very great, but certainly that of Fernando the Catholic, the grandfather of your Majesty, was greater, when the newly converted Christians offered him 600,000 gold ducats to carry on the Navarrese war. He did not accept their proposals, because he preferred the purity of the Christian religion to all the gold in the world. With all the true devotion of a loyal subject, with the zeal which I must have for the office to which your Majesty has raised me, I beseech you to open your eyes and follow the example of your Majesty's grandfather, and consent to no changes in the proceedings of the Inquisition. All the objections raised by its adversaries have before been refuted, under the Catholic kings of glorious memory. The modifications of even the most unimportant law of the Inquisition could not be made without betraying the honor of God and insulting that of your most illustrious ancestors. If this consideration has not sufficient weight with your Majesty, may it please you to recall the deplorable occurrence which has lately taken place at Talavera de la Reina, when a newly-converted Jew, who had learned the name of his accuser, searched for him and stabbed him. The hatred against these informers is indeed so great that, if the publication of their names is not prevented, they will not only be assassinated in private and public, but even at the foot of the altar. No one will be found in future willing to risk his life by similar denunciations; this would be the ruin of the Holy Tribunal, and the cause of God would be left without a defender. I live in confidence that your Majesty, my King and Lord, will not become unfaithful to the Catholic blood which runs in your veins, but be convinced that the Inquisition is a tribunal of God, and an excellent institution of your Majesty's ancestors." [3]

Charles delayed his coming to Spain, and Ximenes had to reassume all the burdens of the regency. Yet those who expected to deal with an old and doddering prelate were surprised to find him as cool, decisive and energetic as he had been at fifty. Nothing was too small or too great for his keen attention. He saw the last printed sheets of his Polyglot Bible, and the newest buildings of his University of Alcalá. He patronized men of science and of letters. He carried out the wishes of Queen Isabel, neglected under Philip and Fernando, to have the Indians of the New World treated humanely; and to this end he gave his support to the reform of Bishop Las Casas; indeed, he went even further than Las Casas, for he forbade negro slavery, which Las Casas, champion of the red men, condoned; and he sent a Jeronymite mission to America to aid the Indians. But the most important and unrelenting task imposed upon him was holding together the lifework of Fernando and Isabel until young Charles was ready to rule.

The obstacles were enough to frighten a far younger and sturdier man. The great nobles were nearly all against him. They saw what might be a last opportunity to regain the almost regal freedom that Fernando and Isabel had curbed, and many resented the regency of an ascetic monk of lowly origin. Don Pedro Giron, son of the Count of Urena and one of the many noble descendants of the prolific Jew Ruy Capon, organized a league of grandees, who demanded that the Cardinal hand over the regency to them. The *Conversos* generally had no love for the man who had twice prevented them from weakening, if not destroying, the Inquisition. The former King and Queen of Navarre, seeing an opportunity of regaining the kingdom taken from them by Fernando the Cath-

---

[3] Canon Dalton gives an English translation of this letter in his rendering of Hefele's life of Ximenes, from Carnicero, t. II, pp. 289-293.

olic, stirred up a formidable uprising in the north. Some of the old
military orders strove to get out of the grip of the crown. The
household of Prince Fernando, younger brother of Charles, was
a centre of discontent and of intrigue, where plans were laid to trip
up the old Cardinal, and where even the absent heir was spoken
of contemptuously.

Charles was loitering in the Low Countries, surrounded by
Flemish favorites who traded upon his youth and inexperience as
much as they could, and did everything possible to "protect" him
from the influence of Ximenes, which they knew would be irresistible to him and fatal to them. Chief among these crafty and
avaricious men were two men with French names: Chièvres and
Sauvage, both of whom conducted a lucrative business selling
offices in Spain to the highest bidders. Knowing that Ximenes was
old and frail, they staked everything on the probability of his dying
before he could exert the magnetic powers of his genius upon the
Prince. Charles, however, was beginning to show that he had a
mind of his own, and in the main he followed the advice of the
Inquisitor who had been the wise and unselfish counselor of his
father and his grandparents. Once he disregarded it, and the
result was the revolt at Málaga. Meanwhile the tax gatherers of
Spain, encouraged by the Flemish party who were waiting to loot
the country, as others had looted it before the rise of the Catholic
Sovereigns, were growing bold and fat again. Everywhere were
symptoms of disintegration that would have discouraged an
ordinary regent, thrust suddenly into a crisis by the death of his
king.

Ximenes was no ordinary man, though eighty, and he met the
challenge so magnificently that even his enemies had to admit that
never in his prime had he been more alert, more daring, more
resourceful, more kingly in his own quiet way. For twenty-three
strenuous months, the last of his life, it was Ximenes against the
world. With all his old time subtlety and skill, all the more to
be feared because it went with a childlike innocence and incor-
ruptibility, he disposed of each emergency as it arose. He sent
Villalba to seize the vital pass at Roncevaux and crush the armies
of the Albrets. He had the walls of every fort in Navarre razed

to the ground; and when some one taunted him with being an accomplice in the unjust seizure of the country by King Fernando, he replied that being only a subject, it was not his business to inquire whether or not the acquisition of the country by his former king was legitimate or not, but to defend the kingdom committed to him as regent. He restored peace in Málaga with troops from Córdoba. As for the nobles, he saw clearly that Charles, the lawful heir, was the only leader under whom Spain could remain one; and he proceeded by a series of adroit and often surprising moves to fortify the authority of that Prince against all who threatened it. His master stroke against the restless aristocracy was the organization of a militia or national guard of some 30,000 loyal men. "These troops," he wrote to a friend, "will make the king king and justice justice; and neither Frenchmen nor Turks will dare to challenge them, even in thought." Ximenes was an expert in military preparedness. He had an emissary buy the arms and armor of his new force in Flanders. "See that the corselets are made by the best masters," he wrote, "and are very cheap." There was resistance in some places, but most of the country welcomed an organization which meant peace and order. The *gente de la ordenanza,* as they were called, had some new cannon, brought from Flanders, which they used to call, in honor of the Cardinal and his order, *San Franciscos.* When several grandees appeared before him with some rather insolent demands, and met his refusal with a remark about the legal powers they had, the Cardinal drew aside a great curtain, revealing a row of well-armed soldiers. "These," he said, "are *my* powers." He made sweeping financial reforms. He removed rapacious tax gatherers. He restored property alienated from the Crown. He eliminated many unnecessary pensions, including that of Peter Martyr, who thereafter liked him less than ever. He did away with the sale of offices. He reported to Charles that Prince Fernando's residence was a hotbed of opposition to the regency and a menace to the Crown. Charles ordered the removal from his brother's household of nearly all the sycophants and parasites who surrounded him; one notable exception being Alfonso Castillejo, who "excelled in poetry, and as he did nothing else, he was suffered to remain." Fernando was furious. He fairly raved at the Cardinal: he said he would not obey the orders from Flanders, he would turn the whole world upside down.

"That is as may be," answered Ximenes quietly. "But before the sun sets tomorrow, the King shall be obeyed, though all Spain be against me. And Your Highness shall be the first of all to obey."

Next morning Ximenes had a guard posted at the doors of the Prince's house, and the orders from Charles were carried out to the letter.

All through those tireless months the old statesman was carrying on a long-distance duel of wills with the Flemish courtiers; and in this too, he advanced from triumph to triumph. He swept away their corrupt system of distributing offices. He prevented Chièvres, who had no scruples against making a profit on human flesh, from sending 500 negroes from Africa to work as slaves in the silver mines of America. He brought grandees over to his side one by one; first he would make friendly overtures, then, if necessary, he would use force, but only enough to accomplish his purpose; finally, he would use conciliation. To one *magnifico* who boasted, "I obey no one except my God and my King," Ximenes replied, suavely, "In that case you owe me double allegiance. I am your God's Inquisitor General, and your King's viceroy." Finally, by dint of many letters and embassies, he impressed upon Charles the necessity of returning to Spain at once. Nothing else, Ximenes was convinced, would save the country. Charles at last consented. The powerful will of Ximenes seemed to be drawing him, whether he would or no, to the Peninsula, in spite of all the other wills that sought to keep him away. The Prince left Flanders September 7, 1517, and several days later landed in northern Spain, at Tazones, near Villaviciosa. With him were his sister Lady Eleanor, Chièvres, Sauvage and other Flemish courtiers.

Ximenes was ill. All his life he had suffered from violent headaches, the cause of which was discovered only when his tomb was opened in 1545, and the skull that had ruled Spain was found seamless. All that summer of 1517, he had been failing noticeably. In July and August, he had received from Pope Leo X a letter which, in spite of its benevolent intentions, brought an acute disappointment. Incidentally, it also casts a light upon Ximenes at this period:

"We have learned," wrote the Médici Pope, "that though you are eighty years old and exhausted by the fatigue of church and state affairs, you continue, against the advice of your physicians, not only to observe the fasts and abstinences ordained by the Church, but to practice all the austerites customary to the Order of Saint Francis: that you wear the habit and the girdle, and sleep fully clothed on a hard bed, without linen and clad in a woolen tunic. Although this manner of life, my dear son, is most edifying, and although we recognize thereby that in the evening of your days you are striving nobly to attain the eternal crown which the just judge will give you, yet having regard for your great age and your labors, and to your irreplaceable services to Holy Church and to your country, we, in virtue of the obedience which you owe and have always shown us, and under penalty of our displeasure, do of our own will order and command that you relax your manner of life during the time that is left to you, in accord with the advice of your physicians. We order you, namely, to lay aside your habit, to sleep comfortably and in linen, in order that your health may be maintained."

On reading this, Ximenes turned to a friend and said, "What a command! Worldly men consider it an honor to die in the habit of Saint Francis, and I, who am dying, am ordered to put it away, after wearing it all my life!"

Obedient to the last, he laid aside the only thing he had ever wanted for himself, and went on with his work. The news of Charles's landing seemed to revive him, and he celebrated the feast of St. Francis, October 4, at Aguilera with other monks of his order, right joyfully. He could be jolly on occasion, and kept a favorite dwarf whose jokes amused him. He wrote the King, advising him to go to Segovia, to avoid the plague in Valladolid. Charles, however, went to the latter place, fighting to the last, it would seem, against the unconquerable will that sought to draw him to his own good. The Flemings did all they could, of course, to delay his meeting with his minister. Well informed about Ximenes' condition, they had reason to hope that he would die in a few days. They

are said to have induced Charles to write the famous letter in which
he is alleged to have treated Ximenes coldly and ungratefully.
About this there is some doubt; whether Charles wrote it, and
whether the Cardinal received it. Apparently Ximenes did not.[4]
Various studied insults were offered him, however, by his Flemish
enemies.

Ximenes was not the man to be troubled much by such trifles,
nor even by the ingratitude of princes. He left the monastery
at Aguilera October 17, wrapped in furs, in obedience to the Pope's
orders, to protect him from the cutting Castilian wind, and travelled toward Valladolid to meet Charles, who had meanwhile
gone to Tordesillas to see his mother. The meeting was to be held
at last at Mojados.

Ximenes meanwhile had got as far as Roa. There at last his
physical strength failed, and he died November 8, gazing serenely
and affectionately upon a Crucifix.

Charles never met him in this life. Yet it is quite possible that
the victory belonged to Ximenes, and that the future Emperor was
a better ruler for the example of such a minister. For Spain had
never had, nor has since had, a greater ruler than the simple
Franciscan monk who wanted nothing but a burlap covering and
a cell in which to pray; who made gifts like a king, but was too
wise to give away the king's power; who kept his humility and
simplicity even in the possession of great wealth and authority.
Ximenes held very dear the medieval Catholic conception of Kingship: the King represented all the people against any section or
faction or interest, and he had the right to their obedience; yet he
himself received his awful authority from God, and must constantly keep before his eyes the eternal truth, the eternal justice,
the eternal mercy. This was the notion that Fernando and Isabel
reëstablished. It is no disparagement of them to say that he carried
it further, and served it even more faithfully, without wearing a
crown. No loftier or sounder conception of human government has
ever existed.

[4] Ruiz, for example, his closest friend, said that he never received the letter
that is supposed (in the pages of Prescott and many others) to have hastened his
death.

Eight days before the death of Ximenes, Martin Luther nailed his ninety-five theses on the door of Wittenberg cathedral. It was the first overt and decisive step toward the fatal confusion of western Christendom, which has continued to this day. The two events seemed unconnected, and it is likely that, although Luther must have heard of Ximenes, the Cardinal did not know of the Augustinian monk's existence. Yet the spirit of Luther, in essence, had been one of the things he had fought as Inquisitor General; and long after his death, the forces he set in motion would stand between Lutheranism and the conquest of Catholic Spain.[5]

[5] The earliest life of Ximenes, on which most later works have been based, was that of Gomez (Alcalá, 1569). There followed those of Robles (Toledo, 1604) and Quintanilla (Palermo, 1633). Of modern works, the biography by Hefele (*Der Cardinal Ximenes* etc., Tubingen, 1844, is the best known in English, as translated by Canon Dalton, and in spite of some mistakes and omissions, is still in the main reliable. There had been several lives in French: Baudier (1635); Marsollier (1684); Fléchier (1694) and Richard (1704). The excellent work of the Conde de Cedillo, *El Cardenal Cisneros, gobernador del reino,* Madrid, 1921, is indispensable, especially for the last regency. Of the many popularizations, one of the most readable and honest is that of Mr. Reginald Merton, though it is woefully inaccurate and misinformed on the Inquisition and its background, and other matters of Catholic interest. For Ximenes as a statesman, and his ideal of the kingship, see the profound study by Miss Marie R. Madden, *Political Theory and Law in Medieval Spain,* New York, 1930.

VII

Some Sixteenth Century Victims

DURING the spectacular and fateful reign of Charles the Fifth, the Spanish Inquisition became so inactive that its enemies began to take its early death for granted. Charles, who was elected German Emperor soon after becoming King of Spain, and while still a youth crowned an extraordinary good fortune by marrying the most beautiful woman in Europe, seemed too powerful a monarch to have to worry about a few heretics here and there; moreover, he was by nature trusting, tolerant and magnanimous to such a degree that Cervantes has been suspected of drawing a sublime caricature of him in Don Quixote. Master of the New World, whose gold came by galleons to Sevilla, he was always in need of money and dependent upon the favors of usurers. Lover of peace, he was always fighting, now defeating Francis I at Marignano, now performing the prodigies of a paladin in Africa, now warring against traitorous barons in Germany and Austria. Lover of Christ and of the Catholic Faith, he saw through the fallacies of Luther; yet he made fatal compromises (his famous *Interim,* for example) which permitted Lutheranism to pass from the sectarian to the political plane, and so to destroy the unity of Christian Europe for centuries; and he heard with shame, in 1527, that his armies, composed in great measure of German Lutherans and of secret Mohammedans (Moriscoes) from eastern Spain, had sacked Rome, besieged and all but killed the Pope, and filled the capital of Christendom with the horrors of butchery, rape, and desecration even of the Blessed Sacrament. Charles considered himself the great champion of the Church, and was sincerely anxious for the reform

214

of the existing abuses against which the Lutherans in the north were clamoring, yet he allowed his aunt, Catherine of Aragon, to be cast aside for a royal concubine by Henry VIII, as a prelude to the crafty destruction of the Catholic Faith in England; and he saw his rivalry with Francis I constantly prevent, and finally interrupt, the deliberations of the Council of Trent, which alone could restore health and discipline to the human organization of the Church. A cool and skilful statesman, a keen judge of men and motives, and on the whole, a better man than either Francis or Henry, he was in the main outwitted from first to last by more subtle and unscrupulous individuals. At a time when Europe needed a man of single purpose, a Saint Ferdinand, a Saint Louis, a Catholic Moses, to insist always that the soul of western civilization was the Christian Faith, on which, in the nature of things, no compromise was possible, there were two conflicting men in this Habsburg potentate: an ascetic and a sensualist. During the lifetime of his wife, to whom he was faithful apparently until her death, he promised her that when their son Philip was old enough to rule, they would retire from the world, he to a monastery, she to a convent, to meditate and pray. After the death of the Empress Isabel, however, circumstances seemed to demand that he retain his power; and the animal in him, which had always manifested itself in his huge feeding and drinking, gained the ascendancy for a time. By one of his mistresses, the blond termagant singer Barbara Blomberg, he begot Don Juan of Austria, about the time when he was advising his legitimate son and heir, Philip, to live chastely, and to beware of politicians who would seek to gain influence over him through the wiles of women. The contrast was characteristic, and it continued to the end. An old man at forty-nine, he handed over the government of Spain to Philip, and retired to the monastery at Yuste to prepare for death, to flagellate himself for his sins, to curse at choristers who sang off key, to gorge himself with meat and wine and then to pay with spasms of the gout, as the dregs of his earthly life seeped miserably away.

Charles seemed unaware, most of his life, that he was surrounded by the agents of an international conspiracy to destroy everything that his heart loved and revered. Most of his councillors were

Catholics in name only, or very lax Catholics; many of them, in key positions, were of Jewish descent. Charles saw no danger in this. His favorite chaplain was Doctor Constantino Ponce de la Fuente, an eloquent preacher whose voice is said to have had something like the effect of music on his congregations, and whose book on Christian doctrine (dedicated to the Emperor, who read it faithfully) gained him a great reputation as a theologian—though at the very time he was in secret communication with Lutherans in Germany, and had two wives living. The chief minister of Charles, the wily Gattinara, had adopted the principles of the Erasmian heretics then industriously undermining Catholicism in Spain, while Erasmus himself, alarmed at the turn events were taking, was denouncing Luther. Even Alonso Manrique, the Inquisitor General, was said to have Erasmian tendencies. The Emperor intervened to save Juan Gil, who was secretly propagating anti-Catholic doctrines at Alcalá, from the Inquisition; and he wanted to make him bishop of Tortosa. Another court preacher in high favor was the secret Protestant, Father Augustin Cazalla. Michael Servetus was secretary to the Emperor's confessor, Juan de Quintana. Propagandists were at work to draw the whole Imperial family away from the Church Catholic. Charles's brother Fernando remained faithful in his rather stupid way; but their sister Mary of Hungary was a Lutheran for a time; and Fernando's son, Maximilian (who later became Emperor) was notoriously Protestant in his views and in his friends. Even the children of Charles were in grave danger of perversion. Some one skilfully suggested that young Philip II take as his confessor the great Doctor Constantino; but Philip, warned against the man, chose some one else. Philip's sister María (later Empress) was not so wary. Her confessor was Fray Vicente de Rocamoro, who later threw off the mask of Catholicism and joined the Hebrew community at Amsterdam as Isaac of Rocamoro.

The Expulsion of the Jews from Spain had been only a temporary misfortune for that energetic and resourceful race. Already, in various parts of the world, they had built up new political and commercial empires. Even before the Spanish calamity, their control of international trade, and of almost the entire economic life of

Europe, had been broken by the organization of the medieval
Catholic workmen's guilds: but they had gone a long way toward
repairing the misfortune, and scattered from Spain and Portugal,
were soon controlling the overland trade between the West and the
Indies, at Ferrara, Venice, Ancona, Salonika, Constantinople, Cairo
and Suez. A Portuguese Jewish family named Mendes, with relatives in Spain, the Netherlands and England, formed a powerful
syndicate which became known as the Spice Trust, whose owners
collected toll on goods consumed in every country in Europe, maintained an elaborate intelligence or spy system, indulged in usury on
a vast scale, gradually pushed into the background such Catholic
bankers as the Fuggers, and threw the huge weight of their wealth
and influence on the side of any movement aimed against the
Church of Christ.[1] Joseph Mendes, one of the spice magnates, went
to Constantinople and there became virtually master of the policy
of the Sultan; it was he, for example, who instigated the great
threat to Christendom which was stopped by the fleet of Don
Juan of Austria at Lepanto. All the powers of international Jewry
were allied with, if not actually the motive power of, the vast
conspiracy which produced the Protestant revolt. In fact, it was
the famous Battle of the Books, a dispute over the Jewish Talmud
and Kabbala, which set the stage for Luther. Erasmus's friend
Reuchlin, the defender of the Jewish books, assembled around him
a party of revolutionaries without whose instant support the
Augustinian monk's voice might have had no more effect than
Huss's or Segarelli's. Once the landslide began, the wide-spread
wealth and power of Talmudic Jewry was organized behind the
new movements in England, Germany and France, and probably
gave them their permanence. International finance gave the
Protestant Revolt a world capital at London. Many good things
came to an end: medieval hospitals and charities; the unity of
Europe; the Catholic guilds of workmen, from which the modern
labor movement still has much to learn.

Charles apparently had no insight into the real significance of
all this revolution that was going on around him and in his very
household. For many years he retained a pathetic belief in the

[1] These statements are elaborated and documented in my *Philip II*.

efficacy of physical force and, even more, of political intrigue. As he had compromised with the Lutheran movement in Germany, so he attempted to outflank the Anglican position by compromise and finesse. He arranged for Philip (whose Portuguese wife had died) to marry Mary Tudor, with the hope that they would have a son who would inherit both England and Spain, and thus bring England back into the Catholic fold. This in part was to be Philip's recompense for having lost the Empire. The whole international anti-Catholic ring had seen to it that the Imperial succession would pass not to the Spanish prince, whose unyielding devotion to the Catholic Church was well known, but to his cousin Maximilian, whose lukewarm Catholicism was believed to mask a Protestant heart. Philip, however, would still be the most powerful ruler in Christendom: he would have, besides England and Spain, the control of Italy through Milan and Naples; Burgundy, the Low Countries, and the New World. The recovery of England would make the victory over Protestantism decisive.

This beautiful dream dissolved in the light of actuality. Charles and his obedient son made the fatal mistake of not following the advice of the Pope and Cardinal Pole on the restoration of the immense properties of the English Church, stolen by Henry VIII and passed on by him to crafty upstarts who supplanted the ancient nobility. These men, under the skilful and unscrupulous leadership of William Cecil, were resolved at all costs to suppress the Catholic worship in England, for the sake of the loot they held. They were so cowed at the accession of Mary that a bold stroke then might have forced them to restore the monastery lands and other properties to the rightful owners. But Charles and Philip advised Mary not to insist too much on the point; counting, of course, on the birth of a Catholic heir, and the healing effects of time. The heir was not born, however, and time proved unfaithful. When Mary died without issue, Philip felt sure that her bastard sister Elizabeth would keep her oath to be a good Catholic if crowned. It had been within his power to exclude her; he even toyed with the idea, doubtless with encouragement by Elizabeth, that he could marry her if he chose, and thus keep England within his hand. Philip did not know that William Cecil had secretly arranged matters with Ann Boleyn's daughter, and would control her by his powerful will, and the weapon of fear, for nearly all her life. She had hardly been crowned when she broke her oath, revealed herself a Protestant, and made Cecil her chief minister. Thus Philip, with the best of intentions, and it must be admitted, as victim of his father's opportunist policies, had set up a power which would become the rallying point of the new Protestant world, shield the ancient hatred of the Catholic Church, and plague him to the day of his death. Thanks to his father's political advisers, too, he had been drawn into a costly and foolish war with Pope Paul IV, who on his side was deceived by a scoundrelly nephew; and it was a sorry satisfaction when the Spanish troops, under the Duke of Alba, took Rome.

Charles, meanwhile, on returning to Spain to prepare his soul for death, had had more than one rude awakening. With no Ximenes beside him to give wise and disinterested advice, the prematurely old Emperor was shocked especially to learn that while he had been neglecting the Inquisition founded by his ancestors, and making clever compromises with the heretics of Germany and England, Lutheranism had not only appeared, but had made considerable headway, in Spain.

Even after the reforms of Ximenes, there was some danger that an anti-Catholic movement might take hold in Spain. The reforms of the great Cardinal had not yet permeated the secular clergy. Also, among the large population of Catholic Jews there were still some who were waiting for any opportunity to embrace a cause which called itself Christian (without demanding the Christian test of sincerity in the confessional) and yet was a solvent of true Christianity. Finally Erasmus had sown the seeds of dissidence. This Voltarian individual, this versatile mediocre man with far more knowledge than wisdom, this sickly misbegotten dispeptic who had an almost irrational hatred of monks because his uncle had forced him to enter an Augustinian monastery, and jeered at Crusaders among whom his puny limbs could never have taken a place, became immensely popular in Spain at the beginning of the *siglo de oro*. He had done some good work on pagan and Christian antiquities, and in patrology; he was skilful in polemics; above all, he attacked clerical abuses at a time when it was fashionable all over Europe to do so. He went even further: he ridiculed rites and ceremonies of the Church, and scoffed at some of her sacred dogmas.[2] He despised such warrior Popes as Julius II (whom Moses would have understood better) and could not find words enough to flatter the Médici Popes, Leo X and Clement VII, under whose pontificates occurred two of the greatest calamities that had befallen the Church: the loss of Germany and the loss of England. His *Praise of Folly* contained in embryo all of Luther's subsequent attack, and even ridiculed texts of Holy Scripture. Good men were taken in by him, believing him to be a sincere Catholic seeking needed reforms. Saint Ignatius began reading his works on the advice of his confessor: but on noticing that his fervor and devotion began to ebb away in proportion, he cast away the book he was reading, and thereafter held all the writings of Erasmus in abhorrence. Juan de Vergaro, though he had been a secretary to Cardinal Ximenes, was less sensitive to spiritual odors; he obtained a Spanish pension for Erasmus. Neither wholly Catholic nor wholly Protestant, this mean-spirited scholar withdrew from the abyss into which Luther had walked, while his disciples became pioneers of the New Religion in England, and even in Spain.

To understand the shock of horror with which the Emperor Charles discovered all this in 1558, just before his death, one must consider circumstances often omitted or overlooked in the modern conspiracy[3] against truth which has poisoned the records of the English-speaking world, but painfully real to men of the time. England, more than ninety per cent Catholic, was quietly taken in hand by a small rich minority of enemies of the Catholic Church, many of them, like Cecil, of very obscure origin. In France, leagued with the English Protestants, another small but rich minority of Calvinists, chiefly nobles and usurers, were beginning the formidable plots which were to lead to the eight bloody Huguenot Wars. These

---

[2] For a more complete and I think definitive portrait, see Menendez y Pelayo, *op. cit.,* t. II, 1880 ed. lib II, cap. 2.

[3] When I use "conspiracy" in this sense, I do not mean necessarily a plot controlled by one man, or a small group: it suffices to notice that men of the same spiritual affinity tend toward a common end.

two groups had very intimate connections with the Lutheran princes of Germany, and with William of Orange, who was already laying the groundwork for the Protestant revolt in the Low Countries, and urging the Turks, through Jewish banker friends who were his heavy creditors, to attack Catholic Spain from the Mediterranean. Not all of this was evident in 1558, but enough of it had come to light to make the last nights of the Emperor very restless indeed. And then to find out that a Lutheran plot was well advanced in Spain—!

Perhaps the Spanish, having fought the battles of Christendom against unbelief so many centuries, had a keener awareness than some of their northern neighbors of the significance of such movements. They had learned that in this world appearances are often deceptive. A Dominican theologian, familiar with the recent activities of the *Alumbrados,* discovered by the agents of Ximenes, and aware of the ideas of the medieval Manichee heretics from which they derived, would not be long in stripping the gospel of Luther of its accidents, which gave it the superficial appearance of something new, and finding in its essentials the same old enemy that the Catholic Church had been fighting so many centuries. Luther professed to be appealing from the Middle Ages to the virgin purity of the first Christian centuries. In reality he was leading the minds of his victims even further back in time, back, in the labyrinth of ideas, to the gospel of despair so elaborately disguised by the *bhikkus* of India, and so craftily revived by the Beghards, Beguins and other secret societies of the thirteenth century.

"Escape from the evils of life (Karma), from desire and action, into nothingness," said the Buddhists in effect. "Join us, look within, and sink into pure contemplation. Once desire is dead, you shall be free from sin, rebirth and misery."

"Life is evil, the work of the devil," said the medieval Manichees. "Do not listen to Pope or priest, but join our sect of the Pure and the Perfect; then, no matter what you do, you are free from sin, from the torment of conscience, from the evil of living."

"Be illuminated by a divine feeling from within," said the *Alumbrados.* "Obey no one but God. Once you have become perfect and left desire behind, no carnal act you happen to perform can be sinful."

"No human works are of any avail," said Luther. "Only faith can save you. If you have faith, it does not matter how much you sin; in fact, the more you sin the more you prove your faith. Therefore be a sinner, sin strongly, sin a thousand times a day."

Was not Luther's doctrine of salvation by grace alone a restatement, with a somewhat different emphasis, of the old despairing dogma of the *Alumbrados,* the Manichees, the Gnostics, the Buddhists? Did not he and Melancthon, in the name of reform, revive that other heresy of the *Fraticelli:* the detestable error that the state had absolute power over the individual and the Church, that the State was the supreme judge and master of human affairs? There was a familiar Manichean smell about all this Lutheran business, and in the nostrils of the Dominicans it was not good.

Spain had a reminder of the implications of Illuminism in 1544, when the Inquisition, in one of its few moments of activity under Charles V, astonished the country by arresting the famous *beata,* Sister Magdalena de la Cruz, who had been a nun for forty years at the convent of Saint Isabel of the Angels in Córdoba, and had had such a reputation for holiness that even members of the royal family went to solicit her prayers, while the Empress Isabel, wife of Charles V, gave her in gratitude the robe in which her son, Philip II, had been baptized. It was said that the saintly woman performed dreadful penances and vigils, that she lived only on the Host received in Holy Communion, and that she had received the stigmata of Our Lord on hands, feet and side.

Under examination by the Dominican inquisitors, however, Sister Magdalena made some very different revelations. She admitted that she was not a Catholic at all, but one of the sect of the *Alumbrados;* that when seven years old, she had been persuaded by the devil to pretend sanctity; that at eleven she had made a pact with two *demonios incubos,* named Balban and Pitonio, who used to have intercourse with her by night, disguised in various ways— now as a Jeronymite friar, now as a Franciscan, now as a black bull, now as a camel. In obedience to them she made wounds on her hands, feet and side so cleverly that even holy persons were deceived; she went into "trances" in which she seemed insensible even to the prick of needles; she imposed even upon princesses and the Empress.

The Inquisition imprisoned this foul impostor for life. Yet her evil mission had a certain measure of success even after her death. Her example made good people afraid of all who manifested any of the phenomena to which she laid claim; so that when Saint Teresa of Ávila experienced real raptures and visions, she was suspected by pious persons of being just one more Magdalena of the Cross, and endured unspeakable persecutions in consequence, even after the Inquisitors declared her free from heresy and deception, and a true mystic.

Whether Magdalena was an impostor, a paranoiac, a lunatic, or one possessed, is beside the point here. It was intolerable that such a person should be allowed to represent the Catholic religion and impose upon the Catholic people. It was one of the functions of the Holy Office to protect the faithful from such deceptions; and although Luther was a very different sort of person from the nun of Córdoba, there was a certain similarity between his doctrine and that of the secret society to which she belonged. They too, used Christian terminology, though with esoteric meanings; they spoke of "contrition for sin," "the cross of the Christian," "the warmth of the Holy Ghost" and so on; and all their emphasis was on feeling as opposed to reason, and on private judgment as opposed to the authority of an ordered Church.

The discovery of the Lutheran conspiracies in several Spanish cities came about through the jealousy of the wife of a goldsmith named Juan García, who lived at No 13 *Calle de Platerías* in Valladolid. She noticed that her husband was behaving rather strangely. He seemed absent-minded and morose. He began going to bed very early, but on certain nights, when he thought the whole household was asleep, he would arise and slip out, to be gone for hours. One evening his wife quietly followed him out of the house and through the dark and narrow streets, until she saw him stop before a residence near the *plazuela* of Saint Michael; it was still called the house of Doña Leonor de Vivero, though that lady was dead. A wicket opened, and a voice within asked for the password.

"Cazalla," replied the silversmith. The door opened and closed, and darkness swallowed him.

The jealous woman, concealed in the shadows, heard other persons approaching from both ends of the little street, and saw both men and women admitted, as her husband had been admitted, on saying the magic word. Finally there came a devout-looking and demure *beata*. Plucking up courage, the wife of García followed her to the door, gave the countersign, and was promptly admitted through a passage into a hall where some sixty persons of both sexes were gathered, listening to the famous Father Agustin Cazalla, doctor of the University of Salamanca and one of the favorite chaplains of the Emperor, expounding some of the Lutheran ideas he had brought with him from Germany.

There are different versions of the details of this incident, one being that the silversmith's wife told her confessor, who did not take the matter very seriously; but she, being a devout Catholic, could not rest until she had reported what she had seen and heard to the Inquisitors. Another is that the confessor sent her to them. At all events, the Holy Office got enough information from her to commence an investigation which resulted in the arrest of a large number of rich and socially prominent persons. The ramifications of the conspiracy, for such it proved to be, extended to various other cities, to convents and monasteries, to circles influential in Church and State. Doctor Cazalla admitted his Lutheranism and was very defiant about it, even in the prison of the Inquisition, where he is said to have remarked, "If they had waited four months to persecute us, we should have been as many as they; *and in six months we would have done to them what they are doing to us.*" The lootings and burnings of Catholic churches in Germany, and the murders of priests and nuns there by the apostles of the New Freedom, convinced thoughtful Spanish Catholics that they were not dealing with a small and helpless minority of dissenters, but with part of a well-armed international anti-Christian force that aspired to nothing less than world dominance. As Professor Merriman says, speaking of the Protestant movement in the Netherlands, "Before long it became evident that some of the revolutionists would not be content with liberty to exercise their own faith, but were even intent on the destruction of Catholicism." [4]

The sensation in Spain was tremendous. The Emperor Charles, at his retreat in Yuste, wrote his daughter, the Princess Juana, then acting as regent, and the Inquisitor General, Don Fernando Valdes, Archbishop of Sevilla, that the thing discovered must be put down decisively. King Philip was notified in Flanders, and he, horrified in his turn, wrote similar instructions to Juana.

The result of all this was an impressive revival of the activities of the Inquisition. Not since the days of Fernando and Isabel had there been such a sensational *auto* as the one held at Valladolid on May 21, 1559.[5] The prominence of several of those found guilty and unrepentant, and the fact that the court was then at Valladolid, ensured a huge attendance by the aristocracy and the *hoi polloi* alike. The Regent, Princess Juana, a gentle and pious soul, felt it her duty to attend with her nephew, Don Carlos, the hapless child who was heir to the throne. A few days before the event, she sent an affectionate note to Doña Magdalena de Ulloa, wife of Luis Quijada, inviting her to come to see the *auto de fe,* and suggesting that she bring "the boy she had with her." This boy was Jeronim, about whom the Princess had heard strange rumors lately. She was about to learn that he was her own half-brother.

Early on the morning of May 21, more than 200,000 persons began to assemble. They came from as far as Aragon, Estramadura and Andalusia; and already the *familiares* of the Holy Office were making their way on horseback, through the crowded streets, shouting that no one could use arms in Valladolid that day, under pain of excommunication; and that carriages, litters, chairs, horses and mules were prohibited on the streets where the procession would pass, or in the *Plaza Mayor,* where the *auto* was to be. Never had Valladolid seen such a crowd. Think of it—rich people to be humiliated, fifteeen men and women to be executed! The mob doubtless had already looked over the preparations in the *Campo*

---

[4] *The Rise of the Spanish Empire in the Old World and in the New,* New York, 1934, Vol. IV, p. 254.

[5] In the first edition of my *Philip II,* the date is erroneously given as *March* 21.

Grande, sometimes called the Field of Mars, outside the city limits; there they had seen fifteen little scaffolds around the open space called the *quemadero,* and under each one a great pile of chopped wood, grimly significant of what was to happen; while over each was a garrote, by which the *reo* was mercifully strangled, as a rule, before the flames were lighted under him. Only obstinate impenitents or blasphemers were burned alive. Today there would be only one, a well known official who had had charge of the contraband court in a northern seaport—the Bachelor Herreruelos. One was enough; and already the friars of various orders were moving among the crowds, their voices rising above the sea of murmurs and cries, imploring God to grant the man the grace of repentance lest he die in his sins and be buried in Hell, and begging the people to pray for his soul. The crowd answered with groans and supplications to the blue sky. Here and there pious people were weeping, or falling on their knees to ask God's mercy for the poor blind soul that so far had rejected it.

The *Plaza Mayor,* where the *auto* itself was to be held, was full of people at five o'clock that morning, waiting for the sound of the sad music that would announce the forming of the procession. The crowd extended all the way to the *Campo Grande,* where the grim finale would be, and to the street now called the *Calle del Obispo,* where the prisons of the Holy Office were. Not a few inhabitants made a good profit selling seats or standing room to the curious, some of whom paid the equivalent of three, four and even five modern *pesetas* for the privilege. In little squares and corners of the streets, members of various orders had set up temporary pulpits, where they preached over the heads of the multitudes on how vile and horrible a thing heresy was, being an offense to the divine Majesty, and what a misfortune it was to lose the Faith. This went on all morning.

It was already afternoon when the sermons stopped, and a death-like hush fell over the mighty crowd. A distant solemn music was heard. The procession of the Green Cross must have started at last from the chapel of the Holy Office.

The *Cruz Verde* was the ordinary symbol of the Inquisition. Like every institution in Medieval Spain, the Holy Office had its own coat of arms; a green Cross on a black field. On the right was a branch of olive, on the left a sword; and underneath a burning bramble bush—with the cross of Saint Dominic on the reverse side. Everything on this blazon was symbolic. The black field represented the sorrow of the Church for the apostacies and crimes of the heretics, and the persecutions she endured at their hands. The green cross stood for her hope that they would repent before it was too late, and save their souls; it represented also the eternity, truth and purity of the gospel of Christ, and its vivifying effect upon human society. The olive branch suggested the peace and clemency offered to heretics who repented; and that good olive tree to which St. Paul had so eloquently compared the divine revelation. The sword of justice reminded one of the punishment in store for the obstinate and the impenitent. The burning bramble bush signified the one in which Moses had seen the Lord God, and the faith of the Catholic Church, whose fundamental truths he handed down, and whose prophet and forerunner he was.

At the head of the long line, that May day in 1559, walked the members of all the religious communities in Valladolid and the nearby villages, the monks in their various habits passing two by two, each holding a burning wax taper in his hand. Next came the commissaries, consultors, and various other officials of the Holy Office, with their secretaries, the *alguacil* mayor and the *fiscal;* and these all carried lighted candles of huge size. Then came a Dominican friar bearing, under a pallium of black velvet, a large green wooden cross, covered with mourning crape. Behind this symbolism of sorrow and of hope came the musicians of the chapel of the Holy Office, chanting the *Vexilla regis,* the ancient and magnificent hymn so often sung in the Good Friday processions:

> Forth comes the Standard of the King:
> All hail, thou Mystery adored!
> Hail, Cross, on which the Life Himself
> Died, and by death our life restored. . . .
>
> O sacred wood, in Thee fulfilled
> Was holy David's faithful lay,

Which told the world that from a tree
The Lord should all the nations sway. . . .[6]

Slowly and sadly, as if it were a repetition of the journey to the Mount of Calvary, the procession passed, with many solemn pauses, through all the principal streets of Valladolid, until, when the sun was low in the west and the shadows were long across the city, the head of the column began to file into the *Plaza Mayor*. There draped in black was the great platform, and on it an altar, before which twelve candles, watched all through the night by Dominican friars, were burning. At the right and at the left were rows of steps where the condemned would sit. In front was a pulpit for the preacher.

The people looked on, almost breathless with curiosity and dread, as the condemned appeared, in two long files, bearing lighted candles in their hands, while the bells of the Holy Office tolled dismally. Between the two rows walked officials of the Inquisition, at several paces apart: one carrying the parochial cross of the Saviour; the *fiscal*, Jeronimo de Ramirez, with the standard of the Holy Inquisition, made of crimson damask, with the white and black escutcheon of the order of Saint Dominic, and the royal arms embroidered in gold; and on the ends of the great flag were the words, *Exurge, Domine, et judica causam tuam*.

It was toward the prisoners themselves, however, that all eyes were turned. They walked twelve to fourteen paces apart, each guarded by two *familiares* of the Holy Office and four soldiers. First of all came a man of fifty who in other days had heard friendly and flattering salutations as he crossed that square, but now seemed to have grown old and emaciated, after his months of incarceration, and hardly able to drag himself along. He wore about the upper part of his body a yellow garment called a *sanbenito*, something like a priest's short chasuble, with a green cross of Saint Andrew on the breast. (This by the way, was one of the reforms of Cardinal Ximenes, who did not think that secret enemies of the Church should be allowed to wear the Saviour's cross, and so de-

---

[6] I have taken the translations of these two stanzas from the Daily Missal of Dom Gaspar Lefebre, O. S. B. p. 681. The classic English translation, a very free one, is that of Blount.

creed the diagonal one.) On his head was a pasteboard conical hat, painted over with flames and devils. The famous Doctor Agustin Cazalla, whose sermons had made thousands weep, had come to this sorry state; not because some of his ancestors were said to be Jews, still less because he was a believing Jew, for he was not, but because, as a member of the Catholic Church, he had tried to destroy it from within. Many people along the way probably looked on him as little short of a devil incarnate, while the friars kept reminding them that he was a human soul about to face his God, and in need of their prayers that he might with all his heart accept the sacrifice that Christ had made for him on the cross.

After him came his brother, Francisco Vivero, another Catholic priest found guilty of betraying his office and his flock. This man is said to have uttered such horrible blasphemies that he had to be gagged along the way. Then came their sister, Doña Beatriz; then the Maestro Alonso Pérez, a priest of Palencia; then the unfortunate silversmith García, whose wife had brought about the arrest of them all; then Cristóbal del Campo; then another man who was bound and gagged, and people said with horror that he was the Bachelor Antonio Herrezuelo, who had refused to retract his heresies, and had uttered things too shocking to be heard; then Doña Catalina Ortega, widow of a captain; then the Licenciate Calahorra, *alcalde mayor* of the houses of the Bishop; then Catalina Roman, Isabel Estrada and Juana Velazquez; and finally, in this group, Gonzalo Baez, a Portuguese condemned not for Lutheranism but for judaizing. Of these persons, Herrezuelo alone was to be burned alive. All the others were to be strangled first, and burned dead. The house of Doña Leonor de Vivero, where they had discussed their plans to destroy Christian Spain, was to be razed to the ground, and the site strewn with salt.

A second, less terrifying section of the melancholy parade now filed up to the platform. Here were sixteen men and women who had got off with lesser penalties, and therefore did not have to wear *sanbenitos* or caps decorated with flames or devils. The men walked bareheaded, and each woman was allowed to wear a piece of cloth over her hair and face to hide her shame. In this group were some notable personages. There was, for example, Don Pedro

Sarmiento, *comendador* of the Order of Alcántara and a relative of the Admiral of Castile. He was deprived of his uniform and office and condemned to life imprisonment, wearing a *sanbenito* as long as he lived; he must hear Mass and a sermon every Sunday, and communicate at Christmas, Easter and Whitsuntide; never was he to use silk, gold, silver, horses or jewels—such were the rules of the Holy Office for serious offenders not judged worthy of death. His wife, Doña Mencia de Figueroa, who had been a lady of the royal palace, also was to spend her life in prison.

There was also a very gay young aristocrat, the Marqués de Poza, whose sentence was to be exiled forever from the Court and deprived of all the honors of a *caballero*. Another prisoner in this group was a very beautiful girl, Doña Ana Enriquez, daughter of the Marqués of Alcanices. Her sentence was lighter still: she was to go to the platform wearing a *sanbenito* and carrying a candle; then she was to fast for three days, in her home; then she was to return in her penitential habit to the prison, and then go free. On hearing her sentence read, she fainted.

When all were seated, there was a flourish of music down the street, and the murmur that the Court was coming. Presently appeared the Royal Guard on foot, opening a way through the crowd for the notables; then came the grandees of the Council of Castile, followed by the Constable and the Admiral, the Marquéses of Astorga and of Denia, the counts of Asorno, Nieva, Módica, Saldaña, Monteagudo, Ribadeo and Andrade; the Duke of Lerma; Don García of Toledo; the Archbishops of Santiago and Sevilla and some bishops. Then, in two files, came some ladies in waiting of the Regent, all dressed in mourning, richly relieved with jewels. Following them walked the Marqués of Sarria, *mayordomo mayor* of the royal household, and that stately and holy Portuguese lady, Doña Leonor de Mascareñas, who had been a friend of the Empress Isabel and governess of young Philip II.

Then came all the august trappings of the majesty of Castile: two *maceros* with gold-studded maces on their shoulders; four kings-at-arms wearing dalmatics of crimson velvet, embroidered before and behind with the royal arms; the Count of Buendia, with the great sword of justice, unsheathed, which was carried only before God's anointed rulers; and immediately after, the Princess Juana herself, and her nephew Don Carlos. The slender Regent wore that day a black skirt of rather coarse material, with a black mantle and toque of crape, and a little Russian jacket; white gloves, and in one of her dainty hands a black fan bordered with gold. Don Carlos, who was then about thirteen, with a great head and a small hump on his back, came limping along beside her (for one leg was slightly shorter than the other) and showing his sad yellowish face to the curious crowd—poor Don Carlos, son of double first-cousins, and born to live a short unhappy life. At that moment, however, it seemed possible he might be King of Spain, with all that implied; and observing eyes noted that he was dressed, like his aunt, in coarse mourning clothes—a black cape and jacket, with half hose of wool and velvet breeches, with a sword at his side. Behind the representatives of the absent King Philip came other members of the Royal Guard, on horseback, attended by the shrilling of fifes and the booming of drums.

When all were assembled and seated, a white-robed Dominican father mounted the pulpit and preached, according to one account, "with marvelous eloquence and energy," on a text taken from the warning words of Christ, "Beware of false prophets, who come to you in the clothing of sheep, but inwardly are ravening wolves. By their fruits you shall know them. Do men gather grapes of thorns, or figs of thistles? Even so every good tree bringeth forth good fruit, and the evil tree bringeth forth evil fruit. A good tree cannot bring forth evil fruit, neither can an evil tree bring forth good fruit. Every tree that bringeth not forth good fruit shall be cut down, and shall be cast into the fire. Wherefore by their fruits you shall know them. Not every one that saith to Me: Lord, Lord, shall enter into the kingdom of heaven; but he that doeth the will of My Father who is in heaven, he shall enter into the kingdom of heaven." [7]

After the sermon came the real *auto de fe,* the act of faith on the part of princes, officials, people and penitents. All, from highest to lowest, presented themselves before the Inquisitor General Valdes,

[7] *St. Matthew,* VII: 15-21.

who held a jeweled cross of gold, the Inquisitor Vaca of Valladolid, who bore the Missal, and the secretary who held up the parchment with the ancient formula illuminated upon it. First of all the Princess and the Prince swore on the cross and the gospels that as Catholic rulers they would defend with all their power and their lives the Catholic Faith held by the Holy Apostolic Mother Church of Rome, and to the end that it might be preserved and increase, they would give all aid and favor to the Holy Inquisition and its ministers, that heretics, perturbers of the Christian religion which they professed, might be punished in accord with the apostolic decrees and sacred canons, without fear or favor, or the exception of any persons whatever. Finally, after all the notables had sworn, the parchment was read to the crowd, who were asked by an official if they were willing to swear, and who answered, in a thunderous shout that rumbled like the echo of a passionate sea through faraway streets,

"*Sí, juramos!*"

Then the sentences were read, beginning with Cazalla's. The sixteen penitent *reos* were absolved by the Archbishop, who welcomed them back to the bosom of the Church, and they were taken back to their prisons to begin doing their penance. Immediately afterwards the fourteen who had been relaxed to the secular arm were taken in charge by the civil officials, and started, some on foot and some on mules, for the last tragic mile to the *Campo Grande de Marte*.[8] The *auto de fe* was finished.

Toward the end of the *auto,* the Princess was seen to kiss, very affectionately, the blond page boy who had come with Doña Magdalena de Ulloa—much to his surprise, as well as that of the spectators. Presently the word spread like fire that the Emperor, lately deceased, had had another son, who had just been discovered. When the condemned and their gloomy escort had departed for the place of execution, the crowd surged around the royal party, some climbing on the shoulders of others, some being trampled, in their anxiety to see the new Prince. Finally, to appease them, the Count

---

[8] These and other details are to be found in a very vivid account by P. Gabriel, *La Santa de la Raza,* Vol. III, pp. 125-145. See also Menendez y Pelayo, *op. cit., lib.* V.

of Osorno held up, for all to see, the gallant boy to be known henceforth as Don Juan of Austria. Not all, perhaps not many of the spectators at the *auto* went to the executions. Royal persons ordinarily did not.

Philip II heard of the renewed activity of the Inquisition with approval, and hastened his departure for his native land that he might complete the work that his dying father had begged him to do. Charles on his death bed had regretted sincerely that he had not had Luther put to death years before, when he had power to do so; and he urged Philip to stamp out the heresy as he would the plague. The young King already had the beginnings of the revolt in the Netherlands on his hands, and rightly distrusted the bland and shifty William of Orange; however, he sailed as soon as he could, and finally arrived in Spain in September of that year, 1559. Meanwhile the Inquisitors had been following up some of the leads of the Spring investigation, and as a result, were ready for a second great and memorable *auto,* which the King graced with his presence October 8, with his nephew Alexander Farnese, the future Prince of Parma, and Don Carlos.

Again the Holy Office showed it was no respecter of persons, and terrified the huge crowd of spectators, by relaxing to the secular arm members of some of the richest and most influential families in the land. It was astonishing to see in the line of those condemned to death such persons as Don Carlos de Seso, Fray Domingo de Rojas, Pedro de Cazalla, the parish priest of Pedrosa; Juan Sanchez; Domingo Sanchez, licenciate and presbyter. There was also a nun twenty-one years old, Doña Catalina de Reinoso, of the Cistercian convent at Belen, daughter of Jeronimo de Reinoso, lord of Astudillo de Campos and his Jewish wife Doña Juana de Baeza. This nun was sister also of Don Francisco de Reinoso, who was later bishop of Córdoba. There was also among the condemned another nun of the same convent, Doña Margarita de Santisteban; and another named Doña Marina de Guevara, a relative of the Bishop of Mondonedo and the great family of the Tellez-Girons (even an Archbishop had tried in vain to save her). And there was Doña María de Miranda, a young and beautiful nun of Belen; and there were two men, Pedro Sotelo and Francisco de Almarza.

A *beata* named Juan Sanchez was to have been in the procession, but had cut her own throat in prison, and died impenitent and without confession. Her effigy and bones were carried along by one of the servants of the Holy Office, to be burned at the *Campo Grande*.

Some other women were to be penanced and reconciled—Doña Francisca de Zuñiga y Reinoso, sister of Catalina, also a nun of Belen, and two other nuns, besides the wife of Don Carlos de Seso.

The name Reinoso, recurring in these lists of Lutheran heretics or judaizers, suggests powerful contrasts and paradoxes in the history of Sixteenth Century Spain. Some members of this New Christian family were executed, some sent to prison; yet others became illustrious in Church and State. Don Francisco de Reinoso was the trusted friend and majordomo of Saint Pius V, who nominated him to be canon of Toledo. Philip II opposed that appointment, because the rules of the Holy Church of Toledo excluded *Conversos;* but the absence of any racial prejudice in the King, or any prejudice against the *Conversos* as such, is illustrated by the fact that he offered Reinoso a compensating benefice elsewhere, and later nominated him to be bishop of Córdoba, where the relative of judaizers became a great reforming prelate. His nephew, Don Jeronymo de Reinoso, noted for his holy life, and goodness to the poor, was at one time confessor to Saint Teresa of Ávila, and rendered her invaluable services in the founding of her convent at Palencia in 1580.[9] Further light on the situation in Spain, and on the feeling of the best Catholics toward the Jews, is contributed by a remark that Saint Teresa adds to this little anecdote:

"I was delighted that the foundation was made on that day, for it was the feast of King David, to whom I am devoted." [10]

Twelve of the fourteen condemned that day were strangled before being burned; fourteen others were reconciled. Philip II and his son apparently attended the *auto,* but not the executions. Vari-

---

[9] St. Teresa, *Foundations*, cap. XXIX.

[10] *Yo guste mucho se fundase aquel dia, por ser el rezado del rey David, de quien yo soy devota."—Ibid.* cap. XXIX, B. M. C., Vol. V, p. 273. The date was December 29. There is an office of King David for the date, and the Spanish Carmelites have kept it faithfully.

ous historians have conveyed the impression that he was a spectator of the horrors which Prescott, for one, confuses with the *auto* itself.[11] Philip has been directly connected with only five *autos* in his entire reign. One was in Portugal. In a letter he wrote his two little daughters from Lisbon, after his conquest of that country, he said, "Today my nephew and I went to the *auto,* and we saw it from a window, and we could hear everything very well. They gave each of us a paper on which was written the name of those who were going to be in it. First there was a sermon, according to custom. We stayed until the sentences were read, but then we went away, for in the house where we were the secular judge was going to sentence those delivered by the Inquisitors to be burned. We went at eight o'clock, and came back to eat about one."[12] In another letter Philip wrote, "No, I wasn't very tired from the *auto,* for it didn't last as long as most of the ones they have here, at least the ones I have seen—it was less than four hours."[13] Perhaps he was a little bored by the long performance, which he must have attended as a public duty; but there is no trace here, or in any of Philip's vast correspondence for that matter, of the gloomy bigot of a false tradition, gloating over the agony of his victims.

After the *auto* of October, 1559, there were several others in various places: a very large one in Sevilla, where fifty were executed— and there the Inquisitors found a Dominican priest, eighty years old, who had secretly been teaching Lutheranism to his many noble penitents, under cover of his reputation for holiness. In Toledo a certain cavalier accused his wife of being a heretic, to get rid of her. The Holy Office, employing its usual efficient if somewhat disagreeable means, discovered the truth, proclaimed the innocence of the woman, had her husband publicly flogged, and sent him to the galleys to pull an oar in the hot sun for three years.[14]

The next national sensation after the arrest of Doctor Cazalla and his friends was that of the Emperor's favorite preacher, Doctor

---

[11] Cf. Prescott's *Philip the Second,* Vol. II, p. 325 *et seq.*

[12] *Lettres de Philippe II à ses filles, les Enfantes Isabelle et Catherine, écrites pendant son voyage en Portugal,* etc., ed. by Gachard, Paris, 1884, page 159.

[13] *Ibid.*

[14] *Venetian Calendar of State Papers,* Vol. VII, p. 302.

Constantino, who committed suicide in prison rather than face the stake that awaited him. How different Spanish and world history might have been, if young King Philip had not been warned against taking him for a confessor!

In a few months, by energetic measures, the Holy Office had the situation well in hand, and Lutheranism, at least, was no longer a serious danger to Church and State in the peninsula. Throughout the reign of Philip II there was, however, a constant watchfulness, though never the necessity of such severity as both the dying Emperor and his son had demanded in 1558. There were, however, several of those borderline cases which are as interesting to the historian as they were often perplexing to the Inquisitors and harrowing to the victims. Whole volumes could be written, and have been written, on each of these *causes célèbres*. The three most famous were those of the Archbishop Carranza, primate of Spain; Fray Luis de Leon, distinguished professor at the University of Salamanca; and Antonio Pérez, confidential secretary to King Philip.

Carranza, as the historians have agreed to call him, was commonly known in Spain for many honored years as Maestro Bartholomé de Miranda, from the place of his birth. He was the son of Pedro de Carranza, a gentleman of Miranda de Arga, in Navarre, where he was born in 1503. At the age of seventeen he entered the Dominican order, and began acquiring a wide reputation for holiness and learning. During the famine of 1540, he went begging in the streets for the victims who came flocking from the northern mountains in Castile. For more than twenty years he served as an advisory official of the Inquisition, and in 1542 preached at an *auto* after which Francisco de San Roman was burned. He was censor of books for the Inquisition. When Charles V offered to nominate him archbishop of Cuzco, he declined the honor, but offered to go and preach in America, if the Emperor so desired. He was one of the theologians sent by Charles to the first Council of Trent in 1545. The following year, by order of the Pope's delegates, he preached before members of the Council on the text, *Domine, si in tempore hoc restitues regnum Israel,* and lamented the persecution of the Church by the heretics so feelingly that many of his hearers wept. This was the first Sunday of Lent; on Palm Sunday he preached again before all the Spaniards and some of the French and Italians, and was commended on all sides for a very Catholic exposition which many said was quite in accord with the views of Saint Thomas.

Maestro Miranda returned to Spain in 1548. He was elected prior of the Dominican Convent at Palencia, where he remained for two years, during which time he declined, out of humility, to be confessor to the Emperor and to young Philip II, and refused to be made bishop of the Canaries. In 1550 he was elected provincial of his order. The next year he returned, at the instruction of Charles, to the Council, where he voted, like the other delegates, in favor of the Catholic view, against Luther's dogma of justification. As censor for the Council, he had many Lutheran books burned. In 1553, after the second suspension of the Council, he returned to Spain, and preached frequently at the royal chapel. When Philip II sailed for England in 1554 to marry Mary Tudor, he entrusted Maestro Miranda with the duty of giving 6,000 ducats, on his behalf, in alms to orphans and hospitals. A little later the King sent for him to come to England, where his eloquence and sound orthodoxy were depended upon to do much to bring the heretics back to the Church.

The services that Fray Bartolomé Carranza de Miranda rendered the Catholic Church in England were great. He helped to rectify two of the worst blunders of Charles V by using his influence to have Cardinal Pole admitted as legate of Julius III, and to have part at least of the stolen church property restored. His sermons in the royal chapel in London were moving. He obtained alms to support three houses of his own order, one of the Carthusians and one of the Benedictines. He caused religious processions and the public veneration of the Blessed Sacrament to be restored in a country where well over ninety percent of the people were still Catholics.[15] He became the trusted confessor of Queen Mary. When King

---

[15] Doctor Nicholas Sanders told Cardinal Morone in 1558 that ninety-nine percent of the English people were still Catholics—*Report,* C. R. S. Vol. I, p. 5. There is some confirmation of this in the Lord Keeper's speech in Cobbett, *Parliamentary History,* Vol. I, p. 683.

Philip went to Flanders in September, 1555, he left Carranza in England to look after religious matters. The following spring the Spanish Dominican made an inspection, with thirteen colleagues, of various sees and universities. They found Oxford still Catholic in spirit, and while there, had the bones of the heretical wife of Peter Martyr Vermigli, buried in the main chapel of the Cathedral, disinterred and burned. Cambridge they found quite different. There, as a matter of record, the English Protestant Revolution had had its origin, on the intellectual side, in the lectures of Erasmus as Lady Margaret Professor in 1511, and in the secret deliberations of a little group of students who used to enter the White Horse Inn by the back door to conspire against the Church. The other students called the Inn "Germany," in derision, and dubbed the conspirators "Germans." Some of their names, indeed, sound less English than others. They included Barnes, Hugh Latimer, Ridley, Cox, Skip, Harmann, Frier, Akars, Sygar, Nicholson, Shaxton, Dominick and Matthew Parker.[16]

Carranza was one of those who urged the execution of Latimer, and considered it an excellent thing for England. Indeed, he showed himself so hostile to the heretics that they called him *The Black Friar,* and plotted more than once, it is said, to kill him. After spending three years in England, in such activities, he went to Flanders and reported to the King that some Spanish students at the University of Louvain were suspect in faith, and that some Protestant fugitives from Sevilla were bringing Lutheran books into the Low Countries, by way of Germany, and selling them even in the royal palace.[17] There was a great traffic in Protestant bibles all over Europe, apparently from Ferrara and other places where the Jews had acquired almost a monopoly of the new printing industry, and were assiduously using it for international propaganda purposes.[18] Antwerp was one of the great centres of intrigue. "From an early period," as Dr. Lucien Wolf remarks, "the Mar-

[16] On the beginnings of Protestantism at Cambridge as a sort of international conspiracy see J. B. Mullinger, *The University of Cambridge from the Earliest Times,* Vol. I, p. 553 *et seq.;* Cooper, *Annals of Cambridge;* Henry Eyster Jacobs, D. D., *The Lutheran Movement in England,* Philadelphia, 1890.

[17] Menendez y Pelayo, *op. cit., Lib.* IV, cap. 8, p. 17, 1928 ed.

[18] So Cardinal Aleander reported to Rome as early as 1521.

ranos in Antwerp had taken an active part in the Reformation movement, and had given up their mask of Catholicism for a not less hollow pretence of Calvinism. The change will be readily understood. The simulation of Calvinism brought them new friends, who, like them, were enemies of Rome, Spain and the Inquisition. It helped them in their fight against the Holy Office, and for that reason was very welcome to them. Moreover, it was a form of Christianity which came nearer to their own simple Judaism. The result was that they became zealous and valuable allies of the Calvinists." [19] The chief minister of the Calvinist Synod at Antwerp in 1566, when the beautiful Catholic churches of the city were wrecked and looted by a mob who sang Calvinist hymns, but had all the appearances of a small well-trained gang of thugs— indeed, an English diplomat [20] recognized some London criminals among them—was a Spanish Jew named Marcus Pérez, whose wife was quite friendly with the wife of William of Orange.[21] One of the good "Calvinists" who passed over from Antwerp to London about this time was the famous Jewish Doctor Rodrigo Lopez, who was to be hanged on a charge, now believed to be unjust, that he planned to poison Queen Elizabeth. In Poland and other parts of Europe, the first Calvinists and Unitarians who showed such intense proselytizing activity, all acting as one man, were everywhere called *semi-Judaei*.[22] Cabrera, contemporary biographer of Philip II, went so far as to write that "most of the heresiarchs and heretics of this present century have been of those people." [23]

Against all this seething revolutionary activity Carranza showed a firm and watchful hostility. He engaged in Inquisitorial functions in Frisia. He explained that the vast traffic in heretical and distorted versions of the Bible by the Jews of Ferrara and elsewhere was the true reason why the Catholic Church discouraged her children from reading copies of the sacred work in the vernacular, except in approved versions. He had the pleasure of burning many of such

---

[19] In *Transactions,* Jewish Historical Society of England, Vol. XI, p. 8.

[20] See Clough's letter of August 21, 1566, in Burgon's *Life of Sir Thomas Gresham,* Vol. II, p. 133.

[21] For evidence of this, and further details, see my *Philip II.*

[22] Graetz, *History of the Jews,* IV, p. 624.

[23] *Felipe el Segundo,* t. II, p. 240.

books, as he had burned copies of William Tyndale's Bible, which Saint Thomas More denounced as "the father of all heresies, by virtue of his false translating."

Carranza showed himself so zealous in fighting against the whole unseen army of international agitators against Christendom that when Archbishop Siliceo of Toledo, primate of Spain, died in 1557, Philip the Second insisted on nominating him for the office. Three times Carranza refused, each time naming some good man who he said would be more fit for so exalted a dignity. But the King persisted, and finally had his way. Such was the reputation of Carranza that the Pope and the Cardinals approved of his appointment on the very day they received the King's nomination, dispensing with the usual inquiries about his manner of living, reputation, orthodoxy and so on. Arriving in Spain in August, 1558, the new Archbishop began to discuss with other good Catholics the means for getting rid of the Lutheran infection discovered at Valladolid. The following month he visited Charles V at Yuste. A few weeks later he was present at the deathbed of the Emperor. He then began to tighten up the discipline of his archdiocese, to preach at various parish churches every Sunday, and to impress observers generally as an exemplary prelate.

In August, 1559, while King Philip was still absent in Flanders, all Spain was aghast at the news that the Archbishop of Toledo, primate of Castile, had been arrested by officers of the Inquisition and committed to prison. It seemed impossible. Yet so it was. A Dominican Inquisitor General had ordered the trial of a Dominican prelate.

The sequel, as related so often by the historians to whom this world has given most credit, is too well known to need more than a hasty summary. Carranza, we have been told, was the victim first of the jealousy of the Inquisitor General Valdes, who had craved the primacy for himself, and secondly, of the general ignorance, superstition, bigotry and tyranny of Sixteenth Century Spain under the heels of Philip II and the Inquisition. The Archbishop was kept in prison at Valladolid—and what a prison!— for several years, while the ponderous machinery of the Holy Office ground over him. Finally Saint Pius V insisted on his being sent to Rome for trial, in accordance with the canons which exempted bishops from the authority of the Inquisition. Philip II, after a losing fight, reluctantly complied with the Pope's wishes, and Carranza, followed by cartloads of testimony and records that had accumulated in this strange case, at last reached Rome. Pius V never believed much in his guilt, according to the popular version, but was reluctant to offend the Majesty of Spain; hence he allowed the Archbishop to remain in pleasant confinement, and never made a decision. Finally Gregory XIII pronounced a sentence, which, though "much milder than the Inquisition desired" (to quote a Harvard authority [24]) brought an end to "the king's persecution of Bartolomé Carranza, archbishop of Toledo, who was unjustly suspected of Protestant leanings." [25] The same historian, who generally follows the lead of Lea on the Inquisition, adds that "there was not the slightest basis for the charge" [26]— though he does not quote any of the verdict of Pope Gregory XIII, leaving his readers to assume that it was virtually an exoneration, and probably would not have come forth at all save for ecclesiastical politics. Carranza died shortly afterwards, as a pious Catholic, still in nominal incarceration, but revered by most of those who knew him, including the Pope and many Cardinals.

This most widely accepted version has managed somehow to suggest (1) a cynical venality and political opportunism on the part of the Popes; and (2) a variation of the usual picture of the Spanish Inquisition, which, instead of being merely cruel and bigoted in persecuting innocent dissenters, becomes inexplicably stupid as well, in hounding a perfectly orthodox Catholic to his death. It is rather amusing to find the liberal historians defending Carranza from the accusation that he was a liberal!

The picture was painted in passion and ignorance, and must be done over. The first step, so far as this particular case is concerned, is to lay aside all *a priori* conceptions, of whatever nature, and to ask, have we had the true facts, and all the facts necessary for forming a just conclusion? This imposes no small difficulty at the

[24] Merriman, *op. cit.*, IV, p. 481.
[25] *Ibid.*, p. 58.
[26] *Ibid.*, p. 480.

start, for the Process of Carranza filled no fewer than twenty-two folio volumes, besides the documents concerning the hearings in Rome, and the works of the Archbishop himself.[27] Yet in all the great libraries of the United States there is a great deal of material on this and other related subjects, of which almost no use has been made. One does not have to spend years at Rome or burrowing in the Spanish archives to ascertain this much:

The whisperings about Carranza's orthodoxy, which were rife after his return from Flanders in 1558, did not date only from the rivalry of Valdes. The archbishop had even more bitter enemies in his own order. As early as November 19, 1530, when he was a student, he had been delated to the Inquisition by Fray Miguel de San Martin, *lector* at San Gregorio, as *poco afecto* to the authority of the Pope; and several days later (December 1, 1530) he was accused by Fray Juan de Villamartin, *colegial* of San Pablo, of holding opinions similar to those of Erasmus on the sacrament of penance, and of failing to oppose the reasons alleged by Erasmus against the authorship of the Apocalypse by Saint John.

Evidently these complaints were not taken very seriously, or Carranza made satisfactory explanations, for nothing was done about them. He made several enemies by publishing a tract, *De Residencia,* in which he expressed frank views concerning bishops who did not reside among their flocks; but there was no law under which the Inquisition could punish a man for telling the truth.

The inveterate enemy of Maestro Miranda in his own order was Fray Melchor Cano, "the Quintilian of the theologians, the master of the censors, the admiration of the Council of Trent." [28] This man of prodigious learning, this writer of Ciceronian Spanish and Latin, this gusty typical Renaissance scholar who probably knew as much about the philosophy and theology of Saint Thomas as any man living, and had a passionate and single-hearted devo-

---

[27] The *Real academia de la historia,* Madrid, has a complete copy of the Proceso, in 22 volumes. Señor Menendez y Pelayo gives an extended and well-documented summary, of which unfortunately, too little attention has been paid in England and America. (*Op. cit., lib.* IV, cap. 8.) He gives a summary of the contents of each volume of the Process (pp. 8-9, ed. 1928). For Llorente's account, see his *Histoire Critique, etc.,* t. VII, caps. 32, 33, 34.

[28] Menendez y Pelayo, *loc. cit.*

tion to truth worthy of the traditions of his order, was noted for
the intensity of his likes and dislikes. His great fault, as his
friends knew, was a proud and overbearing temperament which,
when aroused, was capable of harshness and unfairness. His reputation as a master of principles was such that Philip II would not
commence his war with Pope Paul IV without getting an opinion
from him justifying his position—though not as unreservedly as
the hasty quotations and summaries of many historians have made
it appear.

Cano and Carranza had taken a dislike to each other when they
were young students at San Gregorio in Valladolid. The rivalry
continued even when they were masters. Students took the part of
one or the other. There were *Carranzistas* and *Canistas,* and doubtless now and then a black eye or a bloody crown. When Carranza was confirmed as provincial of his order in 1550, Cano,
who happened to be *definidor,* could not resist the opportunity to
administer to him a mild correction. Carranza never forgot this.

The choice of his old enemy as Archbishop was probably no
good news to the redoubtable Fray Melchor. He watched the man
more vigilantly than ever. He had always thought him a heretic
at heart, and he felt that sooner or later he would betray himself.
In 1558 he heard that the new Archbishop had been a great friend
of Cazalla and some of the other arrested Lutherans.

When it became Cano's turn to be elected Provincial of the
Dominicans, Carranza did all he could to oppose the nomination,
giving as his reasons before the *Definitorio* "certain words which
he had spoken to the Admiral, with great daring and malice, in
his dishonor." The words he imputed to Cano were that "the Archbishop is more of a heretic than Luther, and favors Cazalla and
the other prisoners." Fray Melchor justified himself before twenty
fathers of the *Definitorio,* and was elected Provincial. The Archbishop then tried to have the election annulled at Rome, through
a skillful agent of his, Fray Hernando de San Ambrosio, who
was *muy protegido* by Cardinal Alexandrino and by the Italian
General of the Dominicans.

This was more bitter than death to Fray Melchor Cano. Backed by the friars of his province and by King Philip II, he went to Rome, fought his own case there, and won it.

He and the other Dominicans who distrusted Carranza now turned their attention upon his *Commentaries on the Christian Catechism,* published in Antwerp in 1558 with the ostensible purpose of warning the faithful against the Lutheran errors. The Archbishop sent some copies to the Marquesa of Alcanices, Doña Elvira de Roja, whose daughter was one of those arrested in the house of Dr. Cazalla's mother. There were many copies circulating in Valladolid when the Bishop of Cuenca, Don Pedro de Castro wrote a letter to the Inquisitor General Valdes, April 28, 1558, expressing doubts about the orthodoxy of the work.

In the *Commentaries* there certainly were many expressions which suggested dogmas of the Lutherans and of the *Alumbrados.* Like the heretical leaders, Carranza announced his intention to "resuscitate in every possible way the ancient Church, because it was the best and purest,"—a statement which, if interpreted in a Protestant sense, would seem to imply a denial of the continuous unity and divine inspiration of the Church founded by Christ. He spoke of faith and justification in terms almost Lutheran. His enemies said that by contact with heretics in England and Flanders and by reading their books, he himself, intentionally or unintentionally, had become infected with their errors, or at the very least, with their ambiguous habits of expression. They pointed to statements like the following:

"Faith without works is dead, not because the works give life to the faith, but because they are a sure sign that the faith is alive."

"Living faith does not tolerate evil works."

"Through the merits of the Passion of Christ, our good works have value before God, and those which do not have their origin there, however good they may be, have no value whatever, nor does God owe us anything on their account; for thence they draw all their worth." [29]

[29] "Por los méritos de la Passion de Christo tienen valor delante Dios nuestras buenas obras, e las que no nacen de allí, por buenos que sean, no tienen valor alguno, para que por ellos nos deba Dios algo; que de allí traen todo su valor."

"The Passion was one complete and accomplished satisfaction for all sins."

"God interposed Himself, throws a mantle over my sins, and puts His Son in my place, and places all my sins upon Him, and I remain clear and free from all of them."

"The first and principal instrument to justify men is Faith, although other causes contribute to our justification."

"God has promised the state of blessedness to all who with faith accept the Redemption made by Jesus Christ." [30]

To many of such statements by Carranza a Catholic interpretation can be given; but as Señor Menendez y Pelayo asks, why did this theologian, instructed in lucid scholastic methods of thinking and writing by the sons of Saint Dominic, express himself so ambiguously, when Lutheranism was attacking the Church all over Europe—and this, too, in a work to be read by simple uneducated persons, unaccustomed to making logical distinctions?

It is possible, however, that the Holy Office would have put the most charitable interpretation on the statements in question, if some of the prisoners arrested in connection with the Cazalla conspiracy had not indicated a belief that at heart Carranza was one of their faction. Pedro de Cazalla, the parish priest of Pedrosa, accused the Archbishop of having been the cause of Don Carlos de Seso's falling into heresy, by giving him a Lutheran opinion on Purgatory. In a hearing held on April 29, 1558, Doña Ana Enriquez said that she had heard Francisco de Vivero say, "The Archbishop will be a big charcoal in Hell if he doesn't become a convert, for he understands these truths better than we"—inferring that Carranza did not declare himself a Lutheran through fear. Then, she said (still reporting what Vivero had told her) the Archbishop said, "For my part, I hold there is no Purgatory."

Don Carlos de Seso related a conversation with Carranza, supporting the testimony of Pedro Cazalla. On the other hand, Fray Domingo de Rojas, another witness, told of a conversation in which he said, *"Pues, Padre; y el purgatorio?"* and the Archbishop replied, *"¡Mal año!"* indicating a belief in it. This friar said also

[30] Señor Menendez y Pelayo gives several other similar examples, *loc. cit.*, pp. 22-23, and others having an *Alumbrado* flavor.

however, that he had heard the Archbishop in a sermon say that he was sure of his salvation, and that he considered works of little importance, compared with the beneficence of Christ.

Two of the Lutheran prisoners, Doña Isabel de Estrada and Doña Maria de Miranda, a nun of Belen, told their physician, according to his testimony, that "they greatly desired that the Archbishop would come, for he knew a great deal about these matters, and as a *letrado* he would know how to understand and to deal with these gentlemen," meaning apparently the Inquisitors.

There were several other statements, made independently by various witnesses, that pointed toward the Archbishop. Yet the Holy Office waited and watched for something more substantial. Ambiguity was deplorable, but it was not a crime.

The next report about the Archbishop had to do with his conduct at the bedside of Charles the Fifth. The Emperor's confessor testified that the Archbishop came in the day before His Majesty died, and without raising any question about his contrition for his sins, or penance, absolved him several times. This seemed to the confessor, Fray Juan de Regla, to be making a mockery of the sacrament. Charles himself showed his displeasure when the Archbishop kissed his hands and said, "Let Your Majesty have great confidence, for if there is any sin or has been any sin, the Passion of Christ alone suffices."

About two weeks after the Emperor's death, corroboration of this statement was given by Don Luis de Ávila y Zuñiga, *comendador mayor* of Alcántara and historian of the wars in Germany, who said that Carranza held a crucifix before the eyes of Charles, saying, "Here is the one who pays for all; now there is no more sin, all is pardoned." Luis Quijada partially confirmed this.

Fray Marcos de Cardona quoted the Emperor as showing his distrust of Carranza by saying, "When I offered Maestro Miranda the bishopric of the Canaries, he did not want it, and now he has accepted the archbishopric of Toledo. Let us see what his sanctity will amount to."

It was even said that the Emperor's confessor and some of the nobles had refused to permit the Archbishop to enter the room, and that Carranza had finally gone in without permission, to the obvious displeasure of Charles.

Álvaro Lopez, a priest of Ciudad Rodrigo, quoted Francisco de Vivero as saying, "God forgive the Archbishop, for if it were not for him, not so many of our good people would be in prison."

Two Franciscan friars reported that in a sermon at Saint Paul's, Valladolid, August 21, 1558, the Archbishop had defended or exculpated the *Alumbrados*. Others reported that some of his sermons in London, though publicly praised, had caused no little scandal among devout Catholics. After one sermon there he was warned through a friend by a Franciscan father to watch out what he was saying, for he had uttered certain Lutheran phrases.

One of the letters of Carranza to Dr. Agustin Cazalla contained this expression, "I grieve for the troubles you have had; but this is the way to glory, and God, who gives the fatigue, helps with his favor to endure it, and helps to bring about the remedy." Asked in prison what troubles the Archbishop had referred to, Cazalla said it was the death of his brother-in-law, who left thirteen children, and a lot of debts for him to pay.

So the *indicios* piled up, and still no formal action was taken against the Archbishop. He himself was apparently informed what was going on, for he began seeking opinions favorable to his *Commentaries*. The Archbishop of Granada told him there was no heresy in the book. The University of Alcalá agreed, but advised that in view of the dangerous times, it might be well to clarify certain statements. The Bishop of Leon was less favorable.

Meanwhile Valdes sent the famous Catechism to various theologians, for their opinions. The first one was Cano. It is safe to infer that it was probably a great moment in Fray Melchor's life when the book of his old enemy was placed in his hands with a request for an official opinion.

He wrote one with great gusto and vigor, first in Latin and then in Spanish, at considerable length, and, needless to say, in a frame of mind far removed from the juridical ideal set up by Bernard Gui, Eymeric, Torquemada and other Dominican lawgivers of the Inquisition. The document was a violent blast, scattered with hyperboles, from beginning to end. The lion of the reforming

Council of Trent seemed to forget at times that he had been asked for his judgment only on the theological questions involved. He could not resist disputing an opinion which Carranza had put forth with the good intention of persuading women not to use cosmetics. "True beauty," the Archbishop had written, "consists in the good composition of the parts, and hence it follows that color has nothing to do with it." Cano gravely explained the importance of color as an element in beauty, and observed that the remark illustrated well the Archbishop's lack of common sense. He went on to list 140 propositions in the catechism alone which he said were false, ambiguous or of heretical flavor. In summarizing, he made six general indictments against the work: (1) it gave to untutored people, in the vulgar tongue, difficult and complicated ideas; (2) it profaned and made public the mysteries of religion; (3) its statements concerning justification by faith were dangerous, considering the controversial times, and should have been explained more fully, or annotated, to make the meanings clear, instead of following Lutheran ways of speech; (4) there were ambiguous statements whose expression suggested the evil rather than the good sense in which they might be taken; (5) it was dangerous to place some of the Lutheran disputes before the public, especially in Spain, where books of heretics were not in circulation, "and the remedy is worse than the disease," (6) the book contained many rash, scandalous and ill-sounding propositions, others which savored of heresies, others that were erroneous, and some that were even heretical, in the sense they seemed to make.

It has been the fashion in our language to exploit the obvious bias and rancor of Cano's opinion, and to neglect the truth of a great deal of what he said. Many years were to pass before his essential criticisms of the Catechism were to be vindicated by the final judgment of Pope Gregory XIII. Meanwhile, as that sane and wise scholar Señor Menendez y Pelayo has noticed, Fray Melchor's farrago contained a magnificent defense of the rights of the human reason against the traditionalism of Carranza. The Archbishop resembled many of the heretics, from the Manichees to Luther and from Luther to Buchmanism, in at least a tendency to emphasize feeling, intuition, emotion, and to set up a fictitious conflict between religious sentiment and cold reason. The Catholic Church, whose best theologians looked askance at Ramón Lull when he seemed to be claiming too much for human reason, was always the defender of that faculty against those who despised it; she always maintained the supremacy of the human reason in its own field. The Nineteenth Century rationalists who spoke so loftily about monkish antipathy to reason in the Middle Ages were often so ignorant of what the great monks actually said and wrote that it never dawned upon them that the situation was exactly the reverse of what they imagined: it was usually the heretics and infidels who attacked reason, and the monkish theologians who defended it. And in the Sixteenth Century it was the ambiguous, if well-meaning Carranza who was disparaging reason, and the orthodox champion Cano who defended it.

"To Christians," wrote Carranza, "it is necessary to lose this North of the reason and to navigate by faith and rule our works by it, especially in matters which concern Christian Religion and the Sacraments." In another place he said, "Reason and natural intelligence, although they may be pure and well-ordered, condemn the article of faith as false." [31]

"This proposition," replied Cano, "is not only injurious to the reason of man, but is blasphemy of the wisdom and power of God, who gave man reason; for if the order of nature and reason contradict faith, then, seeing that faith always speaks the truth, it would follow that the order of nature and reason are contrary to the truth; and as this natural order and reason proceed directly from God, God would be contrary to Himself. . . . And so Saint Paul referred the knowledge of God, which the philosophers through discourse and natural reasoning attained, to God Himself, as to a first principle. . . . For this reason Saint Thomas and the other theological doctors teach that faith is over reason and over nature, but not contrary to them." [32]

Meanwhile Fray Domingo de Soto had written to Carranza,

---

[31] *"La razon y seso natural, aunque sea limpio y ordenado, condenan al artículo de la fée por falso."*

[32] Menendez y Pelayo quotes this from the *Vida de Melchor Cano,* folio 548; *op. cit., lib.* iv, cap. 8, p. 36.

praising the Catechism; and the Archbishop wrote him November 24, 1558, begging him to say the same things officially. The whole affair, he said, was an effort on the part of the Archbishop of Sevilla to discredit him and all friars, and exclude them from public offices. "I have studied as much theology as Maestro Cano," he added.

Perhaps de Soto had read meanwhile the opinion of Melchor Cano. At any rate, his enthusiasm for the Catechism had cooled, and he was reluctant to give an opinion, when asked for one by Valdes. The Inquisitor General then ordered him to give one within fifteen days, under pain of excommunication. De Soto then rendered a cautious one, granting the good intentions of the author, but observing that certain phrases were questionable, considering the dangers of the times.

Carranza now wrote de Soto a bitter letter of protest, complaining against his opinion, and arguing that Saint Augustine and Saint John Chrysostom could be condemned by such rigorous criticism, and that heresies could be found in Saint John the Evangelist by the same token. The Archbishop was now thoroughly alarmed by the storm that was gathering over his head. He wrote the Licenciate Gulielmo, Inquisitor of Valladolid, a very careful letter, which began by praising him and dispensing him from residence in a certain benefice he held in the diocese of Toledo (though Carranza had denounced such absenteeism in the past) and went on to express regret that Fray Domingo de Rojas, cradled in the Order where the truth had always been taught, should have fallen so foully as to testify falsely against one who did not deserve it. The Archbishop said he hardly knew Don Carlo de Seso, and had never spoken to him more than once, when they were at the college of San Gregory in Valladolid with Pedro Cazalla. "I warned him to look to how he spoke, and not to think he was in Italy where they punish works, but in Spain, where they punish works and words . . . thinking there was no more harm in him than a certain exuberance of speech they have in this country. . . . He admitted to me—saying with many words that he was not a theologian, nor did he know letters—that he had learned that doctrine from two prelates who were at the Council of Trent. . . . Seeing him so humble and making such protestations, I said to him, 'I knew the prelates you mention at Trent, but never have I heard them speak of this matter, except as Catholics and as the Church teaches.' " Seso listened with all humility, and as he seemed harmless and promised to amend, the Archbishop did not think it necessary to report him to the Inquisition.

Carranza then set the Jesuit Father Gil Gonzalez and Fray Juan de Villagarcia to work translating his Catechism from the Spanish; this they never finished. In November he wrote the General Council of the Inquisition that he was having the work shortened, to be read by the common people, and had ordered a merchant at Antwerp not to send any more of the first edition to Spain—though there were only a few in the country, seven or eight which he had in a box, and a dozen at Saint Stephen's, Salamanca, and San Gregorio, Valladolid. He asked meanwhile that they refrain from condemning the book or putting it on the Index, without hearing him on the subject; for if there were anything wrong in the book, he would be the first to burn it.

He wrote explanations to King Philip, the Inquisitor General Valdes, to the Pope, and to other prominent persons. Indeed, it may be that he hastened his own fall by making so many unsought explanations, before he had been publicly accused. King Philip was ready to protect him, if innocent; but kept an open mind. Valdes gave an evasive reply. Knowing that the Inquisition had no jurisdiction over an archbishop, he had sent his nephew to Rome to get a brief from Pope Paul IV, and was waiting for the messenger's return.

Finally Valdes got the brief, April 8, 1559, authorizing him to proceed, for a period of two years only, against any bishops, patriarchs and primates, in matters concerning heresies. Accounts of any such proceedings, however, were to be sent to the Pope at once, and any prelate arrested must be sent to Rome for sentence.

This was enough for the present, and Valdes prepared to act, but with the deliberation characteristic of the Holy Office. Not until May 6 did the *Fiscal,* the Licenciate Camino, demand the arrest of the Archbishop and the confiscation of his goods for having "preached, written and dogmatized many heresies of

Luther." On the same day Valdes assembled his *consultores,* including various bishops and theologians. On May 13 he wrote a letter to Carranza, summoning him to appear and answer the charges against him.

The permission of King Philip, still in Flanders, was considered necessary, and a courier was on the way to ask him for it. He gave it June 26, telling the Inquisitors to respect the dignity and person of the Archbishop. At the same time he wrote his sister and regent, the Princess Juana, instructing her to summon the Archbishop to Valladolid, as if to consult him on important business, to avoid scandal, and unnecessary indignity to Carranza. This the Princess did August 3.

Carranza received her letter August 6. He replied next day that he would go, and set out from Toledo, traveling by slow stages, perhaps hoping that before he reached Valladolid, King Philip, who had long deferred his departure from Flanders, would have arrived in Spain, and would save him. By August 14 he had got only as far as Alcalá de Henares. He remained there two days, leaving on the sixteenth.

On the seventeenth the Fiscal made a second demand for the Archbishop's arrest, this time on the ground that there was reasonable fear that he might flee, and Valdes, growing impatient, granted the request. When the Archbishop reached Torrelaguna August 20, he was met by some officers of the Inquisition, who took him into custody.

The rest of this sad and complicated story has been better publicized. The Archbishop was kept in the new prison of the Holy Office, apparently not as agreeable a house as the old, and in a room which he complained was badly ventilated, smelled like a stable, and was so dark that he often had to light a candle at nine in the morning. He received his meals on broken plates, and his dessert on a book.[33]

The great process began. There were innumerable delays, many of them caused by the Archbishop's appeals to rules of the Inquisition protecting his rights, others, we must infer, by the unrelenting pressure of his foes. Meanwhile Pope Paul IV died; but his

[33] *Documentos inéditos para la historia de España,* V, pp. 540, 549, 552.

successor, Pius IV, repeatedly demanded that the Archbishop be sent to Rome for trial, and delegates at the second and triumphant Council of Trent, who had known Carranza at the first, interceded repeatedly for him in 1562 and 1563, while the Congregation of the Index at Trent gave a favorable report on the Catechism. The Spanish Inquisition refused to yield up its prisoner, and the King would not interfere until the investigation was ended in 1564. At that time Philip suggested that judgment be given in Spain by judges to be appointed by the Pope. Pius IV agreed, and appointed four, all of whom were in their turns to sit upon the chair of Saint Peter: Cardinal Buonocompagni, Ippolito Aldobrandini, the Franciscan Father Peretti, and Archbishop Castagna of Rossano. They arrived in Spain in November, 1565. Unable to proceed without interference from the Spanish Inquisition, backed by the King, they were obliged to give up the task.

With Pope Pius V, a Dominican monk of humble origin, Philip had a vastly different man to deal with in Rome, a man who added to great abilities and energies the irresistible power of saintliness. Philip had matured slowly, even though he had ruled Spain in his 'teens; it was not until 1569 or later that he reached his full stature as a Catholic King with the exalted medieval (and, it might be added, ancient Jewish) ideal of a responsibility to God for ruling justly, and a complete independence of all human beings except as advisers. At the period in question he was still very much under the influence of the Duke of Alba, one of the greatest military commanders of all time, but a mediocre opportunist as a statesman; and later he was to be taken in for a dozen years by a secretary, Antonio Pérez. At one time during the short pontificate of Saint Pius V, the King's government trampled so ruthlessly on the rights of the Church that the Pope, in 1569, offered prayers that the Church be freed from the tyranny of the Spanish government, and declared—this when Philip was fighting the Moriscos in the south and the Calvinists in the Low Countries—that Kings who refused obedience to Christ's vicar need not be surprised if they were punished by the rebellion of their own subjects; while the President of the Royal Council went so far as to assert before the Nuncio, "There is no Pope in Spain."

Nevertheless when Pope Pius V, tired of the infinite delays in the Carranza case, commanded in 1567 that the Archbishop be sent to Rome, he made known his determination in such terms that Philip, always Catholic at heart, complied rather than risk excommunication or a new schism. So Carranza went to Rome at last. He was received with great kindness, and given the papal chambers in the Castle of Sant' Angelo for his residence during an imprisonment that was made as light as possible in every way. The huge masses of evidence followed him from Spain; the case had grown to such mammoth proportions in that respect that it is hardly to be wondered at that it was before the Curia for nine years. Pius V died before he could arrive at a decision. Not until April 14, 1576 did Pope Gregory XIII, who had tried to settle the matter as Cardinal Buonocompagni eleven years before, render judgment, after a ballot of all the Cardinals and many theologians.

The writings of the Archbishop, said the Holy Father, did contain various heretical opinions, similar to those held by Luther, Melancthon, and other Protestants. He specified sixteen of these in particular—among them the one attacked by Fray Melchor Cano eighteen years before: "That natural reason in affairs of religion may be contrary to faith," and another attacked by Eymeric centuries before, to the effect that those in mortal sin could not understand divine Scripture or judge in matters of faith. "And so now We command," wrote Gregory, "that he detest, anathematize, withdraw and abjure in Our presence all the aforesaid errors and heresies." This done, the Archbishop was to be subject to no further penalties on their account; "but that such excesses may not have to be punished in future, and that he may proceed more carefully, we determine that the said Bartolemé, Archbishop, be suspended from the administration of his church of Toledo for five years from this day . . . and must live in the monastery of the Dominicans in the city of Veyano, which city we designate as a prison, from which he cannot go during the period mentioned without Our express permission." The Archbishop was obliged, before leaving Rome, to visit the seven basilicas and to say a Mass solemnly at each. At Veyano he must say certain Masses within three months. Then, for five years, he could say Mass only on Christmas Day and certain other feasts.

All those heavy years the Archbishop had borne his cross with patience and resignation that touched many hearts. Now he received the sentence in the same spirit. He was seventy-three, a broken weary old man. He died that year, receiving the sacraments on his deathbed and protesting to the last that he had never intended to be anything but a good Catholic.

This was believed by all except perhaps a few of his bitter personal enemies. Pope Gregory XIII, like his predecessor, held a high regard for the Archbishop, and had a handsome monument erected to his memory in Rome. In Spain the chronicler Morales, at the command of King Philip, wrote an account of the whole case which is surprisingly compassionate and without animus.[34]

A later Congregation of the Index put the Catechism of Carranza back on the list of forbidden books; and Catholics are prohibited from reading it to this day.

In a world where orderly thinking has become more and more rare, men are likely to say, "Why so much persecution of one whose intentions were admitted to be good? Why so much fuss about a mere dogma or two? Are a few words so important that they are worth the sacrifice of a human life, or of human liberty?"

A Dominican Inquisitor, or the great Franciscan Inquisitor Ximenes, would have answered gravely, without hesitation, "Yes, they are. Words convey truth or falsehood. They lead men to action which is good or bad, according as it supports one side or the other of the struggle between opposing spiritual forces, which is the reality behind all the shifting appearances of history." The words of Luther begot the Peasants' War and its cruel suppression, the inexpressible miseries of the Thirty Years' War, and out of the wretched ruin of Christian Europe, a false and decaying semblance of peace and security, destined to end in our century with the butchery and starvation of millions of human beings, and the threat of slavery in one form or another to a bewildered world. These Catholic theologians well understood the inexorable opera-

---

[34] For this, the sentence of Gregory XIII and the sixteen condemned propositions, see the *Coleccion de Documentos inéditos,* etc., V, pp. 482 *et seq.*

tions of the law of cause and effect. These Dominicans loved truth so sincerely that they were willing to sacrifice even one of their own distinguished members to safeguard the divine revelation which alone could give peace to men and health to society. This is not to defend everything they did, for they had the faults of human beings; it is only to suggest that the Inquisition, like our own courts, is entitled to be judged not by its incidental evils, but by the far greater evils it prevented. Granting that Erasmus meant well, his disciples founded upon his careless words a movement disruptive of orderly society. Granting that Carranza had even better intentions, and was the victim in part of human envy and spite, the fact remains that his disciples (if the Holy Office had permitted him to have any) might easily have given Spain a Peasants' War and a Thirty Years' War.

About the second year of Carranza's imprisonment in Spain, the attention of the Holy Office was called to the fact that an Augustinian friar, thirty-four years old, had made a speech, on his election to a chair of theology at the University of Salamanca, criticizing the Dominicans, and calling attention to the recent discovery of various heretics among them. This, coming from a member of Martin Luther's order, was a bitter draught for those whose ranks had borne the brunt of the fight against heresy for centuries, and who had never hesitated to condemn their own when truth so commanded. From that time on, Fray Luis de Leon probably did or said very little that was not observed by watchful eyes.

He soon proved to be one of the greatest lecturers at the Athens of Spain in the time of its most brilliant intellectual achievements. Himself a graduate of the University, he was one of the most learned men then living; a master of Latin, Greek and Hebrew, a sound and thorough theologian, and in addition to all this, one of Spain's great lyric poets. His lecture hall was always crowded to the doors and windows. As a teacher he was always "stimulating, personal, living and extremely lucid." [35] His most profound discourses were made more interesting to his students by a quotation from a pagan poet, a reference to contemporary events, a homely remark about "a bullfight, or fishing, or gambling among students" . . .

[35] Aubrey F. G. Bell, *Luis de Leon,* Oxford, 1925, p. 111.

and "he always made his hearers feel that he was interested in them, as when in discussing free will he says, 'I see you writing and am not mistaken in this, yet I do not make you write, you do it of your own free will.' " [36] A great dialectician, with some of the Renaissance combativeness of Fray Melchor Cano, he was saved from arrogance by a profound humility, and by the quiet sense of humor which helped to make his lectures a memorable delight to all who heard them. A thin, frail man with a long nose, sunken cheeks, and piercing eyes of a greenish color, he was reputed to be an exemplary religious, transparently honest, chivalrous and magnanimous, compassionate to the poor, calm and courageous before the rich and the powerful. There was something in this Augustinian college professor that could not stomach lies, hypocrisy, or tyranny in any form.

Such a man, of course, was bound to have enemies, and Fray Luis de Leon had bitter ones, especially among his less successful rivals at Salamanca. The two who had most to do, by his own account, with having him denounced to the Inquisition were Leon de Castro, a self-centered, pompous, intolerably dull pedant, who blamed the failure of one of his books in 1570 on "Luis de Leon and the Jews"; and Fray Bartolomé de Medina, a good theologian, but cold and heartless enough to try even the angelic patience of Saint Teresa, when she was founding her convent at Salamanca: it was of him she wrote, "As for Father Medina, never fear that I should distress myself about him even were he far more embittered against me: indeed, he makes me laugh." [37]

His intolerance might amuse Saint Teresa, but it was no laughing matter for Fray Luis de Leon. In March, 1572, the famous professor was arrested by officers of the Holy Inquisition and taken to the prison at Valladolid where Carranza had spent seven years. Apparently the quarters of Fray Luis were better; at least he made no complaint of them; but his jailers sometimes neglected to bring him food. There he remained month after month. Perhaps his

[36] *Ibid.;* from Luis de Leon's *Opera,* VII, 129.
[37] Letter to Mother Mary Baptist, May 14, 1574—*Letters of Saint Teresa,* Stanbrook Abbey edition, I, p. 146.

enemies thought that so impulsive and imaginative a man would little by little incriminate himself in anger.

Fray Luis fought back valiantly. He named his enemies and demanded that they be punished for causing the arrest of an innocent man. But he furnished them none of the evidence they expected, and in fact needed. They had caused his arrest on grounds that they themselves felt to be not quite sufficient for a conviction. He was suspected of judaizing, on the following grounds: (1) He had made a translation of the *Canticle of Canticles* for a nun, a relative, who could not read Latin; (2) he was said to have given the Hebrew text of the Scriptures more authority than the Vulgate; (3) he was of Jewish descent—indeed, his great-grandmother Leonor de Villanueva and her sister had worn *sanbenitos,* and had been reconciled to the Church as judaizing heretics.

He was indeed of Jewish descent, and a fine example of that noble type of humanity, the sincere Catholic Jew. In fairness to the Inquisition it must be noticed that the matter of race was considered only an *indicio* of judaizing when accompanied by other alleged *indicios,* and was immediately dropped when these latter were discarded. Discarded they were, but only after Fray Luis had remained in prison about four and a half years.

When the news of his release reached Salamanca, there was a great outpouring of professors, students and gentry on the afternoon of Sunday, December 30, to meet him on the road from Valladolid. With trumpets braying and drums booming they escorted him in triumph back to the University, where the next day, a Commissary of the Holy Office publicly declared his unconditional acquittal, and the Rector of the University expressed the delight of the faculty and students over the event. Fray Luis was given a better chair than the one he had before (at least it paid about three times as much salary) and quietly resumed his old life of teaching and writing. There is a delightful story (not supported by contemporary evidence but so characteristic of the man that one hopes it is true) that he walked into his lecture room after an absence of nearly five years, and began,

"As I was saying when interrupted—"

In 1582 he was again denounced to the Inquisition, but this time the charge was not taken seriously. After the death of Saint Teresa of Ávila (whom he revered, but never met in life) the Royal Council commissioned him to edit an edition of her works. He helped in the reformation of his order. In 1590, old and ill, he defended the Carmelite nuns, and he defended the Pope's authority against the pretensions of the King's ministers, who would not allow papal bulls to be published in Spain.

Even after his release from the prison of the Inquisition, Fray Luis continued to speak the truth as he saw it, and sometimes with a bit of rashness, but with impunity. He had the courage to say that the legal fiction by which the Holy Office, in handing over an impenitent heretic to the secular arm, begged that he be treated mercifully, was pharisaical. For his attitude on the Inquisition generally, and on the Jewish Problem so intimately bound up with it in Spain, I cannot do better than quote from Mr. Bell's excellent work: [38]

"Against the error and delusion of the heretics he speaks frequently in his works. As to the Jews, his writings contain many very remarkable passages. He continually dwells on their blindness, but believes that they are nevertheless especially loved by God, and in lectures delivered after his imprisonment declares that the flower of the aristocracy of the Jews had taken refuge in Spain (*'in Hispaniam confluxit Iudaeorum nobilitatis pars maxima'*). He is persuaded that before the end of the world the Jews will be reduced to the Christian fold. In a significant passage, a few years after his release, in 1582, he declares with great boldness that, although the enemies of the people of God now seem to flourish, yet they will be blotted out and the people of God will ultimately prevail over all, to the confusion of those who have acted unjustly and impiously towards God and towards His people, persecuting the just and good as well as the sinners with a personal hatred. He speaks of the services rendered by Jews as missionaries in the pagan lands to which they were dispersed, and reminds his readers that Christ was a Jew. Another passage of the *In Cantica Canticorum* is applicable, perhaps purposely, both to converted

---

[38] *Op. cit.,* pp. 272-3. For further details, see this scholarly book, to which I am indebted for most of the details here given on Fray Luis.

Jews and Old Christian hypocrites, while elsewhere he makes the unpalatable statement that before the end of the world the faithful will be rooted out for their great sins and replaced by *fideles ex Judaismo*. Meanwhile the Jews were a difficulty in the State. Luis de Leon fully acknowledged the authority of the Inquisition and believed in its utility. He had himself before his arrest described in a lecture the various kinds of heretical propositions. Heretics and Jews were in fact incompatible with that harmony and unity which formed the basis of his whole conception of life. That wonderful harmony of the stars, of the Universe, was to enter into men's lives, as a harmony of the body with itself, in health *'como musica concertada';* of body and soul, in subjection of the senses to reason; between the one and the many, each thing containing within itself all other things, which is *'avecinarse la criatura a Dios';* harmony of the relations between man and man, and between the soul and man and God. . . Each man must perform his part as in a play, and the three kinds of men (agricultural, commercial and landowners) which form a State must constitute separate parts of an ordered whole. . . ."

Fray Luis never manifested any bitterness or resentment over his unjust imprisonment. In his old age he paid a visit to King Philip II, by invitation. Unfortunately no record has been left of the conversation between the Jewish-Catholic scholar-poet and the monarch who considered himself, as chief protector of the Church Catholic, a sort of successor of King David; and who, "like Solomon, with lofty meditation, gave infinite thanks to God" as he contemplated the setting up on the façade of his palace of San Lorenzo the gigantic statues of the six Kings of the tribe of Juda and the family of David, all crowned and sceptred above the spacious greenery of El Escorial.[39]

Philip, contrary to the northern legend about him, was undoubtedly the greatest ruler of his country. His sometimes excessive concern for his authority and prerogatives, even against Popes, was part of a studied policy inaugurated by Fernando and Isabel. By nature, however, he was simple, unassuming, affectionate and considerate as husband, father and friend, and inclined, if any-

[39] Cabrera, *Felipe el Sugundo,* III, p. 198.

thing, to be too trusting. The confidence he reposed in his life-long friend Ruy Gomez, Prince of Éboli, was never broken. In 1566 he took into his Council of State a young protegé of that facile diplomat, and gradually extended to him the same absolute confidence. When Ruy Gomez died, leaving a young and volatile widow and ten children, young Antonio Pérez was ready to succeed him as the King's closest confidant. The Princess, in the first excess of her grief, rushed to Saint Teresa of Ávila and arranged to enter the new Carmelite convent at Pastrana. It was not long, however, before she was back in the palace, still beautiful in spite of the fact that she had lost an eye in early life and wore a patch, and more spoiled than ever without the restraining influence of Ruy Gomez. Soon this emotional widow was the mistress of Antonio Pérez. For a long time the guilty pair managed to keep their relationship a secret from the King, who hated adultery as he hated all deception. Meanwhile Pérez was gradually poisoning Philip's mind against Don Juan of Austria, making it appear as if the hero of Lepanto aspired to supplant his brother on the throne. He falsified despatches from Don Juan, then in Flanders, as he decoded them for the King.

Shortly after the death of Don Juan in the Netherlands, Philip discovered that Pérez had been deceiving him. He quietly watched the favorite, and learned other facts about him: his liaison with the Princess of Éboli, some said a criminal correspondence with the enemies of Spain and the Church in Constantinople and the Low Countries. When he had all the information he needed, and had a man ready to take the important office of Pérez, the King, after months of patient dissembling, had both his corrupt minister and the widow of his old friend arrested on the same night. The outlines of the rest of the story are too well known to bear much repetition. The King accused Pérez of the murder of Escobedo and an astrologer who knew too much. The case dragged on for six years. In 1585 Pérez was banished from court for ten years, condemned to prison for two years, and ordered to pay a fine of 30,000 ducats in restitution for his thefts from the Treasury. Pérez, with valuable state papers still hidden where the King could not find them, escaped and fled to Aragon. In 1591 the Inquisition made inquiries among people who had known the fallen minister well, and received some shocking charges: one of sodomy, which was not corroborated, and several of disloyalty to the King, and of heresy—a cousin of Pérez, for example, quoted him as saying that he hoped Philip would be defeated, and that he intended to "go to Geneva and live among the heretics." To this was added the alleged *indicio* that he was of Jewish descent—a "charge" from which the sons of Pérez later obtained a certificate of acquittal from the Holy Office.

Arrested in Aragon, he escaped from prison disguised as a woman, but was recaptured and lodged in the royal jail at Zaragoza. There, with the help of some lawyers from Italy, he prepared a skilful defense, appealing to the ancient *fueros* of which the Aragonese were so proud, as the *Conversos* had done in the time of the *reyes católicos*. His friends went about stirring up the people on his behalf, saying that the King was persecuting him for no reason at all, and making an especial bid for the sympathies of the women. The King had the case transferred again to the Inquisition, and a formal charge of heresy was lodged against Pérez. A mob of about 200 armed men, carefully prepared for their work, seized him from the hands of the officers of the Inquisition, crying "Liberty! Liberty!" and killing the King's viceroy, Almenara, who had forbidden the Inquisitors to give up their prisoner. Pérez found safety in Aragon. Later he went to Paris, and from there to London, where he received a pension from Queen Elizabeth, and consorted with Doctor Lopez, the half-Jew Don Antonio of Portugal, and other refugees from Catholic countries, who were acting as spies and propaganda agents for Cecil. Quarreling with Lopez, he is said to have instigated the false charge on which the physician was hanged, drawn and quartered.

The case of Pérez remains mysterious to this day. The anti-Spanish, anti-Catholic historians have represented him as a martyr to the sinuous policy of Philip and the intolerance of the Inquisition—and of course quite innocent of the charges made against him. Pérez himself, however, admitted having falsified the letters of Don Juan; his lechery was notorious; and his later conduct certainly lent a large measure of confirmation to the accusation of the

Holy Office that while acting as Philip's secretary he was secretly a part of the huge, invisible international conspiracy that extended from London to Constantinople. He was received with open arms by the persons then most active in the campaign to discredit and destroy the Catholic Faith in Europe—by Henry of Navarre, by Jewish agents in Paris, in London, by the Cecils and their minions. The revolt which was the pretext for his escape had all the appearance of being engineered by some secret society lead by a dissolute man named Heredia. A Dominican monk, Fray Agustin de Lebata, testified in the investigation of the affair that "all has proceeded from the doings of those who know a great deal of the mutinies present and past of Flanders and of Italy, to avenge themselves in this manner for the injustice which they say the king has done him." [40] As Prescott remarked, "The Protestants of that time constituted a sort of federative republic, or rather a great secret association, extending through the different parts of Europe, but so closely linked together that a blow struck in one quarter instantly vibrated to every other." [41] In the next century the descendants of many of the leading Protestant conspirators would be found in the ranks of Freemasonry.

"The sixteenth century in Spain, when Spain stood at the head of the nations of Europe, is all the more interesting to study because it bears a strong resemblance to our own age," observes Mr. Bell very sensibly. "If we substitute heresy for Bolshevism, and Luther for Lenin, and the discovery of America for the development of flying, we shall obtain a good insight into the various influences at work in men's minds. . . . The gloom and fanaticism in sixteenth century Spain have been greatly exaggerated. . . . If we inquire into the special characteristics of the Spanish Renaissance we find foremost a sanity, moderation and balance scarcely to be found elsewhere in the sixteenth century. . . . The profound and original Vives, Sepulveda, Fox Morcillo, Gomez Pereira, Benito Pereira, Huarte, all maintain the utmost freedom of thought and rigorous examination of authority, thus laying the foundations of the induc-

---

[40] *Doc. inéditos*, XII, p. 267. Further details of the Perez case, with references, are given in my *Philip II*.

[41] *The Reign of Philip the Second*, I, 474.

tive method. . . . A third characteristic of the Spanish humanists is their practical sense, very marked in Vives. The Renaissance in Spain always retained a certain ethical purpose, characterized by clearness, energy, and sincerity of thought, without necessarily excluding a passionate love of beauty, evident in Luis de Leon and other writers. . . . It is precisely when a horror of great darkness is supposed to have fallen upon Spain that we find there ecclesiastics such as Arias Montano, Luis de Leon, Luis de Granada and José de Sigüenza, to whom poetry and beauty were the very breath of life." [42]

England, which had become the stronghold of the international opposition to the Church of Christ, was remarkably successful, through hundreds of propagandists, in discrediting Spain; especially in attributing to the Catholic country faults which were far more in evidence along the Thames. When Elizabeth's government was brutally suppressing every opposition, hounding authors with spies and censorship from which Marlowe, Jonson, and even Shakespeare suffered, writers in Spain made some very frank criticisms of Philip II, and with impunity. If Fray Luis de Leon had been in England, and had written of Elizabeth some of the strictures he made of certain policies of Philip, he would at least have had his ears cut off. While the bastard daughter of Ann Boleyn was claiming absolute power not only over the State but over the Church of England, Philip's confessor was rebuked by the Holy Inquisition for daring to say, in a sermon, that the King had absolute power and was accountable to no one; and Luis de Cabrera, poet and historian, was only one of several who told His Majesty to his face that he was a fool to send the Armada against England, and would regret the venture. Yet many generations have heard of free England and despotic Spain; and in the Tower of London, as if to symbolize the vile hypocrisy of this propaganda, thumbscrews used to torture Catholic priests under Cecil's tyranny have been shown, until very recent times, as instruments used by the Spanish Inquisitors.

The age of Philip II was the golden age of Spain. The Inquisition, with all its human blunderings, was one of the chief devices

[42] *Op. cit.,* pp. 41-43.

by which the peace, prosperity and freedom of that age were secured. It may well be, as Mr. Bell conjectures, that Philip, by this and other means, built up reserves of spiritual and moral strength which would enable his country, even in our own day, to cast off foreign poisons and to renew its strength in its true source, the revealed truth of Catholicism. Never again, however, would the Holy Office manifest the alertness and energy with which Philip had inspired it.

VIII

Llorente

THE man who gave the *coup de grâce* to the Spanish Inquisition, and wrote its epitaph across the slowly darkening skies of the modern world was, by a paradox significant and saddening, both a Catholic priest and a Freemason, Juan Antonio Llorente. A great many influences had converged to produce him two centuries after the death of Philip the Second; and it goes almost without saying that some were influences which would never have been permitted to worm their way back into Spain, if the successors of the Dark Demon of the South (as Philip's enemies called him) had been men of his kidney.

Philip left Europe more Catholic than he had found it, and this through a policy on the whole firm, patient, unselfish and Christian. He supported, with all the force of his royal authority, the completion of the true Reformation in Spain, begun by Cardinal Ximenes, and he had contributed hugely to the Reformation of the whole Church at the Second Council of Trent. When the Huguenots and compromising Catholics (*Les Politiques*) of France were preventing the publication of the Council's decrees in that country, Philip insisted on having them published in Spain and the Netherlands, even though he was advised that some of them curtailed his own royal prerogatives.[1] At a tremendous cost to Spain and to himself, he made sure that France and a good part of the Low Countries should remain Catholic; while the Jesuits, whom he

---

[1] Many modern historians have asserted the contrary. But see Philip's letter to his sister Margaret in Gachard, *Correspondance de Philippe II*, Vol. I, pp. 326-8, for a glimpse into the very Catholic mind of this slandered King.

had employed to reform other orders in the Peninsula, reclaimed Poland from the Unitarians and Calvinists and Bavaria from the Lutherans, and shed their blood even in England and the New World. It was this Spanish King David who drew across the map of Europe the eternal limits of Protestantism. He had failed to recover England, and a terrible failure it was; most of Holland and Scandinavia also were lost. These misfortunes, however, might not have been irretrievable, but for a less dramatic defeat that Philip endured in France: the accession of the House of Bourbon, following the conversion of Henry of Navarre.

Perhaps the choice was inevitable. Perhaps a Catholic Europe, controlled by Habsburgs even in France (as Philip II desired) would have proved even worse than what actually followed. Nevertheless the Bourbon ascendancy (added to the fact, we must admit, that so many Habsburgs in Germany, Austria and Spain were inferior as men and as Catholics to their illustrious ancestor) was to make impossible the attainment of Philip's dearest hopes. The rivalry of Bourbon against Habsburg, with Protestant England waiting to take advantage of the errors of both, repeatedly sacrificed the best interests of the Church and of the people of Europe. The tendencies of the Bourbon kings toward Gallicanism, their neglect of public interests for sensual indulgence, Richelieu's fatal mistake of ranging France on the anti-Catholic side for nationalistic advantages, the alliance of Habsburg Austria with Protestant England against the Bourbons—these are only a few of the blunders and crimes that led directly, step by step, toward the loss of Catholic political power, the dechristianizing of the masses, the French and Russian Revolutions, and the state of the world today.

The clique of usurers and their hirelings who had ruled England since the time of Henry the Eighth, had struck a deadly blow at the medieval concept of monarchy by the judicial murder of Queen Mary Stuart. They struck another when they cut off the head of Charles I. At the same time consolidating their power over Catholic Ireland, they were prepared, in the Eighteenth Century, to loot and destroy the Catholic empire of France, taking over, by brute force, both Canada and India, but losing, by a stupidity destined to prove very costly in the long run, the colonies which are now the United States of America.

One of the instruments used by the rulers of England to undermine the powers of France was Freemasonry. There is much evidence that something like this secret society, or at least its parent organization existed in the Sixteenth Century, and had a great deal to do with coordinating the international conspiracy against the Catholic Church. The Freemasons themselves claim even greater antiquity; but whether this is true or not, the thing certainly existed in the Seventeenth Century and in something like its present form. It was first brought to America as early as 1658, when fifteen Jewish families arrived at Newport, R. I., from Holland, and proceeded to confer upon one Abraham Moses, in the house of Mordecai Campanall, the three Blue Lodge degrees.[2] After the Hanoverian Revolution of 1688 (and the degradation of the British monarchy to its present state under the aegis of the Freemason William of Orange, financed by a Jewish banker in Amsterdam) the English lodges, which had taken a Jacobite direction little to the taste of their invisible masters, were carefully reformed and reorganized under the direction of a Huguenot parson, Desaguliers, imported for the purpose. Old records were destroyed, and by 1717 all the brothers were safely marshalled under a new Constitution and the leadership of a Grand Lodge, which from then on became a pillar of the figurehead monarchy and the *nouveaux riches* nobles who had risen on the ruins of English Catholicism.[3]

As thus reorganized, the lodges appeared as a definitely anti-

[2] Peter Wiernik, *History of the Jews in America*. New York, 1931, p. 111.

[3] This tendency has continued. On July 1, 1937, King George VI was invested as Past Grand Master of the Grand Lodge of England, at a ceremony attended, according to the United Press, by more than 9,000 Freemasons, representing 3,500 lodges *"all over the world."* The King then invested the United States Ambassador, Robert Worth Bingham, with the rank of Past Grand Senior Warden. President Roosevelt was a Mason of the thirty-second degree when he took office in 1932 (according to the *New York Times* of the morning after the election of that year). It is notorious that Freemasons hold a great many "key positions" in American politics, business and education. American Masonry is far more closely connected with European Masonry than is commonly believed. In a book published in New York in 1930, Sir Alfred Robbins put forth in guarded language what was virtually a proposal for the control of the world through a union of the Masons of all the English speaking countries! (*English Speaking Masonry*, p. 366.)

Catholic force, which pretended, however, to reconcile and amal-
gamate the Catholic faith with all other religions, in a sort of
super religion. They were actually one more secret heretical society,
in its effects dissolvent of real Christianity; and like the secret
Manichee clubs of the Middle Ages, they derived ideologically from
the Gnostics and the Buddhists, even to their Great Architect of
the Universe, who was a sort of secondary god in the quaint
theology of Mani and not by any means the Creator adored by
Hebrews and Christians. Much of this has grown vague in
Masonic lore, and has been replaced by elements borrowed from
Buddist, Jewish and Christian sources, to concoct the all-inclusive
religion of Humanitarianism.

In France the secret force became far more active and more
virulent. It made especial efforts to enlist persons of power, wealth
and influence. Prominent Catholic laymen joined. Even some priests
became members, in a society already weakened by Gallicanism
and Jansenism. The Princess of Lamballe belonged to an order of
female Masons. A second reorganization then occurred, under the
direction of the Grand Orient. The details are naturally obscure,
but certain facts stand out as incontrovertible: (1) Frederic II,
grand master of the Prussian lodges, had a great deal to do with
the matter. (2) The French lodges were "illuminized" by members of a sect organized in Bavaria by "Sparticus" Weishaupt under
the name of the *Illuminati*. This was a revival of the Manichean
secret society of the *Alumbrados,* discovered by the Inquisition
under Cardinal Ximenes and driven out of Spain by Philip the
Second. While the infamous Anacharsis Clootz, who called himself
"the personal enemy of Jesus Christ," went from Germany to
France to get himself elected to the French Assembly, Mirabeau and
other agents of Illuminism carried to the Grand Orient lodges the
pseudo-mystical impulse which was to give a fanatical and bloody
turn to the movement.

The objective of the Grand Orient was the destruction of Catholicism, first in France, and secondly in all Europe. Before the
thunders of revolution could be loosed, however, there were certain
obstacles to be removed. One of the most formidable was the
Society of Jesus. This organization, in spite of perpetual vilifica-

tion and slander, had proved immune from outward corruption or intimidation. The Jesuits were ready if necessary to lay down their lives for the Church of Christ, and did so in countless places. They established schools and colleges so excellent that even Protestants and Jews felt obliged to send their children to them, if they were to get the best possible education. They were the confessors of the kings of Spain and Portugal, and naturally did all they could to keep those countries Catholic, and to guide the consciences of their royal penitents in accord with the revealed truth of Christ and His Church.

Another obstacle was the Spanish Inquisition. True, that institution had never been very active since the death of Philip the Second. Philip III was pious and weak; Philip IV self-indulgent and weak. The Count of Olivares, who had been insolent to Popes in Rome, proved himself, as prime minister, a friend of the Jesuits, but let the Holy Office languish. There seemed no danger of Protestantism in Spain; was it not beginning to decay even in the north? The Inquisition, therefore, became almost an anachronism. In the Seventeenth Century it had punished the quietist Molinos, who had taught the old Manichee hypocrisy which allowed the Perfect and the Pure to commit any carnal act whatever, without sin. Under Philip IV there was only about one *auto* a year, with even fewer executions. Under Philip V, according to Llorente, there were 54 *autos,* while 79 persons were burned alive and 829 penanced, most of them for judaizing—but these figures, like most of Llorente's, are highly exaggerated. One of the famous cases of the eighteenth century was that of two disciples of Molinos. Father Juan de la Vega for several years was confessor and biographer of an abbess named Agueda de Luna, who professed to have ecstacies and visions, but who, on investigation, was shown to be the mother of five children by him, while in the interims he had corrupted other nuns, also members of his little sect. Agueda confessed her deceptions under torture, and died as a result of the *tormentos* (it was one of the rare occurrences of the kind). The other nuns were scattered to various convents, under close surveillance and penance, while Father Vega was kept in prison until his death.[4]

[4] Menendez y Pelayo, *op. cit.,* VI, pp. 107 *et seq.*

The Holy Office did not display the same vigilance toward Jansenism and Freemasonry, which were already making inroads in high circles. The latter was at first of the English variety, particularly after the British navy ruthlessly seized Gibraltar, with the treacherous connivance of Spanish Masonic officers ashore. Finally, the Count of Aranda, prime minister of Charles III, quietly put into effect a "reform" by which all the York Rite lodges, of which he was Grand Master, became affiliated with the French Grand Orient.[5]

Aranda was warmly admired by the Freemason Voltaire, friend of Frederic of Prussia. In his *Dictionnaire philosophique*, Voltaire spoke in eulogistic terms of the Spanish prime minister who had "begun to cut off the heads of the hydra of the Inquisition," [6] and in verse likewise praised the modern Hercules who was cleaning the Augean stables:

> *"Tu verras en Espagne un Alcide nouveau*
> *Vainqueur d'une hydra plus fatale,*
> *Des superstitions déchirant le bandeau,*
> *Plongeant dans la nuit du tombeau,*
> *De l'Inquisition la puissance infernale."* [7]

Voltaire congratulated Aranda on his decree of February 7, 1770, which struck a blow at the Holy Office by depriving it of its jurisdiction over bigamy cases. "All Europe ought to congratulate you on it," he wrote. Pope Pius VI, however, observed that the ministers of Charles III were men without religion.

The Inquisition, next perhaps to the Jesuits, was the *bête noire* of the Masons, Jansenists, Encyclopedists, "broadminded" or political Catholics seeking the favor of men in high places, and all the rest of the shameful crew who were preparing miseries for the Church and for humanity beyond the power of their puny minds to imagine. It was the Company of Jesus, however, that they attacked first. As Voltaire wrote to Helvetius, "Once we have destroyed the Jesuits, we shall have it all our own way with *l'infâme*." A

---

[5] Tirado y Rojas, *La francmasoneria en Espana.*
[6] *Oeuvres completes,* t. xxxiii, p. 421; 1821 ed.
[7] *Ibid.,* t. iv, *Poésies,* p. 172.

thousand lesser and noiser scribblers, many of whom, as Burke noticed, were in the pay of "the monied interest," [8] laid down a barrage from one end of Europe to the other in preparation for the main assault. A remarkable intrigue was set in motion in all the important capitals of Catholic Europe. In Portugal, the prime minister Pombal, whose family name Carvalho had often appeared among lists of judaizers punished by the Inquisition in days gone by, expelled the Jesuits, almost without warning and on a pretext so flimsy that only the most rabid anti-Catholic propagandists still endeavor to defend it. This was in 1759. In France, the Jansenists founded The Merchants Bank to finance books and pamphlets vilifying the Jesuits, and in 1764 the anti-Catholic minister Choiseul obtained (by the aid of the concubine of Louis XV) a parliamentary decree giving the Jesuits the choice of repudiating their Institute and their vows or leaving the country. Only five of the 4,000 French Jesuits shrank from the bitter test. Two years later, the Count of Aranda, champion of royal absolutism over the Church, champion, in short, of the ancient aberration of the *Fraticelli,* and forerunner of the modern totalitarian state—persuaded the Bourbon king Charles III to sign a decree expelling the 6,000 Spanish Jesuits on trumped up charges without a hearing, much less a trial.

The stage was now set for the final *coup.* All the influence of the Bourbon courts was exerted at Rome to induce Pope Clement XIII to suppress the order founded by Saint Ignatius. This the holy pontiff refused to do. When he died in 1769, the influence of the Bourbon kings, that is to say their Masonic ministers, supported the candidacy of a known enemy of the Jesuits, Cardinal Gangan-

---

8 "For the same purpose for which they intrigued with princes, they cultivated, in a distinguished manner, the monied interest of France. . . . Writers, especially when they act in a body, have great influence on the public mind; the alliance, therefore of these writers with the monied interest had no small effect in removing the popular odium and envy which attended that species of wealth. These writers, like the propagators of all novelties, pretended to a great zeal for the poor and the lower orders, whilst in their satires they rendered hateful, by every exaggeration, the faults of courts, of nobility, and of priesthood. They became a sort of demagogues. They served as a link to unite, in favour of one object, obnoxious wealth to restless and desperate poverty."—*Reflections on the Revolution in France,* p. 109. Everyman Library ed.

elli, who was elected as Pope Clement XIV. Although he had previously told the French Ambassador that he favored suppression of the Order, he now saw the matter from a different perspective, and put off the decision which the enemies of the Faith desired. Finally the Bourbon ministers threatened him with a schism, and a new disruption of the Christian unity; and thinking to avoid this evil, Clement signed the brief which deprived 22,000 Jesuits, in all parts of the world, of the organization and direction which the enemies of the Catholic Church so feared.

In a France weakened by the wars of Louis XIV, the blunders and extravagances of Louis XV, and the broadminded folly of many Jansenist priests, some of whom were Freemasons, the obscure international forces so long at work were now able, in a few years, to produce the hideous butcheries of the French Revolution. Then, out of the dragons' teeth so liberally scattered, arose the legions of Napoleon, which became a threat to the very men who had planned the evil sowing; to Protestant England and her international bankers as well as to Catholic Spain.

When Napoleon invaded the peninsula and set his fatuous brother Joseph on the throne of Fernando and Isabel, the Spanish people were suffering from a deadly moral sickness. For several decades anti-Catholic influences from France had been at work. Freemasons, Jansenist priests holding fat benefices, *literati,* encyclopedists seeking popular applause, members of economic and philanthropic societies based upon philosophies purely materialistic and hence anti-Christian, political pensioners of the conqueror of Europe and of the lodges, all formed a demoralizing party who would now constitute a "Fifth Column," but in Spain were called derisively the *Afrancesados*—"the Frenchies," or more accurately, "the Frenchified."

Their patient boring within opened a way for the most powerful military machine then existing. Napoleon, convoking a rump Cortes at Bayonne, proclaimed, "Spaniards, your monarchy is old, my mission is to renew it! I will improve your institutions and let you enjoy, if you aid me, the benefits of a reform without which you will experience great losses, disorders and convulsions." His brother Joseph, philosopher-king of the lodges, promised religious toleration; and when Madrid capitulated in December, 1808, it was on condition that the Catholic religion be preserved, and that the lives, property and rights of the. Church and the clergy be respected. "Religion," said Joseph expansively to the Inquisitor General Ethenard, "is the foundation of public morality and prosperity."

The Spaniards had hardly laid down their arms when Napoleon decreed the abolition of the Holy Office, and the suppression of two thirds of the convents of Spain. He suppressed the historic monastery of the Dominicans at Valladolid, on the pretext that various Frenchman had been assassinated in it—a charge utterly without foundation. As soon as Joseph was enthroned, he did away with the monastic orders and confiscated their property, and some of that of the seculars, for the benefit of the royal treasury.

This was the opening wedge of a policy which, if it had continued, would have left Spain as helpless as France against the Nineteenth Century intrigues of the atheists and communists who would presently be revealed as directors of the Grand Orient. But the Spanish people, thanks perhaps to the reserves of strength stored up by the heroic labors and sacrifices of *los reyes católicos* and Philip the Second, were able once more to regain their moral balance and to cast out foreign and oriental venoms, dissolvent of the Christian culture and traditions that alone had made them great. Seeing the Voltairian abbots and scribblers, the bad friars and libertine priests flocking to the French cause, hearing of the barbarous shooting of the eighty-five-year-old Bishop of Coria by order of Marshal Soult, the burning of the Cathedral of Solsona, the raping and murder of the nuns of Uclés by French troops in 1809, and the shootings *en masse,* by command of Marshal Suchet, of friars and theological students in Murviedro, Castellon and Valencia (not to mention the pillage of priceless works of art, and of the archives of Simancas, some of which have never been returned)—the Spanish people reacted against the neo-pagans from the north as their ancestors had reacted against the Mohammedans and Jews. The good Spanish priests and monks, that is to say the vast majority, placed themselves at the head of the war of liberation against Napoleon and fought him off for four years, until victory was achieved.

In the Napoleonic conflict, however, the Spanish Inquisition came to an end; and the instrument of its death was Father Llorente.

He was born March 30, 1756, at Rincon del Soto, near Calahorra, in one of the families discreetly referred to by official biographers as of noble origin but reduced circumstances. Left an orphan, he inherited a modest fortune at sixteen, and was educated by his paternal uncle, a priest of Calahorra, who sent him to study law at Zaragoza. He then went to Madrid to seek his fortune, and there began to publish *"essais dramatiques,"* and even two or three pieces for the theatre, which however, remained unpublished.

He had received the tonsure at fourteen. At twenty-four he became a doctor, and (by dispensation) received Holy Orders. Soon after this he became an advocate for the Supreme Council of Castile, and a member of the royal academy of ecclesiastical history. The Bishop of Calahorra then appointed him *promotor fiscal* of the Holy Inquisition, and vicar general of the diocese.

Up to this time he had accepted the Inquisition, like most Spaniards, as a good and necessary institution. But he was soon to part company with it. It was about this time that he lost his faith in the Holy Roman Catholic Church, by reading the subtle and destructive sophistries of Descartes, and conversing with a "foreign savant" who was then in Calahorra; and by a coincidence not surprising, he began to take a different view of the Holy Office.

There is some lack of agreement in French and Spanish accounts of all this. Michaud tells us, for example, that Llorente "separated from the Spanish clergy," and "gave up ultramontane principles and scholastic and peripatetic doctrines," for the foreign savant persuaded him "that a great part of his knowledge rested on prejudices, and that there is no authority outside of us competent to judge the reason." In 1785 however, he compromised with his new principles to the extent of accepting a lucrative post as commissary of the Holy Office of Logroño; and about then he began to explore the mystery of the iniquity of the Inquisition, which meanwhile "gave to its young minister many hours of leisure which he devoted to literary and historical works." He won favor with the Count of Florida Blanca, the wily choleric old man who had persuaded Pope Clement XIV to suppress the Society of Jesus, and through him became a friend of the duchess of Sotomayor, first lady to the Queen of King Charles IV, who got him a post at court. He was one of the executors of this noblewoman's will, and tutor of her nephew. Thanks in part to her influence also, he became Secretary General of the Inquisition (1789), canon of the Cathedral of Calahorra, member of the Academy of Sevilla, and literary censor. The intrigues of his rivals forced him out of Madrid, we are told, in 1791.[9]

The Spanish version is that he had become a Freemason, even while taking a salary from the Inquisition and when bound by oath to maintain the Holy Roman Catholic Faith. Possibly the "foreign savant" at Calahorra had something to do with that. The young liberal then attached himself to the forward-looking, pro-French party of Jovellanos, a talented and probably misguided Catholic, the political foe of Godoy. When the latter came into power, Llorente, the apostle of freedom, sued for his favor and won it by publishing an historical essay attacking the liberties of the Basque provinces. True to the same instincts, he gravitated into the party of King Joseph Bonaparte, and after the French occupation put forth various *folletos* in which he branded the Spanish Catholic patriots as vile common *canaille,* paid by English gold, though he himself was not ashamed to be paid by French gold and subsidized by the French Freemasons. It was the French, oddly enough, who removed him from office as Secretary of the Inquisition, accusing him of a "subtraction" (the modern euphemism is "irregularity") of 11,000,000 *reales.* The crime was not proved, but Llorente did not return to his old office. On leaving, he gathered up all the priceless records of the Inquisition, burned those which were favorable to it, and put aside those that would be useful later for his *Histoire Critique de l'Inquisition.* He then turned to various literary works until his political star should rise again.

The first two of these were revealing. Llorente's ability as a writer was on a par with his character as a man and a Catholic. In a dry and graceless style, this propagandist for freedom exemplified a fact often confirmed in history: that liberals who cry out that the Church should be stripped of her functions for the

<hr>

[9] Michaud, *Biographie Universelle Ancienne et Moderne,* t. xxiii, p. 629.

sake of human liberty almost invariably end by conferring the same powers on some form of political despotism. As the *Fraticelli* fawned upon the medieval Emperor, so the liberal Freemasons flattered the omnipotent state of Napoleon, as they would later exalt the tyrannies of Socialism and Communism. It was perhaps inevitable, then, that Llorente's *Colección diplomatica de varios papeles antiguos y modernos sobre dispensas matrimoniales y otros puntos de disciplina eclesiastica* should prove to be a regalistic, jansenistic tract urging the thesis that "the supreme civil power is the only one which can originally [10] impose impediments to matrimony"—a principle that the councillors of King Joseph began to apply by ordering the few bishops who obeyed them to dispense from all sorts of impediments. Llorente next wrote a tract attempting to justify the interference of the State in matters of ecclesiastical discipline by appealing to antique Visigothic precedents.

In 1812 he read, in the Academy of History, a *Memorial* seeking to prove that the Inquisition (which had been overwhelmingly supported by public opinion for more than three centuries, else it could never have endured in that country of individualists) was a tyranny imposed in opposition to the popular will. This was used as a springboard on which a Commission of the Cortes, appointed to consider constitutional changes, took the bold leap that had long been in preparation in the lodges. Admitting that "it is the general will of the nation that the Catholic religion be kept in its purity, protected by wise and just laws, without permitting the profession of any other cult in the realm," the Commissioners reviewed the history of the Holy Office, cited the documents of Llorente, asserted that the institution had been founded illegally and had been inimical to the bishops' jurisdiction. This concern of the Freethinkers for the rights of the bishops was extremely touching; but even more ironic was the invocation of the very argument which Fernando and Isabel, in establishing the Inquisition, had used against its first victims: the Holy Office, said the Commission, was a sovereignty within a sovereignty, a state within the state, a jurisdiction exempt from the laws of the land and depending on the Roman Curia. They proposed to restore the ancient

[10] *Sic: "originalmente."*

law of the land, but were careful not to say—and many of the public did not notice the omission—that the old *Partidas* had furnished the fundamentals of the legislation of the Holy Office regarding heretics.

A tremendous debate followed in the Cortes. In the end the Freemasons and the *Afrancesados* had their way. The Holy Office was temporarily and feebly revived, but came to a definite conclusion with the Revolution of 1820.

Llorente meanwhile was taken unawares by the withdrawal of the French in 1813, and had to pick up his stolen papers and depart in a great hurry for France. He had finished only two volumes of his *Histoire Critique de l'Inquisition,* and was compelled to forego his plan to publish it first in Castilian. This did not prevent his selling the archives of the Holy Office of Aragon to the *Bibliothèque Nationale* of Paris, where Spanish scholars must go for such important *dossiers* as those of Antonio Pérez and the murderers of Saint Peter Arbues. The book finally appeared in French, and of course was hailed by the liberal foes of Spain and of the Church everywhere as a monumental and conclusive piece of scholarship.

Nothing but the highly controversial nature of the subject, and the service rendered, under the name of liberty, to the foul cause that controlled so many professors, reviewers and lecturers of the world, can explain the influence of this work in crystallizing the false legend of the Inquisition which is invoked by enemies of the Church even to this day. Señor Menendez y Pelayo has well remarked upon the contemptible erudition of the man, his puerile judgment, his dry pedantic style without vigor or grace; his bad arrangement, which, dealing with material rich in dramatic scenes, atrocious crimes, and terrible passions and conflicts, is incapable of doing more than string together papal briefs, royal decrees and letters of councillors, in the manner of a lawyer's process, obscure, turgid and incoherent. "His philosophy of history reduces itself to a long Masonic sermon . . . and to the high and transcendental idea that the Inquisition was not established to maintain the purity of the faith, nor even perchance by religious fanaticism, but to enrich the government with confiscations." [11] It is full of exaggerations and inaccuracies; it even contains a chapter on the unfortunate Don Carlos, who had nothing whatever to do with the history of the Inquisition—though for some reason, which may be significant, he has been commemorated by the Spanish lodges in modern times as a martyr of Freemasonry.[12] Among the other "victims" of the Holy Office, Llorente places Clemente Sánchez de Vercial, who died about a hundred years before it was established in Castile.

The anti-Catholic and prejudiced tone and purpose of the *opus* were so evident that when it was published in Paris, the Archbishop there suspended Father Llorente's faculties of preaching and hearing confessions, and forbade him to teach in colleges or private houses. Llorente thereupon threw himself openly into the arms of the Freemasons with whom for years he had secretly been cooperating. For some time he lived on money they furnished. Yet it was characteristic of this sly and grovelling man to make one more effort to regain his post as canon of Toledo and his benefices at Calahorra and Rincón de Soto, by flattering King Ferdinand VII, even to the extent of forging, "in the manner of a hungry king of arms," a genealogical family tree in which he claimed the relationship of His Majesty, in the thirty-fourth degree, with Sigerdus, King of the Saxons in the Fifth Century.[13]

Ferdinand had the good sense to pay no attention to him, and Spaniards generally treated his attempts to repair his fortunes at the expense of the Church he had betrayed with the scorn they deserved. Llorente then turned to the profitable field of American filibustering. To fan the revolutionary ardor of the Masonic conspirators who were preparing to rob Spain of her glorious American empire he published a new edition of Las Casas, with a memorial by the French revolutionary bishop Gregoire.

For the benefit of the new American republics, he then produced a work so obviously Protestant from A to Z that he did not have courage to sign his name to it, but represented himself as editor for

---

[11] *Op. cit.,* Vol. VII, pp. 17-20.

[12] The relation of Don Carlos to some of the anti-Catholic conspirators in the Netherlands, probably as their dupe, is discussed at length in my *Philip II.*

[13] Menendez y Pelayo, *loc. cit.*

an anonymous author. This was his *Discourses on a Religious Constitution Considered as Part of the National Community* (Bordeau, 1821); *Its Author, an American; given to the light by Don Juan Antonio Llorente, Doctor in Sacred Canon Law, etc.* With it he printed the censure of the Vicar General of Barcelona, and his own reply. He acknowledged that the plan of "an American" was based upon the Civil Constitution of the Clergy in France, and that it went hand in hand with the Protestant systems. Like the heretics of the Middle Ages and those of the Sixteenth Century, Llorente denied all hierarchy in the Church, and asserted that "the legislative power of the Church belongs to the general congregation of all Christians." He would limit dogma to the Apostles' Creed, allow the civil power to dissolve marriages, reduce confession from a precept to a counsel, forbid the Church to compel her members to receive Communion at Easter or any other time, annul the perpetual vows of religious communities, allow the marriage of priests and bishops, and finally, have the church ruled by the Supreme National Government, under whom the archbishops would be only public servants, having nothing to do with the Pope.

Llorente was now in his sixties. Nothing remained for him but to befoul his old age with a *Political Portrait of the Popes* (in which he not only swallowed the oft-discredited myth of the Popess Joan, but gave the months and days of her pontificate, and made Princess Matilda the concubine, God help us, of Saint Gregory); and a Castilian translation, to which he signed his name, of Louvet's pornographic French novel, *The Adventures of the Little Baron de Faublas.*

These last two exhibitions from a sexagenarian priest were too much even for the Parisian government; and Llorente was officially requested to leave the country. Fortunately for him, he was able to take advantage of the amnesty granted to political exiles by the liberal Spanish government in 1820. Early in 1823 he returned to his native land, only to die a few days after reaching Madrid.

With this contemptible modern Judas there passed forever the institution on which he had lived as long as he could, and which he had hated, one must infer from his works in general, not so much for the rigors that he exaggerated or imagined, as for the support it lent to the imperishable doctrines of that true historic Christianity which in his twisted and darkened soul he despised and sought to pervert. The Spanish Inquisition was dead, and dead forever. It belonged to phases of Catholic history in Spain just as definitely as the slaughter of idolaters and blasphemers belonged to a certain epoch of the ancient Hebrews.

Today the Roman Inquisition still persists as the Congregation of the Holy Office. Some such tribunal is necessary to a Church which believes in the distinction between right and wrong, true and false, black and white, and which is charged with the duty of protecting its members from deception, even by impostors pretending holiness within their own ranks. Such functions of the Medieval Inquisition are permanent, and will always be exercised by the Holy Office and the Bishops. The other functions, cast as a reproach against the Church even today, were incidents of time and place, and are not peculiarly or essentially Catholic. They existed vigorously only in comparatively short periods of the Church's long history, and in a few of the many Catholic countries. I have never met a Catholic who wanted the medieval Inquisition reëstablished anywhere; if I did, I should suspect him of being *non compos mentis*. Not even the Ku Klux Klan can really expect that the procession of the Green Cross, the *auto de fe,* and the victim strangled or screaming on the funeral pyre, will ever again appear upon the stage of this world.

Many other horrors have appeared instead, and will appear; and in justice to the memory of the men who thought they were doing their duty to God and humanity in carrying on the Inquisition, it is to be noticed that they are precisely the aberrations and iniquities which that maligned institution suppressed wherever it could. Consider some of these devils of our own time: every one of them has been condemned by the Catholic Church for centuries, and was fought tooth and nail by the Inquisition:

(1) *The isolation of the human soul from God.* The indifference and godlessness of our day are directly traceable to the triumph of Manicheanism under the guise of Sixteenth Century Protestantism. Many thoughtful Protestants are now beginning to see that the Revolt inflicted a ghastly wound upon Christianity without add-

ing anything to it. Such positive Christian elements as the Reformers taught were already in Catholicism. As for the aberrations—Luther's doctrine of grace, Calvin's predestination—how
many who call themselves Protestants today believe in them? An
Episcopalian will tell you he does not believe in the divinity of
Christ; a Methodist will say he believes in the existence of some
vague Life Force, not a personal God. With each generation the
descendants of the men and women who were led from the Catholic fold by plausible reformers promising them primitive Christianity, become less and less concerned with any religion, and more
the prey of Communism, Fascism or some other panacea with new
false hopes of creating something permanently good on the frail
structure of human nature alone. These will not even listen to the
ancient wisdom of the Catholic Church; as Mr. Chesterton wrote
somewhere, "They are tired of hearing what they have never
heard."

(2) *Moral confusion and nihilism.* There is and can be no objective and eternal standard of conduct, except that of Christ, as
interpreted by His Church. All the old sins and follies that the
Church began to drive into exterior darkness two thousand years
ago, have come back to destroy the peace of individuals and the
harmony of society. Divorce is destroying the family, murder the
individual. The free love of the Beghards and the Alumbrados is
corrupting the young. What is the prevalent craze for self-destruc-
tion but a manifestation of the old Manichean despair of life?
And what is the fatal race-suicide known euphemistically as "birth
control" but the old nastiness of the Manichees, born of cowardice,
sensuality, distrust of life itself and the Author of life? Usury, which
the medieval schoolmen called theft, and capitalism, which in its
reprehensible form they identified as one of the seven deadly sins
(greed), are defended by dull college professors in the name of
economic law; while the enslaved masses everywhere pay tribute
to the modern Mammon.

(3) *Intellectual confusion.* The Catholic Church speaks with
authority in our world in defense of the human reason against
a thousand sophistries having their origin in obscure feelings or
prejudices. It has become the fashion in certain academic circles

to speak disdainfully of logic itself, and of the law of cause and effect, as if these were relics of medieval barbarism. It was not merely a coincidence that a Manichean thought, or rather feeling, has appeared extensively in our literature, and in some of the best of it, wherever the Protestant Revolt has prepared for the return of darkness and slavery. Consider the Manichean attitudes in some of Thomas Hardy's work—especially in *Jude the Obscure,* in *The Return of the Native,* and in that frightful sneer at the end of *Tess;* in Ibsen's *Master Builder* and *Hedda Gabler;* in Shelley's *Defense of Poetry;* in the *Autobiography* of Mark Twain; in such plays as *The Piper* of Josephine Preston Peabody, *The Scarecrow* of Percy Mackaye, and a great deal of O'Neill's work; even in that calm Victorian, Tennyson, who puts into the mouth of a Catholic King a sentiment that would have set Bernard Gui on the trail of any Albigensian:

> "For why is all around us here,
> As if some lesser god had made the world,
> But had not force to make it as he would,
> Until the High God enter from beyond . . . ?"

Not to press the point too far—for some liberty must be allowed the fancies of poets!—this and much more that could be mentioned is clearly symptomatic of the sickness which afflicts a world which will not turn to Christ.

(4) *Totalitarianism.* Is not the present evolution of government a retrogression toward heresies that the medieval Inquisitors combatted with all their might? Communism, first propagated by the Freemasons on the ruins of Protestantism, finally set up in Russia the absolute state which the *Fraticelli* had invoked (in so far as the state of science and communications would permit them to envisage it); it was a perversion also of their concept of primitive Christianity, without private property. The Nazi State, set up partly in imitation of Mussolini's Fascism, as a natural reaction to Communism, had also another parentage. The ideal of the omnipotent absolute state, for whose sake the individual exists, was expressed in very similar terms on behalf of Kaiserism by Bernhardi, in 1911; and Bernhardi's teacher was Treitchke, who in turn

acknowledged his indebtedness to Martin Luther.[14] Thus in two different directions we trace the origins of the Totalitarian State, toward which, by imitation or reaction, the governments of the whole world are tending, to breaches made by medieval heretics in the walls of the City of God, in despite of the watchdogs of the Inquisition.

The list could be extended. All the evils that the Inquisition sought to repress, and did in great measure repress, have returned to the modern world, grown great and ravening, to feed upon our children. What then of the evils incidental to the Inquisition itself—torture, loss of liberty and even life, occasional deceit and hypocrisy? Are we better in those regards? Can any one think of the torture cells maintained by the Reds in Spain in 1936-7 to drive their victims mad,[15] of the unspeakable butcheries of civilians and priests by both Germans and Russians in Poland in 1939, of the unrestrained villainy of modern warfare, of all our nightmare of hypocrisy, abortion, child-suicide, unpunished murder, and what is worse even than all these monstrosities, disdain for the Deity Himself, without wondering whether we have really progressed to a point where we can look patronizingly upon the memory of a Torquemada?

All the worst miseries which men everywhere endure today, while they begin "withering away for fear and expectation of what shall come"—famine and pestilence and civil wars whose shadows

[14] I have developed this idea further in an article published in The Sign, with quotations from Luther and others, in February, 1940.

[15] The cells constructed by the "Loyalist" Reds "were described as hollow cement blocks four feet high and containing a cement chair and bed, built in a slanting position so that it was impossible for a prisoner to sit or lie down for more than a minute at a time. Raised cement blocks were arranged in a crazy-quilt fashion on the floor to prevent prisoners from standing up. The prosecutor (in the Cik trial) charged that the Loyalists placed rings in the eyelids of prisoners to keep them open in the glare of powerful lights. Some of the witnesses testified that prisoners were denied food and water and were flogged, sometimes while suspended head down from the ceiling or while cold water was showered upon them. Witnesses said the cells were painted with hundreds of yellow diagonal lines, large and small white-red-blue and yellow spots, broad black lines and scores of black and white cubes."—Associated Press despatch from Barcelona, June 13, 1939, published in the New York Sun and other newspapers. Torquemada would have shrunk from the very idea of such diabolical ingenuity.

may already be discerned on the dim walls of the future—all these have been foretold by the Popes of modern times, one after another pointing out the causes that must lead to such effects, and pleading with mankind to turn away from them to the only possible remedy, held forth by Christ in the Catholic Church. Against all the progressive steps in the disintegration of the European Order, from the Manichees to the Communists and other state worshippers, the Vicars of Christ have uttered solemn and deliberate warnings, based upon ample information. Very soon after the reorganization of the Freemasonry by the Grand Lodge of England, in preparation for the slow poisoning of Catholic France and Catholic Spain, the situation was clearly seen at Rome; and in 1738, Pope Clement XII uttered the first formal denunciation of this particular heresy, this oriental dissolvent in modern guise. "If they were not doing evil, they would not fear the light," he said of all societies, without any exception, of the Masonic type or affiliation. He forbade Catholics to join them, favor, support, shelter, or defend them in any way, or even to receive the members into their homes. Any Catholic so doing was excommunicated by the very fact, and the ban could be removed only by the Pope himself, save in danger of death. This, as we have seen, did not deter vain, ambitious or stupid Catholics, even among the clergy here and there, from being drawn into an organization which pretended to be social and philanthropic, and masked its real aims and nature from all its neophytes, from all except a few initiates. The Popes of the Eighteenth and Nineteenth Centuries continued to raise their voices against the stealthy advances of this mystery of iniquity. Pius XII accused the Freemasons of being the chief causes of the revolutionary upheavals (antichristian in their direction) of Europe. Gregory XVI said they were guilty of sacrilege, infamy and blasphemy, and promoted heresy and revolution. Pius IX applied to them the words that Christ addressed to the scribes and pharisees who sought His destruction, "You are of your father the devil, and the works of your father you will do." He called them the wolves in sheep's clothing against whom Our Lord and the Apostles had warned the first Christians. In another letter he referred to them as "the Synagogue of Satan . . . whose object is to blot out the Church of

Christ, were it possible, from the face of the Universe." Renewing the condemnations of his predecessors, he explicitly included the Freemasons in America "and in whatever part of the world they may be."

Pope Leo XIII warned the world that Freemasonry was the real source and center of Communist and Atheist propaganda. "In this insane and wicked endeavor," he wrote, "we may almost see the implacable hatred and spirit of revenge with which Satan himself is inflamed against Jesus Christ." In that same magnificent encyclical he cried out to all Catholics, laymen as well as priests, to "tear the mask off the face" of the hidden menace. If not, he said, *"the ruin and overthrow of all things must necessarily follow."* [16]

This tremendous prophecy, deliberately uttered by the Vicar of Christ, and now being fulfilled with terrible literalness as the flimsy structure built on the sands of the great apostasy of the Sixteenth Century comes crashing down about us, has of course been generally disregarded by the world, as the prophecies of Christ were disregarded. Other profound observations from Leo and his successors have met the same characteristically Christian fate; nevertheless they remain as true as truth.

It was Pius XI who pointed out the close spiritual affinity of Liberalism and Socialism, even when they waged a sham battle across the arena of the world. "Let us bear in mind," he wrote in *Quadragesimo Anno,* "that the parent of this cultural Socialism was Liberalism, and that its offspring will be Bolshevism." He had no more regard for one of these antichristian aberrations than for the other. Liberalism, he said, had shown as early as 1891 "its utter impotence to find a right solution of the social question," while Socialism "would have exposed human society to still graver dangers by offering a remedy much more disastrous than the evil it designed to cure." [17]

This great Pope remarked that since the time of Leo XIII the "capitalistic economic regime" had "penetrated everywhere"; and that "it is patent that in our days not alone is wealth accumulated, but immense power and despotic economic domination are con-

[16] Encyclical, *Humanum genus,* 1884.
[17] *Quadragesimo Anno,* 1931.

centrated in the hands of a few, and that those few are frequently not the owners, but only the trustees and directors of invested funds, who administer them at their good pleasure. This power becomes particularly irresistible when exercised by those who, because they hold and control money, are able also to govern credit and determine its allotment, for that reason supplying, so to speak, the life-blood to the entire economic body, and grasping, as it were, in their hands the very soul of production, so that no one dare breathe against their will. This accumulation of power, the characteristic note of the modern economic order, is a natural result of limitless free competition which permits the survival of those only who are the strongest, which often means those who fight most relentlessly, who pay least heed to the dictates of conscience. This concentration of power has led to a threefold struggle for domination. First, there is the struggle for dictatorship in the economic sphere itself; then, the fierce battle to acquire control of the state, so that its resources and authority may be abused in the economic struggles. Finally, the clash between states themselves. . . The state, which should be the supreme arbiter, ruling in kingly fashion far above all party contention, intent only upon justice and the common good, has become instead a slave, bound over to the service of human passion and greed." [18]

Elsewhere, of course, Pius condemned the totalitarian theory which, reacting against the evil here described, rushed to the opposite extreme, and erroneously held that the individual existed for the benefit of the state. None of these panaceas could reach the center of the disorder; they were all, in fact, so many forms of Socialism, one fighting the other, but all tending toward a common end. With characteristic acuteness, Pius noticed that since the time of Leo XIII Socialism had broken up into various forms, of which he condemned even the most moderate.

"The question arises, or is unwarrantably proposed in certain quarters, whether the principles of Christian truth also could not be somewhat moderated and attenuated, so as to meet Socialism, as it were, halfway upon a common ground. Some are engaged by the empty hope of gaining Socialists in this way to our cause. But

[18] *Ibid.*

such hopes are vain. Those who wish to be apostles among the Socialists should preach the Christian truth whole and entire, openly and sincerely, without any connivance with error. If they wish in truth to be heralds of the Gospel, let them convince Socialists that their demands, in so far as they are just, are defended much more cogently by the principles of Christian faith, and are promoted much more efficaciously by the power of Christian charity. . . . Whether Socialism be considered as a doctrine, or as an historical fact, or as a movement, if it really remain Socialism, it cannot be brought into harmony with the dogmas of the Catholic Church, even after it has yielded to truth and justice in the points We have mentioned; the reason being that it conceives human society in a way utterly alien to Christian truth.

"According to Christian doctrine, Man, endowed with a social nature, is placed here on earth in order that he may spend his life in society, and under authority ordained by God, that he may develop and evolve to the full all his faculties to the praise and glory of his Creator; and that, by fulfilling faithfully the duties of his station, he may attain to temporal and eternal happiness. Socialism, on the contrary, entirely ignorant of or unconcerned about this sublime end both of individuals and of society, affirms that living in community was instituted merely for the sake of advantages which it brings to mankind. Goods are produced more efficiently by a suitable distribution of labor than by the scattered efforts of individuals. Hence the Socialists argue that economic production, of which they see only the material side, must necessarily be carried on collectively, and that because of this necessity men must surrender and submit themselves wholly to society with a view to the production of wealth. Indeed, the possession of the greatest possible amount of temporal goods is esteemed so highly, that man's higher goods, not excepting liberty, must, they claim, be subordinated and even sacrificed to the exigencies of efficient production. They affirm that the loss of human dignity, which results from these socialized methods of production, will be easily compensated for by the abundance of goods produced in common and accruing to the individual who can turn them at his will to the comforts and culture of life.

Society, therefore, as the Socialist conceives it, is, on the one hand, impossible and unthinkable without the use of compulsion of the most excessive kind: on the other it fosters a false liberty, since in such a scheme no place is found for true social authority, which is not based on temporal and material advantages, but descends from God alone, the Creator and Last End of all things. If, like all errors, Socialism contains a certain element of truth (and this the Sovereign Pontiffs have never denied), it is nevertheless founded upon a doctrine of human society peculiarly its own, which is opposed to true Christianity. . . No one can be at the same time a sincere Catholic and a true Socialist." [19]

Since Pius XI wrote those words in 1931, the nations of the world generally have taken long steps toward various forms of Socialism, which, however different they appeared on first view, are more and more revealing themselves as essentially the same. Communism, the most radical and patently godless form, was not too remote ideologically from its pretended rival Nazi-Socialism, to lie down beside it in the same foul nest, when it suited both to beget a second great war. Other nations, loving freedom, have been conquered and drawn into the two Socialist orbits. Still others have imitated Socialist regimes by reaction, or by military necessity. Few have been able to maintain fully the sacredness of human personality. The tiny nations of Portugal and Ireland, both thoroughly Catholic, are glorious exceptions. Of Spain I have high hopes; may the Catholic spirit of General Franco prevail, and not certain others, very different and very crafty, which still exist in the country and even in high places, hungry for power. England, while fighting Hitler, has kept a friendly hand mysteriously outstretched toward his partner, Stalin; and whatever the outcome of the present war, is likely to emerge from it shackled to some form of Socialism.

Here in the United States Socialism has made more cautious but none the less evident gains. It is rather amusing, and at the same time depressing, to see that likable Socialist Mr. Norman Thomas denouncing both Mr. Roosevelt and Mr. Willkie as champions of peace-time conscription, which he says (and I think rightly) must lead toward dictatorship, and to realize at the same

[19] *Ibid.*

time that both these gentlemen are fundamentally (that is to say spiritually) as Socialistic as he is. If we judge not by what a man says he is or even believes he is, but by the antithesis set up by Pope Pius XI as a test of spirits, this conclusion becomes inescapable. Mr. Roosevelt has tried to save the country by curtailing production. Mr. Willkie proposes to do it by speeding up production. Yet both these Liberals, as they proudly call themselves, are interested primarily in *production;* in the material, in the things of this world. It is difficult, of course, to see how a politician could wholly free himself from such concerns, and I am not criticizing either, or discussing any issues, political or economic, between them—whoever is elected will be entitled to our obedience, under the Constitution, and no doubt will do his best according to his lights. I would only suggest that neither has the lights necessary to solve the social problem. (It is true that both have spoken reverently in public of Divine Providence; but so, for that matter has Hitler; so have the politicians of every country, except godless Russia.) Not too much must be expected from these well-meaning statesmen. They are children of a Liberalism evolving rapidly into Socialism. Both are high in the ranks of a secret society proscribed and abhorred by the Catholic Church, and denounced by Pope Leo XIII as the true source of Socialism and Communism, and the general corruption of European and world society. They are servants of the same invisible masters, to whose obedience they are bound by oaths—masters who may not even be in America, but in Europe or Asia; masters of whose exact identity they may themselves be ignorant. When they speak of "Democracy," one must remember this background, and the fact that the elastic word has been used by many Liberals to include even the tyranny of Soviet Russia. Can Democracy be anything but a farce among men, when some of them, including the most influential, belong to a secret society whose real aims and principles are concealed from the others and when these aims and principles have been repeatedly disclosed as political and anti-Christian? The French Catholics, in the sad clarifying light of catastrophe, have recently found the answer to this question. As Our Holy Father Pope Pius XII said in welcoming the French Ambassador after the tragedy of last summer, "Like lightning which flashes through heavy clouds, the devastating lights of war . . . have torn from the eyes of all careful and sincere observers that veil of prejudices which for half a century the voice of the Church, and especially the reiterated warnings of the last Popes, Our venerated predecessors, did not succeed in penetrating . . . May the lessons of this bitter period result in acts which permit us to hope in the future for a revival of Christian spirit, particularly in the education of youth . . ." and "the creation of a new Christian order. . . . When will this desired hour arrive? God preserves the secret of it; but We beseech Him to hasten its advent."

All this is part of a universal conflict between the Church of Christ and the Prince of This World. All other conflicts are either subsidiary to this or camouflages for it. Just now there seems to be a deadly strife between international capitalism, intrenched in the United States and gradually leading this country toward a State Socialism or (what amounts to the same thing) toward a State Capitalism, and, on the other side, the seemingly more godless and goldless forms of Socialism beyond the seas. Yet if Nazi-Socialism and Bolshevism, after so violent a sham battle, could so speedily come to terms, for a purpose convenient to both, what is to prevent this American Socialism, now in the making and already accepted and propagated by the dominant educational forces of this country, from arriving at mutually agreeable arrangements with both the Soviet and the Nazi forms of Socialism, whenever it may suit the real leaders on both sides to do so? Within a generation we have seen our Liberal politicians denounce the Soviet, cultivate friendly relations with it, and denounce it again—this time more coyly. As the world grows smaller in time, may not all the forms of Socialism be gathered together by skilful hands into a World State, such as many Masonic writers have advocated, and the League of Nations sought to achieve? It is not only conceivable, but probable; for all forms of Socialism (even if some still call themselves Democracies) will be animated by a single obscure but powerful principle: the worship of the material, which is and always must be the negation of Christianity. Here, then, by a masterly antithesis, Pius XI has cast a strong light upon the shapes of things to come.

It is all the more revealing when it shows us only the recurrence upon a larger stage of a deathless drama that happened long ago. Christ still lives in His Mystical Body, the Church, as truly as in the human body he took from Our Lady; and when the time comes for Him to be crucified again in His Church, depend upon it, Pilate and Herod that day will find a way to patch up their differences, some Caiaphas will cry, "Crucify Him! We have no king but Caesar!" and there will always be found some Judas to give the kiss of death.

Admittedly (perhaps my wish is father to this thought) we may by some miracle escape that fate, here in America. Perhaps despite their affiliations, Mr. Roosevelt or Mr. Willkie, as political Catholic admirers of each will tell us, will be led in the right direction by a divine hand. Again, perhaps not. Only the future can reveal this. Meanwhile this much is certain: the United States, in a very few years, will be either a Catholic country (and therefore a free country) or a Socialist country, (and therefore a slave country). "He who is not with Me is against Me." History demonstrates the unfailing truth of this dilemma.

Here on the last edge and in the twilight of the world, the stage is set for the reënactment of an ancient tragedy—or can it this time be a comedy? Here are all the actors who have appeared over and over again in that tragedy in Europe. Here we have most of the Freemasons of the world, most of the Jews, most of the gold and its masters; Parthians and Medes and Elamites—men gathered together from all nations under the sun, speaking one language, leading a common life; and among them heirs of all the isms and heresies that the Catholic Church has denounced throughout the centuries, and some millions of good bewildered folk who have ceased to believe much in anything, and do not know what they believe, or whether anything be worth believing; and, scattered among these millions with their roots in such movements of the past, some twenty-five millions of Catholics.

Now, either the Catholic body will come into sharp conflict with those about them, or they will not.

If they do not, it will be the first time in history that the Mystical Body of Christ (and American Catholics, like all others, are "cells" of that Body) has not aroused violent and unreasoning antagonism. This has been so uniformly a characteristic of the life of Christ and the life of the Catholic Church, that when persons calling themselves Christian or Catholic do not meet with opposition, and strong opposition, one may well begin to wonder whether they are profoundly Christian and truly Catholic. Perhaps then it is a reflection upon us American Catholics that we have inspired so little antagonism (comparatively) thus far. Perhaps we have not been telling our neighbors the truth, the strong truth, the hard saying they will not like: that the real test of our republican experiment here must ultimately be whether it accepts or opposes the Church of Christ; that it must become either a Catholic state, or a slave state.

A great many Catholics, influenced by the Protestant or Liberal environments in which they have lived, have sincerely and deliberately set out to propagate Christianity in such ways as never to arouse antagonism. They have compromised with Socialism, they have compromised with the economic theory of history, they have overemphasized the importance of various material elements. It is a sad evidence of the lack of unity into which we have been betrayed when a Catholic Justice of the Supreme Court can publicly proclaim that "Democracy" is more important than religion; when a Catholic priest, who taught for some years at the Catholic University at Washington and has filled the country with his disciples, openly goes to address a Jewish Masonic lodge (though Catholics are still forbidden by Canon 2335 to cooperate with or condone Masonry in any way)—and this, according to the press, not to remind his hearers of their true home in the Church Catholic, but to confirm them in their sense of injured innocence; or when a Catholic journalist burns a little incense on the altar of the economic theory of history, or a Catholic college professor condones usury, or defends the Communist cause in Spain.

Now all these gentlemen, these liberal broad-minded Catholics, many of whom are teaching the next generation of American Catholics, no doubt think they are doing a service to God in smoothing out our differences with others, and neglecting to utter the challenge which Christianity has uttered everywhere else in the world, until the opposition gnashed its teeth, and took up stones to cast. Perhaps they hope in this way to avert persecution, and gradually to bring about the conversion of the country they love to the true Faith. I do not impugn their motives or their sincerity; indeed, they are often animated by a great, if misguided charity. But if the history of Christianity teaches anything, it fairly cries out from the stones of desecrated and forsaken and stolen churches that if they have their way, they will do just the opposite to what they intend; and even worse. They will lead us, if we are foolish enough to follow them, to that abyss over which the English Catholics fell, one by one and family by family, in the Sixteenth Century. The English Catholics, a huge majority, were kept comparatively silent and inactive in the face of an intolerable but gradual oppression by a small rich crafty minority, in the hope that if they compromised on this point and that point, they would ultimately prevail, since they were more numerous, and had truth on their side. The result was the almost complete extinction of Catholicism in England for centuries—perhaps forever.

Our position, as a Catholic minority in this country, is of course different from theirs; we have no hoary tradition to lull us to a false security, and we have, thank God, a priesthood of high intelligence and character. Nor are we like the Catholics of the Middle Ages, to whom the Faith was as the air they breathed, and therefore at times familiarly neglected. We are more like those earlier Catholics in the Roman Empire, greatly outnumbered, with neither the power nor the desire to use force or to play any political part save what our duty to the state demands; weak in the sight of this world, and therefore (if we are faithful) strong as only Christ is strong. Our one hope of winning, for their own good, the millions of unbelievers who surround us and lead a life increasingly at variance with ours (and increasingly miserable) is to speak boldly the truth God has given us, in season and out of season, and to resolutely repel any pagan idea or custom that would be the opening wedge for the destruction of our faith. This will inevitably bring persecution upon us. What would be the effect, for example, if every Catholic told the truth about the old Manichean perversion called birth-control, wherever and whenever the subject came up? Undoubtedly the unpopularity with which we are now viewed (some "ministers of the gospel" have denounced us as intolerant and backward in this regard) would be intensified to a fury which would make things very uncomfortable for us. But it was precisely by saying and doing what made others furious and themselves uncomfortable that the early Christians overcame the empire of the Caesars; and it is only by the same means that we shall overcome the empires of the Socialists, whether they call themselves Democrats, Republicans, Communists, Nazi-Socialists or what you please. If we are suspected, ostracized, insulted, starved, beaten, imprisoned, misrepresented, neglected, put to death in a thousand new ways—that is precisely our business as Christians; and it is a method that will prove as irresistible in the twentieth century as it was in the first and second. Or does any one imagine that here in America, as an unique exception, the servant shall be greater than his Lord?

The very fact that the Catholic Church throughout the world has been experiencing a great spiritual revival, evidenced by the Eucharistic Congresses, the vastly increased daily communions, and a remarkable literary resurgency, is certain to provoke antagonism which sooner or later will take the form of persecution. This becomes doubly sure as all the heresies begin to join hands in the Socialist State of the future.

If any one thinks that I exaggerate the danger of some form of Socialism (call it American Hitlerism if you wish) in the United States, let him remember the number of Protestant ministers (including a Methodist Bishop), of Hollywood actors and producers, of college professors, of officers high in federal and state governments, who openly championed the Communist cause in Spain during the late war there, and continued to do so even after the Communist affiliations of the so-called Spanish "Democracy" were abundantly demonstrated. As for Communists here, the revelations of the Dies Committee cannot be brushed aside; there is confirmation of them on every side.

The New York Times of today carried a curious account of a meeting of several hundred members of the Ku Klux Klan with members of the German Bund in New Jersey.[20]

[20] August 19, 1940.

Now, suppose that some dominant personality should play upon the emotions of all these various sorts of totalitarians and bigots, and direct them toward a common end? The impact would be furious; and all history means nothing if the target would not sooner or later prove to be the Catholic Church. A Socialist is a Socialist under the skin, as a Catholic is a Catholic; and when the battle lines begin to form on the left and on the right, those of a secret spiritual affinity will all be found together. "He who gathereth not with Me, scattereth."

It is disturbing these days to re-read Monsignor Hugh Benson's *Lord of the World,* written about 1906, and to notice how much of it has already come to pass. In that superb flight of the imagination—far better than anything of Wells or Huxley—he envisaged the antichrist as a Socialistic President of the United States, a Freemason named Felsenberg, a man with a charming voice and personality, who could talk of Christianity when he meant Humanitarianism, and who, after the Second World War, gathered all the nations into an anti-Christian World State, headed by a sort of Federal Union of the English-speaking peoples. Let us hope—let us see to it if possible—that this prophecy, at least, shall not be realized. Yet, as I read the last proofs of this book, I find in a London dispatch to the *New York Times* of September 19, 1940, another reminder of the actualities behind the false issues and sham conflicts that keep humanity blind. Mr. Montagu Norman, Governor of the Bank of England, and Dr. Walther Funk, Economics Minister of the German Reich, are still directors of the World Bank; and although no meetings of the Board have been held lately, for obvious reasons, Sir Kingsley Wood, Chancellor of the Exchequer, assured the House of Commons that *"the link still exists"* and that *"it is essential that the position be maintained."* The temporary unpleasantness between the two countries—the slaughter of innocent women and children in London and in Berlin—will not interfere it would seem, with the long range plans of the real masters of this world.

The spearhead of the Ku Klux and Bund attacks just now seems directed at Jews. The poor Jews! It is always so convenient to blame them when anything goes wrong! I am not suggesting that they are completely innocent, far less that they alone, of all people, have done no wrong. M. Maritain has said truly that an attack on a Jew as a Jew is an insult to God the Father. He might have added that any sympathy for Jews which tends to confirm them in their rejection of the Catholic Church is an affront to God the Son and God the Holy Ghost. Surely this Chosen People is worthy of nothing less than truth! It is no secret in their own histories that they rejected the Jew who told them, and proved by His Resurrection, that He was the prophet foretold by Moses, and that all through the sweaty centuries they have supported every movement that promised to destroy the Church He founded. The Catholic Church has been saying to them for centuries, as Saint Peter said to the Jews contemporary with Our Lord, "The God of Abraham, and the God of Isaac, and the God of Jacob, the God of our fathers, hath glorified his son Jesus, whom you indeed delivered up and denied before the face of Pilate, when he judged he should be released. But you denied the Holy One and the Just, and desired a murderer to be granted unto you. But the author of life you killed, whom God hath raised from the dead, of which we are witnesses . . . *And now brethren, I know that you did it through ignorance, as did also your rulers.* . . . Be penitent, therefore, and be converted, that your sins may be blotted out." [21]

What Saint Peter offered the Jews in the Church, they have sought, many no doubt with great sincerity from the premises handed down to them, in the heresies of all ages. "Socialism itself," wrote an American Jewish scholar in the rosy years following the first world war, "was largely a product of the Jewish mind. In theory and scientific analysis it was the work of Karl Marx, while as a political factor . . . it claims another Jew, Ferdinand La Salle, as its organizing genius." Elsewhere in the same book he says, "Modern Jewish history, as the term is understood today, goes no further back than the French Revolution. . . . America is the new Jewish wonderworld, a sort of *deus-ex-machina*, made-to-order community which rose into its greatest prominence in Jewish life within the past thirty years . . . The very latest period of Jewish history, stretching for seventy years, from 1848 to 1918, will doubt-

[21] *Acts*, III: 13-17, my italics.

less forever rank in Jewish annals as the most important, and in a large sense the most glorious page in the story of the Jewish people since the destruction of the Second Temple at the hands of Titus . . . The day of complete deliverance finally heaves in sight, and amidst the anguish and suffering of a great world war, the harrowing effect of which no part of the globe is permitted to escape, mankind experiences a new birth, and the Jew, too, at last is about to come into his own . . . A new day is at hand when the weak and the oppressed of the earth will find themselves permanently delivered . . . The beginning of this complete emancipation has already been made in the wonderful change in the status of six million Jews wrought over night, as it were, by the Russian Revolution." [22]

Seven years later, Rabbi Stephen S. Wise demanded of his congregation, "Is Western civilization with its grimmest, grimiest social injustice and wrong, worth saving? Or is it not the function of the Jew to bring about the supercession of that decrepit, degenerate and inevitably perishing civilization, so-called?" [23]

I do not consider such utterances as alarming as I did when they first came to my attention. The Rabbi's strictures on modern civilization have been enlarged upon, in just as vigorous if more measured language, in some of the papal encyclicals. And a little boasting now and then is surely pardonable in a people with such a history as that of the Jews! As for Socialism, many of them had high hopes of it; and their sympathy with Russia, and the Reds in Spain, was obvious enough. But most of their hopes in that direction have proved illusory; and if Mr. Bernard Baruch has been largely responsible for preparing the military and industrial draft laws now being considered for the regimentation of the American people (for which he was a propagandist as early as 1932 or earlier), many other Jews (especially since the cynical alliance of Stalin with their persecutor Hitler) have been turning away in disgust from all forms of collectivism. There are many signs among them of doubt, weariness and bewilderment as they face a future full of uncer-

[22] Max Raisin, B.A., LL.D., *History of the Jews in Modern Times*, New York, 1923, p. 37.

[23] *New York Times*, December 7, 1930.

tainty. Perhaps it will bring the wonderworld of Dr. Raisin's fantasy; perhaps it will be just the same old world of futility, misunderstanding and persecution.

It would not be surprising if a great mass of them shook the dust of Socialism and Communism from their feet altogether, and this very soon. The theory of a Jewish conspiracy to dominate the world has never been proved, and is not likely to be. If indeed the more ambitious of them happened in some way to get control of the globe, they would find it a very disappointing and undesirable responsibility, and I doubt whether their restless souls would cling to it very long. Meanwhile they seem more likely to be constrained and hemmed in by the legions of some new Caesar or Caesars, as they were at the time when Christ walked among them. Perhaps, as the latter days come upon us, there will be a division among them, as there was in that time; and like the thousands baptized by Saint Peter and Saint Paul, other thousands will come into their true spiritual home, the garden desired by their own great prophets, the Holy Roman Catholic Church. I stress the possibility not so much to suggest a course of action to our Jewish neighbors—for at present they would doubtless take it as an impertinence—as to remind myself and other Catholics of our plain duty to pray constantly for their conversion, that is to say, for their true welfare.

This is one more reason, (besides the obvious one of simple justice) why Catholics should not in any way encourage or support those dangerous fanatical movements which are already planning a persecution of the Jews. Those who begin by persecuting Jews will probably end by persecuting Catholics. In any event, I am glad to find almost no tendency among Catholics to blame all the woes of the century upon the sons of Abraham. This is as it should be. Even if they had done to us all that their worst enemies allege (and many have not) it would still be our duty as Christians to love our enemies, to do good to them that hate us. There is no debating on this point: Catholics are obliged not only to tolerate, but to *love* Jews, all the more so if the Jews have done anything to injure them. If we should yield to any such spirit as that of the Ku Klux Klan, which is but a new form of that old temptation of the

Pharisee to thank God that we are not extortioners and adulterers like other men, we may yet see the prophecy of Fray Luis de Leon fulfilled, and our descendants cast into exterior darkness, while the poor despised Jew, bearer of the cross of Christ against his will, comes in with downcast eyes like the Publican, forgiving and forgiven at last, to be arrayed in a wedding garment and set upon a lofty seat, when the Bridegroom returns unexpectedly to a world no longer tolerable without Him.

To the Jew, and to all other men, the Catholic Church is their Father's house. Where else shall human beings turn if they are to keep the freedom and dignity of human beings? As the world we have known passes away, and kingdoms and empires fall, only this unique Institution continues the same; she only, because Christ lives in her, remains a centre and norm of sanity in thought and action. Here is the true and only League of Nations, the true and eternal "Union Now," the true Empire of souls, the Fascism that accomplishes what all the other isms only promise, the Communism that is voluntary and leaves men and women free, the Democracy that respects the sacred personality of human beings, the only possible world organization uniting all men as brothers under the fatherhood of God. To persecute her will always be futile, for she is indestructible as Christ is indestructible, as the God of Abraham, of Isaac and of Jacob is indestructible; and in all the confusion and sorrow, the blood and tears of our day, she advances calmly toward some distant Jerusalem where she will find her final crucifixion, and when the stone is sealed once more upon her tomb, she will rise once more fresh and glorious to scatter and confound her enemies. She alone can face a hostile world, with Christ Himself, and say, "Did not Moses give you the law: and yet none of you keepeth the law? Why seek you to kill me?" And when the Pharisees of the last days reply, as they have replied in every age, "Thou hast a devil; who seeketh to kill thee?" (while they continue secretly to plot for her death) she alone will still be able to utter the astounding words of Christ, Who lives in her and sacrifices Himself daily on thousands of her altars, "Before Abraham was, I AM."

Even when she coöperated, as in the Inquisition, with what the modern world, lacking principles, condemns as intolerance, she was intolerant of no human right as such, of no race or creed in itself; she was intolerant of things that were evil and destructive, things which ought not to be tolerated. For two thousand years she has been intolerant of all error, wherever it has appeared; especially of error insulting to the Majesty of the God who spoke to Moses in the burning bush. Yet intolerance is not her distinguishing or essential characteristic; it is but a defensive weapon committed to her with her divine mission. She much prefers to rejoice on some Mount of Transfiguration with her Lord, or to agonize with Him for all men in some Garden of Gethsemani, while she applies to herself (and with a secret especial tenderness to the mother of Christ) the words written by a Hebrew prophet many centuries ago:

"As the vine, I have brought forth a pleasant odor, and my flowers are the fruit of honor and riches. I am the mother of fair love, and of fear, and of knowledge, and of holy hope. In me is all grace of the way and of the truth, in me is all hope of life and virtue. Come over to me, all ye that desire me, and be filled with my fruits; for my spirit is sweet above honey and the honeycomb. My memory is unto everlasting generations. They that eat me, shall yet hunger; and they that drink me, shall yet thirst. He that hearkeneth to me shall not be confounded, and they that work by me shall not sin." [24]

She is the one true and authentic Christianity, fulfilling the promise of Moses to the Hebrews. She alone can say with Christ, "Thou hast hid these things from the wise and prudent, and hast revealed them to little ones. Yea, Father, for so hath it seemed good in thy sight. All things are delivered to me by my Father; and no one knoweth the Son but the Father; neither doth any one know the Father but the Son, and he to whom it shall please the Son to reveal Him. Come to Me, all you that labor and are burdened . . . and you shall find rest to your souls." [25]

[24] Ecclus., XXIV: 23-31.
[25] St. Matthew, XI: 25-30.

15.00